EUROPEAN PRIVATE INTERNATIONAL LAW AT 50

Series Jura Falconis Libri, nr. 21

EUROPEAN PRIVATE INTERNATIONAL LAW AT 50

Celebrating and Contemplating the 1968 Brussels Convention and Its Successors

Geert Van Calster
Jura Falconis
(eds.)

Ilse Couwenberg
Stéphanie Francq
Burkhard Hess
Thalia Kruger
Arnaud Nuyts
Marta Pertegás
Helena Raulus
Geert Van Calster
Arie Van Hoe

intersentia
Antwerpen – Cambridge

Intersentia Ltd
Sheraton House | Castle Park
Cambridge | CB3 0AX | United Kingdom
Tel.: +44 1223 370 170 | Fax: +44 1223 370 169
Email: mail@intersentia.co.uk
www.intersentia.com | www.intersentia.co.uk

Distribution for the UK and Ireland:
NBN International
Airport Business Centre, 10 Thornbury Road
Plymouth, PL6 7 PP
United Kingdom
Tel.: +44 1752 202 301 | Fax: +44 1752 202 331
Email: orders@nbninternational.com

Distribution for Europe and all other countries:
Intersentia Publishing nv
Groenstraat 31
2640 Mortsel
Belgium
Tel.: +32 3 680 15 50 | Fax: +32 3 658 71 21
Email: mail@intersentia.be

Distribution for the USA and Canada:
Independent Publishers Group
Order Department
814 North Franklin Street
Chicago, IL60610
USA
Tel.: +1 800 888 4741 (toll free) | Fax: +1312 337 5985
Email: orders@jpgbook.com

European Private International Law at 50. Celebrating and Contemplating the 1968 Brussels Convention and Its Successors
Geert Van Calster and Jura Falconis (eds.)

ISBN 978-1-78068-775-9
ISBN 978-1-78068-776-6 (pdf)
D/2018/7849/111
NUR 822

British Library Cataloguing in Publication Data. A catalogue record for this book is available from the British Library.

PREFACE

Esther Maes
Editor-in-chief 2017-2018

Fifty years ago, the Brussels Convention saw the light of day. The European leaders sensed more judicial cooperation was needed if they ever truly hoped to achieve a single market. Businesses and consumers will more easily engage in activities across borders when they have the certainty that a judgment obtained in one Member State will be enforced in another. As there was no legal basis in the Treaties, a classic international treaty was adopted to harmonize jurisdiction as well as the recognition and enforcement of judgments within the European communities.

In fifty years, European private international law has undergone several significant changes: the Brussels Convention has been replaced by regulations, authentic EU instruments; applicable law is no longer disregarded; interpretations of existing provisions have changed; and some fields of private international law previously left for the Member States have been included in the harmonization process. Additionally, there have been some important developments on an international level such as the Hague Judgments Project. Moreover, increased globalization and the emergence of e-commerce has led to an elevated need for and more widespread reliance on private international law.

Each year, the editorial team of Jura Falconis scours the libraries and legal databases for a relevant topic to discuss at the annual Jura Falconis conference. Often we focus on what the future holds for the law student, the legal practitioner, the academic: a new law, a future development, a novel evolution. The 50th anniversary of the Brussels Convention, however, presented itself as the perfect opportunity to pause and reflect on the past, to see how far we have come and how we go from here.

Because of the increased relevance of private international law, most legal practitioners can no longer avoid it in their day-to-day practices. Therefore, a thorough revision of the most important aspects of European private international law is certainly not futile. The goal of the conference, however, was not only to refresh students', practitioners' and academics' memories regarding the history, the application and the implications of European private international law but to also offer a view of tomorrow. What will be the future direction of European private international law? What are, for instance, the possible ramifications of the looming Brexit?

Several experts assembled in Leuven on 23 March 2018 for the Jura Falconis conference 'European Private International Law at 50' to discuss prior developments, draw lessons from the past and offer perspectives for the future of European private international law. This book is the written result of that exercise. In name of Jura Falconis, I would like to thank everyone who has aided in its creation. First, I would like to thank the authors for their spoken and written contributions. Next, I would like to acknowledge Intersentia and the KU Leuven for their unwavering support for Jura Falconis. Last but certainly not least, I would like to express my utmost gratitude to professor Geert Van Calster without whom this conference and this book would never have become reality.

CONTENTS

Brussels I Recast and the Hague Judgments Project

Cross-Border Provisional Measures: Stepping Backwards in the Brussels I Recast

LES GRANDS COURANTS OF 50 YEARS OF EUROPEAN PRIVATE INTERNATIONAL LAW

Geert Van Calster
Professor at KU Leuven
Head of the department of International and European Law at Leuven Law

My fellow authors of this conference handbook have zoomed in excellently on a number of topics relevant to the application of the 'Brussels Regime'. My contribution offers a more bird's eye view on some of the *grands courants* of 50 years of European private international law ('PIL'). Inevitably some of my comments may overlap with, hopefully confirm and equally hopefully contradict some of the comments made by my peers.

1. A SEA CHANGE. FROM UPHOLSTERED FURNITURE TO SHARIA DIVORCE

My institute co-organised the conference in March 2018, which led to current conference handbook. At the end of what was a stimulating and from my point of view also simply a fun day, my co-organisers handed me a bundle of past issues of the journal in which private international law papers had been published. Let me start my contribution by listing the papers that were published in the various issues handed to me. (These were not meant as a complete, exhaustive overview. I suspect the pile would have been too high.)

Marc Huysmans, supervised by prof. Koen Lenaerts (at the time the chair of private international law at the faculty) in 1989 wrote on insolvency in PIL. This paper included a comparative review of substantive insolvency in a select number of EU countries, followed by insolvency in Belgian European PIL.[1] The latter focused on what was then the European Commission draft for a European Insolvency Convention.

1 M. Huysmans, 'Het faillissement in internationaal privaatrecht' (1989–90) 26(1) *Jura Falconis* 77, available via https://www.law.kuleuven.be/apps/jura/public/art/26n1/huysmans.pdf or https://bit.ly/2zCUBde, last consulted 31 May 2018.

In the same 1988–89 volume, Wouter Wils comparatively reviewed surrogacy between the US and Belgium, with a few hints at the difficulties private international law might raise in the discussion (the angle of the paper was mostly comparative family law).[2] In the same issue, Geert Morris published the first part of a two part analysis of the 1980 Rome Convention on applicable law in contractual relations.[3]

Hilde Jacobs in 1990–91 discussed the substantive conditions and the 'formae habilitantes' (the formalities required in the event of the sale of immovable property owned by minors)[4], and Pascale Alerts and Margaretha Wilkenhuysen analysed related issues of guardianship and the sale of real estate belonging to foreign minors.[5]

In the 2000–2001 volume, Eveline Bruynincx analysed the return of looted war under both public and private international law[6] – an issue that exercised the European Parliament only recently.[7] Prof. Hans van Houtte, my immediate predecessor to the chair at Leuven, in the same issue discussed mediation by way of an interview, including a few references to the European context of same (and embedded in the discussion on European civil procedure).[8]

After that 2000–2001 volume, there is a gap in the issues handed to me[9] right up to the current 2017–2018 issue, with a contribution by one of my current

---

2 W. Wils, 'Draagmoederschap, een vergelijkende studie vanuit het recht van de VSA' (1988–89) 25(1) *Jura Falconis* 9, available via https://www.law.kuleuven.be/apps/jura/public/art/25n1/wils.pdf or https://bit.ly/2ujfQfe, last consulted 3 July 2018.

3 G. Morris, 'Het Europees Verdrag van Rome van 19 juni 1980 betreffende het toepasselijk recht op verbintenissen uit overeenkomst – Deel I' (1988–89) 25(1) *Jura Falconis* 37, available via https://www.law.kuleuven.be/apps/jura/public/art/25n1/morris.pdf or https://bit.ly/2Nf4e43, last consulted 1 July 2018. Part II was published in the next issue: (1988–89) 25(2) *Jura Falconis* 171, available via https://www.law.kuleuven.be/apps/jura/public/art/25n2/morris.pdf, or https://bit.ly/2L49fyV, last consulted 13 July 2018.

4 H. Jacobs, 'Het vervreemden van een onroerend goed geheel of gedeeltelijk toebehorend aan een vreemde minderjarige en het internationaal privaatrecht' (1990–91) 27(3) *Jura Falconis* 431, available via https://www.law.kuleuven.be/apps/jura/public/art/27n3/jacobs.pdf or https://bit.ly/2NQeMHA last consulted 31 May 2018.

5 P. Alaerts, M. Wilkenhuysen, 'De voogdij en de verkoop van onroerende goederen van buitenlandse minderjarigen: een praktijkonderzoek' (1990–91) 27(3) *Jura Falconis* 401, available via https://www.law.kuleuven.be/apps/jura/public/art/27n3/alaerts.pdf or https://bit.ly/2LfMiWn, last consulted 7 July 2018.

6 E. Bruyninx, 'Roofkunst uit WOII: To return or not to return?' (2000–01) 37(1) *Jura Falconis* 47, 47–84, available via https://www.law.kuleuven.be/apps/jura/artikels/show/122, or https://bit.ly/2LgaAzr, last consulted 13 July 2018.

7 P. Svoboda MEP, 'Cross-border restitution claims of looted works of art and cultural goods', November 2017, available at www.europarl.europa.eu/RegData/etudes/STUD/2017/610988/EPRS_STU(2017)610988_EN.pdf, or https://bit.ly/2KSYZKs, last consulted 13 July 2018.

8 H. Van Houtte, 'Mediatie: realiteit of toekomstmuziek?' (2000–01) 37(1) *Jura Falconis* 85, available via https://www.law.kuleuven.be/apps/jura/artikels/show/123, last consulted 13 July 2018.

9 Among the articles missing from the printed pile, M. Pertegas, 'Cross-border injunctions in patent litigation: ingenious tactics or misue of private international rules', (2000-01) 37(4) *Jura Falconis* 505-522, available via https://www.law.kuleuven.be/apps/jura/artikels/show/137, or https://bit.ly/2P1QTR8, last consulted 17 October 2018; D. Van Isacker, 'Conflit mobile in het Nederlandse, Franse, Belgische en Europese IPR', (2014-15) 51(1) *Jura Falconis* 77-92, available via https://www.law.kuleuven.be/apps/jura/public/art/51n1/vanisacker.pdf, or https://bit.ly/2P0wax1, last consulted 17 October 2018

PhD students, Michiel Poesen, on the European Court of Justice's *Nintendo* judgment.[10]

Many intervening articles of course will have had a private international law angle to it in some way or another, without having had PIL as the main focus.

Let us remind ourselves of the context in which the first of the papers listed above, would have been written. The institutional context of many of the papers was Article 220 of the Treaty on the European Economic Community – EEC, which reads, in relevant part:

> Member States shall, in so far as necessary, engage in negotiations with each other with a view to ensuring for the benefit of their nationals:...
>
> - the mutual recognition of companies.., the maintenance of their legal personality in cases where the registered office is transferred from one country to another, and [cross-border mergers]; and
> - the simplification of the formalities governing the reciprocal recognition and execution of judicial decisions and of arbitral awards.

Commentators typically reflect upon the relative success of this intergovernmental method, pointing to the 1968 Brussels Convention, the 1980 Rome Convention, as well as to two Conventions which were negotiated but never entered into force: the 1968 Recognition of Companies Convention, and the 1995 Insolvency Convention.[11] However it remains an oddity that a subject-matter (free movement of judgments) with such clear and evident importance to the internal market (cross-border contracts are greatly facilitated by certainty about both applicable law and jurisdiction /recognition and enforcement) should not have been more firmly anchored into what was essentially an economic treaty (the EEC). There would have surely been ground to include it in the treaties and one can only imagine that the founding fathers, many of them lawyers, shied away from inserting into the Treaty a legal basis for intervention into core areas of civil procedure of the Member States.

Now, coming to the title of the current heading: Case 24/76 *Colzani*[12] was one of the earliest, if not the very first case in which the Court of Justice interpreted the 1968 Brussels Convention. Parties' contract in that case concerned the delivery of upholstered furniture. The link to the Internal Market is clear. The relative ease with which the Court of Justice would have discussed the case, too: this is an area firmly within the comfort zone of a court for whom 'commercial' cases would have been a staple diet.

---

10 M. Poesen, 'Level up for cross-border IP litigation: the CJEU in Nintendo /Big Ben' (2017–18) *Jura Falconis* 124.

11 More detail in A. Fiorini, 'The Evolution of European private international law' (2008) 57(4) *ICLQ* 969.

12 ECLI:EU:C:1976:177.

Fast forward 40 years. The CJEU continues to issue many a judgment on commercial litigation. However its action span has widened, together with the scope of the legislative instruments which it interprets. By way of illustration, in Case C-372/16 *Sahyouni*[13], the Court interprets the 'Rome III' Regulation on the law applicable to divorce and legal separation.[14] The Court held that Rome III does not cover divorces which are declared without a constitutive decision of a court or other public authority (it squarely uses the Regulation itself to come to this view, without any assessment of whether the foreign State's courts in private sharia divorces, has any impact on that conclusion). Or take the regular cases of the CJEU on parental kidnapping. Cases like these are a tremendously far cry from the delivery of machinery for upholstered furniture: I do not wish to deny the relevance of commercial litigation, far from it, however the nature indeed the outlook and psychology of a court must be very different when it decides cases in which, to give a concrete implication, the parents indeed the child which is the subject of the custody hearings, are present in the chambers at Luxembourg.

2. BOUNDARIES OF EU PRIVATE INTERNATIONAL LAW?

It is well-known that the CJEU, rightly, emphasises the need for an 'autonomous' interpretation of terminology used in EU private international law.[15] Without it, the harmonious application of the Regulations would be at peril. Yet at the same time many of these private international law concepts are key provisions in the private law of the Member States. How far can the CJEU go in pushing an autonomous interpretation without it amounting to harmonisation of private law via the back door? The further harmonisation of substantive EU law may be, some advocate, the next logical step in the European conflicts resolution. This features

13 ECLI:EU:C:2017:988.

14 Regulation 1259/2010 [2010] OJ L343/10.

15 See e.g. Case C-383/95, *Rutten*, [1997] ECR I-57, para 12–13: '*It is settled law (…) that, in principle, the Court of Justice will interpret the terms of the [Brussels Convention] autonomously so as to ensure that it is fully effective, having regard to the objectives of Article 220 of the EEC Treaty, for the implementation of which it was adopted. (13) That autonomous interpretation alone is capable of ensuring uniform application of the Convention, the objectives of which include unification of the rules on jurisdiction of the Contracting States, so as to avoid as far as possible the multiplication of the bases of jurisdiction in relation to one and the same legal relationship and to reinforce the legal protection available to persons established in the Community by, at the same time, allowing the plaintiff easily to identify the court before which he may bring an action and the defendant reasonably to foresee the Court before which he may be sued.' Note that the Convention having been replaced by the Regulation, the interpretation of the Convention, mutatis mutandis (especially of course where material changes to the text have been made), applies to the Regulation.'*

inter alia in the debate on the Draft Common Frame of Reference.[16] One obvious disadvantage of the current Commission focus lies in its disregard for the benefits of regulatory competition. As the very existence of debate especially on applicable law shows, Member States have differing approaches to a wide variety of issues in private law. Far from merely serving as an obstacle to the Internal Market, this competition is essential in shaping, through commercial trial and error, attractive contractual and other provisions which assist in the creation of an internal market and moreover help European businesses that act on a global scale.

The European Commission (EC) may have reached a limit to Member States' preparedness for harmonisation with the 'Rome III' Regulation on divorce and separation, Regulation 1259/2010[17], with currently only 17 Member States being a party to this very first application of the 'Enhanced Co-operation' mechanism. On the other hand, its proposal on a Common European Sales Law (CESL) may be proof of (ill-informed) tenacity rather than defeat. The potential for this proposal was already referred to in the Rome I Regulation, Recital 14 of which reads

> Should the Community adopt, in an appropriate legal instrument, rules of substantive contract law, including standard terms and conditions, such instrument may provide that the parties may choose to apply those rules.

This is a clear reference to the possibility of a future optional instrument of European contract law, most likely linked to the 'Draft Common Frame of Reference'. One such instrument was proposed by the European Commission in October 2011, for sales[18], on the basis of Article 114 TFEU, the core article for legislation with a view to realising the Internal Market. However, the exact relationship between this proposal and Rome I is far from clear, especially in relation to mandatory rules of Union law. At the time of writing the proposal had not advanced past the European Parliament's First Reading stage – 7 years after its introduction. It is interesting to note the EC's justification for the proposal:

> Differences in contract law between Member States hinder traders and consumers who want to engage in cross-border trade within the internal market. The obstacles which stem from these differences dissuade traders, small and medium-sized enterprises (SME) in particular, from entering cross border trade or expanding to new Member States' markets. Consumers are hindered from accessing products offered by traders in other Member States.
> Currently, only one in ten of Union traders, involved in the sale of goods, exports within the Union and the majority of those who do only export to a small number of Member States.

16 Further discussed below, in particular with reference to the proposed Regulation on a European contract law for sales.

17 Regulation 1259/2010 implementing enhanced cooperation in the area of the law applicable to divorce and legal separation [2010] OJ L343/10.

18 COM(2011) 635 on a Common European Sales Law.

Contract law related barriers are one of the major factors contributing to this situation. Surveys[19] show that out of the range of obstacles to cross-border trade including tax regulations, administrative requirements, difficulties in delivery, language and culture, traders ranked contract-law-related obstacles among the top barriers to cross-border trade.

The need for traders to adapt to the different national contract laws that may apply in crossborder dealings makes cross-border trade more complex and costly compared to domestic trade, both for business-to-consumer and for business-to-business transactions. Additional transaction costs compared to domestic trade usually occur for traders in crossborder situations. They include the difficulty in finding out about the provisions of an applicable foreign contract law, obtaining legal advice, negotiating the applicable law in business-to-business transactions and adapting contracts to the requirements of the consumer's law in business-to-consumer transactions.

In cross-border transactions between a business and a consumer, contract law related transaction costs and legal obstacles stemming from differences between different national mandatory consumer protection rules have a significant impact. Pursuant to Article 6 of Regulation 593/2008 of the European Parliament and of the Council of 17 June 2008 on the law applicable to contractual obligations (Rome I), whenever a business directs its activities to consumers in another Member State, it has to comply with the contract law of that Member State. In cases where another applicable law has been chosen by the parties and where the mandatory consumer protection provisions of the Member State of the consumer provide a higher level of protection, these mandatory rules of the consumer's law need to be respected.

Traders therefore need to find out in advance whether the law of the Member State of the consumer's habitual residence provides a higher level of protection and ensure that their contract is in compliance with its requirements. The existing harmonisation of consumer law at Union level has led to a certain approximation in some areas but the differences between Member States' laws remain substantial. In e-commerce transactions, traders incur further contract law related costs which stem from the need to adapt the business's website to the legal requirements of each Member State where they direct their activity. In cross-border transactions between traders, parties are not subject to the same restrictions on the applicable law. However, the economic impact of negotiating and applying a foreign law is also high.

The costs resulting from dealings with various national laws are burdensome particularly for SME. In their relations with larger companies, SME generally have to agree to apply the law of their business partner and bear the costs of finding out about the content of the foreign law applicable to the contract and of complying with it. In contracts between SME, the need to negotiate the applicable law is a significant obstacle to cross-border trade.

For both types of contracts (business-to-business and business-to-consumer) for SME, these additional transaction costs may even be disproportionate to the value of the transaction.

---

19 The Commission refers to Eurobarometer 320 on European contract law in business-to-business transactions of 2011, p. 15 and Eurobarometer 321 on European contract law in consumer transactions of 2011, p. 19.

> These additional transaction costs grow proportionately to the number of Member States into which a trader exports. Indeed, the more countries they export to, the greater the importance traders attach to differences in contract law as a barrier to trade. SME are particularly disadvantaged: the smaller a company's turnover, the greater the share of transaction costs.
> Traders are also exposed to increased legal complexity in cross-border trade, compared to domestic trade, as they often have to deal with multiple national contract laws with differing characteristics.
> Dealing with foreign laws adds complexity to cross-border transactions. Traders ranked the difficulty in finding out the provisions of a foreign contract law first among the obstacles to business-to-consumer transactions and third for business-to-business transactions.[20] Legal complexity is higher when trading with a country whose legal system is fundamentally different while it has been demonstrated empirically that bilateral trade between countries which have a legal system based on a common origin is much higher than trade between two countries without this commonality.[21]
> Thus, differences in contract law and the additional transaction costs and complexity that they generate in cross-border transactions dissuade a considerable number of traders, in particular SME, from expanding into markets of other Member States. These differences also have the effect of limiting competition in the internal market. The value of the trade foregone each year between Member States due to differences in contract law alone amounts to tens of billions of Euros.
> The missed opportunities for cross-border trade also have a negative impact upon European consumers. Less cross-border trade, results in fewer imports and less competitiveness between traders. This can lead to a more limited choice of products at a higher price in the consumer's market. (...)

The EC's justification for the proposed Regulation is, one fears, a classic example of the dangers and opportunities of data management.[22] The Commission summarises the study upon which it relies in relevant part as

> Surveys show that out of the range of obstacles to cross-border trade including tax regulations, administrative requirements, difficulties in delivery, language and culture, traders ranked contract-law-related obstacles among the top barriers to cross-border trade.

20 Same reference.

21 Here the Commission refers to A. Turrini and T. Van Ypersele, 'Traders, courts and the border effect puzzle' (2010) 40 *Regional Science and Urban Economics* 81, 82: '*Analysing international trade across OECD countries we show that controlling for countries specific factors, distance, the presence of common border and common language [...], similar legal systems have a significant impact on trade [...]. If two countries share common origins for their legal system, on average they exhibit trade flows 40% larger.*'

22 '*There are three kinds of lies: lies, damned lies, and statistics*': potentially unjustifiably credited to British Prime Minister Benjamin Disraeli (1804–1881).

However in the relevant section for B2B transactions[23], 'contract-law-related obstacles' only came among the 'top' barriers to cross-border trade identified by business, after regrouping four of the ten reasons provided to those surveyed. In that group, when looking at replies given at the 'large impact' side of the scale (which one assumes means that business immediately sees it as a serious obstacle), '*problems in resolving cross-border conflicts, including costs of litigation abroad*' came third, after tax regulations and formal requirements such as registration and licensing. Language problems and cross-border channels of delivery came next. Only three in ten respondents felt that '*resolving cross-border conflicts, obtaining legal advice regarding foreign contract law*', and '*difficulties in agreeing on the applicable foreign law*' had some impact on their cross-border trading. Of the four reasons arguably related to contract law, three came in the bottom four reasons that were quoted as an obstacle. The other was the last of the top three. That hardly justifies the EC's summary that '*contract-law-related obstacles (ranked) among the top barriers to cross-border trade.*' Indeed, it does not justify it at all.[24]

For B2C transactions, the justification is even fuzzier: four items the survey asked about were closely related to problems with the contract law sanctioning cross-border consumer transactions. Over half, 55%, of the surveyed enterprises in the EU, indicated that at least one of these four items had at least some – even if minimal – impact on their cross-border retail activity. About one in six of the surveyed enterprises (18%) indicated that at least one of the factors was having a big impact; another 18% felt at least some impact, and 19% confirmed at least a minimal impact of one of the consumer contract law related problems tested. A full 45% claimed that none of these obstacles had any impact on their operations. Moreover, uncertainty in this area is arguably addressed by the 'maximum harmonisation' consumer rights Directive[25], which, having just entered into force (it will have to be applied in the Member States as of 13 June 2014), arguably would militate against introducing an optional law of which the effects are at the least uncertain.

Neither does the Turrini and van Ypersele study support the EC's conclusion that

> Legal complexity is higher when trading with a country whose legal system is fundamentally different while it has been demonstrated empirically that bilateral trade between countries which have a legal system based on a common origin is much higher than trade between two countries without this commonality.

The study was a theoretical one, theorising on the data provided by other studies, and not empirical itself. Moreover, while the study does point to data indicating

---

23 Eurobarometer 320 on European contract law in business-to-business transactions of 2011, p. 15 ff.

24 Especially if one considers what the impact would have been had contract-related issues not figured so prominently in the ten reasons provided.

25 Directive 2011/83 of 25 October 2011 [2011] OJ L304/64.

that if countries share common origins for their legal system, they exhibit on average trade flows 40% larger, it additionally showed that judicial asymmetries were also associated with reduced trade (to the tune of 24%), even between two regions of the same country. Further, these studies do not explain whether it is the differences in the legal systems which cause reduced trade, or rather conversely, whether the absence of trade for non-law-related reasons leads to differences in the law. Finally, the singular focus on flows of goods as opposed to the much wider economic picture (movement of capital, movement of workers...) does no justice to the overall goals of the internal market.

The proposal for a Common European Sales Law, if ever adopted, will have no direct impact on the Rome I or Rome II Regulations. Parties will effectively employ the principle of party autonomy to opt into the CESL. However a large number of contractual issues fall outside of the CESL's remit: this is clarified by the already infamous (proposed) Recital 27:

> All the matters of a contractual or non-contractual nature that are not addressed in the Common European Sales Law are governed by the pre-existing rules of the national law outside the Common European Sales Law that is applicable under Regulations (EC) No 593/2008 and (EC) No 864/2007 or any other relevant conflict of law rule. These issues include legal personality, the invalidity of a contract arising from lack of capacity, illegality or immorality, the determination of the language of the contract, matters of non-discrimination, representation, plurality of debtors and creditors, change of parties including assignment, set-off and merger, property law including the transfer of ownership, intellectual property law and the law of torts. Furthermore, the issue of whether concurrent contractual and non-contractual liability claims can be pursued together falls outside the scope of the Common European Sales Law.

Therefore, if ever adopted the CESL will rest on spurious grounds.

3. THE ROLE OF THE CJEU – 'MUTUAL TRUST'

The 'mutual trust' which the Court of Justice has emphasised in the application of the Regulation, arguably has not in fact led to a high degree of independent application by the courts of the Member States. Rather the opposite: the strict *lis alibi pendens* rule of (now) Article 30 ff (obliging courts seized last to give way to those seized first) has made courts keep a rather beady eye on how their counterparts in the other Member States interpret the Regulation. It often results in lack of confidence of those courts. This helps explain the increasing amount of preliminary reviews to the Court of Justice, spurred on by the insistence of the Court that terminology in the regulation be given an 'autonomous' interpretation, and by its tendency to micro-manage the application of the Regulation.[26]

The theme of mutual trust runs through European PIL, extending from the Jurisdiction Regulation into e.g. the Insolvency Regulation[27] (the CJEU in *Eurofood*[28]). The overall themes running through the CJEU's application of the Regulation, are: recognition and enforcement facilitated by common adjudication of jurisdiction; this adjudication by courts in one Member State not to be second-guessed by courts of other States; and subject to an autonomous 'European' interpretation.

The combination of all these elements is firmly promoted by the Court as the only road to legal certainty. In doing so it arguably equates legal certainty with predictability, an equation which may be debatable. Indeed among practitioners, generally and especially those of common law Member States, there is growing dissatisfaction with the Court's principled disregard for commercial arguments in interpreting the Regulation, and for the aforementioned notion of legal certainty.[29] In *Gasser*, the United Kingdom specifically put forward the argument that the Convention had to be interpreted taking into account the needs of international trade – a suggestion not much entertained by the Court.

4. THE INTERNATIONAL IMPACT OF THE EU'S PRIVATE INTERNATIONAL LAW APPROACH

I have already noted above, that the EC's appetite for further harmonisation of private international law has not wavered. Its approach to the international impact of the regime (discussed in more detail by Thalia Kruger in this volume) in the review of the Brussels I Regulation is a good, and for this contribution final example.

The way in which the EU, through Article 6 of the Regulation[30], condones or, through the enforcement provisions, perhaps even sponsors exorbitant jurisdiction

---

26 E.g. recently in *Wood Floor Solutions*, Case C-19/09, [2010] ECR I-2121. The Court interpreted (then) Article 5(1)(b) of the Regulation. Article 5(1) provides for 'special' jurisdiction (jurisdiction over and above the standard rule of the domicile of the defendant) in the case of contracts, and 5(1)(b) in particular adds a presumption for the determination of the 'place of performance of the obligation'. The Court in *Wood Floor Solutions* not only held that the presumption also holds in the case of services provided in several Member States (as opposed to just one), but went on to instruct the national court in detail where the 'place of performance of the obligation' lies in the case of commercial agency contracts.

27 Regulation 1346/2000 [2000] OJ L160/1, as amended, and now Regulation 2015/848 [2015] OJ L141/19.

28 Case C-341/04, *Eurofood IFSC* [2006] ECR I-3813, para 39; see also C-444/07, *MG Probud Gdynia* [2010] ECR I-417.

29 See e.g. A. Dickinson on Conflict of Laws.net, 8 June 2009 (http://conflictoflaws.net/2009/brussels-i-review-online-focus-group/), last consulted 16 July 2018.

30 *Article 4*

1. If the defendant is not domiciled in a Member State, the jurisdiction of the courts of each Member State shall, subject to Article 18(1), Article 21(2), and Articles 24 and 25, be determined by the law of that Member State.

of some of its Member States has attracted some international criticism. However, most of the EU Member States which previously (for some of them really quite a long time ago) may have employed such wide reach, have since abandoned it. Moreover, other jurisdictions are not averse to similar claims. Consequently it would be fair to say that the theory of 'extraterritorial' EU/Member States jurisdictional claims far exceeds its practice. Indeed in its Green Paper on the review of the Regulation[31], the European Commission's attention to the workings of the JR in the international legal order focuses more on the issue of 'subsidiary jurisdiction' or 'third State defendants', in other words those national jurisdictional rules which do not concern a party domiciled in any of the EU Member States, or the exclusive grounds of jurisdiction in (now) Article 24, or finally the choice of court clauses under (now) Article 25. The concern here is with those domiciled in the EU acting as a *plaintiff*, as opposed to the Regulation's focus on the defendant.

Natural or legal persons domiciled in the EU but not domiciled in the Member State with an 'interesting' and wide jurisdictional claim, could not therefore – at least on the basis of the former text of the Regulation – make recourse to such rules. I do not subscribe to the view that this difference is '*hardly according to the principle of establishing an area of freedom, justice and security as described by Article [67 TFEU]*[32]' which now also seems to be the point of view of the European Commission. The Commissions' view is that

> The good functioning of an internal market and the Community's commercial policy both on the internal and on the international level require that equal access to justice on the basis of clear and precise rules on international jurisdiction is ensured not only for defendants but also for claimants domiciled in the Community. The jurisdictional needs of persons in the Community in their relations with third States' parties are similar. The reply to these needs should not vary from one Member State to another, taking into account, in particular, that subsidiary jurisdiction rules do not exist in all the Member States. A common approach would strengthen the legal protection of Community citizens and economic operators and guarantee the application of mandatory Community legislation.[33]

Hence the Commission invited reflection (but obviously encouraged the development of) upon the necessity and appropriateness of additional jurisdictional grounds for disputes involving third State defendants (subsidiary jurisdiction), albeit with a word of caution on the 'international courtesy'

---

2. *As against such a defendant, any person domiciled in a Member State may, whatever his nationality, avail himself in that State of the rules of jurisdiction there in force, and in particular those of which the Member States are to notify the Commission pursuant to point (a) of Article 76(1), in the same way as nationals of that Member State.*

31 COM(2009) 175, p.3–4.

32 Hess, Pfeiffer, Schlosser, *The Brussels I Regulation 44/2001 – Application and enforcement in the EU*, Oxford, Hart 2008, p.22 *ff.* (generally referred to as the *Heidelberg* report), 158 (p.46).

33 Green Paper, p.3.

implications of such extension (a reference to the international public law issue of 'comity'). According to the Commission in its eventual proposal for amendment, each defendant as well as plaintiff in the EU should have 'equal' (what it means in fact is 'identical') access to the courts. It suggested specific additional jurisdictional grounds:

- The proposal extends the Regulation's special jurisdiction rules to third country defendants.[34] This amendment was likely to have the most impact in the case of contracts (jurisdiction at the place of contractual performance) – but failed later in the process.
- The protective jurisdiction rules available for consumers, employees and insured now also applies if the defendant is domiciled outside the EU.[35]
- The proposal further harmonised the so-called 'subsidiary' jurisdiction rules: i.e. those where the Member States so far had retained their national PIL rules. (Now) Article 6 of the Regulation would have been deleted in its entirety, and two additional fora created for disputes involving defendants domiciled outside the EU. These proposals did not make it.

Given that in each of these cases, there is a likelihood of clashing jurisdictional claims by third countries, the proposal provided for a discretionary *lis pendens* rule for disputes on the same subject matter and between the same parties which are pending before the courts in the EU and in a third country: this '*forum non conveniens*-light' (now Article 33) did make it.

It was the European Parliament[36] which – in my view justifiably – expressed serious reservations with respect to the proposal to extend the jurisdictional reach of the Regulation in cases of defendants not domiciled in the EU. It suggested that changes with such obvious international impact ought to be negotiated with the EU's partners, rather than forced upon them. Its influence meant the eventual text of the Regulation did not go quite as far with respect to the international impact of the rules.

Conclusion. Happy birthday, Brussels Convention! What started as a very muted ambition has now become firmly part of an extraordinary venture. One which no longer just impacts business, but rather has the citizen firmly at the heart of the EU's private international law policy.

---

[34] COM(2010) 748: deletion of '*A person domiciled in a Member State may, in another Member State, be sued*' from Article 5, introductory sentence.

[35] COM(2010) 748: deletion of '*domiciled in a Member State*' in each of the relevant sub-headings.

[36] See inter alia Report of Tadeusz ZWIEFKA MEP of 29 June 2010 on the implementation and review of Council Regulation (EC) No 44/2001 on jurisdiction and the recognition and enforcement of judgments in civil and commercial matters (2009/2140(INI), A7-0219/2010, and EP Resolution of 7 September 2010.

REGULATORY COMPETITION IN CIVIL PROCEDURE BETWEEN EU MEMBER STATES

Stéphanie Francq
Professor at UCLouvain

1. INTRODUCTION

Addressing the question of regulatory competition in civil procedure among the Member States at the time when the Brussels Convention is turning 50 might seem like raising an inexistent problem at the wrong time. First, how could Member States engage in regulatory competition at the civil procedure level when international jurisdiction, parallel procedures, jurisdiction clauses and recognition and enforcement issues are regulated by common rules inherited from the charming grandmother celebrated in this book (i.e. the Brussels Convention, mother of Regulation Brussels I and later grandmother of the Recast, without counting other offspring like Brussels IIa, etc.)?[1] Second, why would Member States engage in regulatory competition, especially at the civil procedure level, in order to attract more litigation to their own courts? Do they really wish to increase the overload of their national courts? These two sensible questions tend to doubt the reality of regulatory competition. And indeed they also raise a more fundamental question: is justice or civil procedure an object that can be submitted to regulatory or normative competition at all?

A few statements collected here and there in policy declarations or in academia tend rather to show that regulatory competition at the civil procedure level is raging.

---

1 1968 Brussels Convention on jurisdiction and the enforcement of judgments in civil and commercial matters consolidated version [1972] OJ L299/32; Council Regulation (EC) 44/2001 of 22 December 2000 on jurisdiction and the recognition and enforcement of judgments in civil and commercial matters [2001] OJ L12/1; Regulation (EU) 1215/2012 of 12 December 2012 on jurisdiction and the recognition and enforcement of judgments in civil and commercial matters [2012] OJ L351/1; Council Regulation (EC) 2201/2003 of 27 November 2003 concerning jurisdiction and the recognition and enforcement of judgments in matrimonial matters and the matters of parental responsibility, repealing Regulation (EC) 1347/2000 [2003] OJ L338/1.

- 'Today, justice has become an instrument to boost economic growth and employment.'[2]
- 'The judicial apparatus is not only destined to defend a citizen's fundamental rights and our society. It may as well provide a catalyst for our companies and by extension, our economy … The setting up of the BIBC has to be viewed in this context. This court will foster Brussels attractiveness for companies and investors (…).'[3]
- 'Effective courts are important for sustained economic development … An obvious implication is that countries with underperforming courts should reform them … There is however another approach to dealing with a dysfunctional court system – one that can go hand in hand with domestic judicial reform. The law can enable litigants from countries with ineffective judicial systems to have their cases adjudicated in the courts of other nations that have better-functioning judicial systems.'[4]

These statements indicate that there is at least a 'narrative' or a 'discourse' about regulatory competition and civil procedure. These statements also identify three core presumptions upon which this discourse is built: (i) a good justice system is attractive for investors and businesses; (ii) a good justice system will therefore prompt economic growth; (iii) for this 'attraction' to practically take place, the law needs to enable litigants/investors/businesses to decide where they want their cases to be adjudicated.

These statements are indeed rather commonplace in contemporary policy statements and academic literature. Since William Landes and Richard Posner published in 1979 their famous paper 'Adjudication as a Private Good', the idea of competition among legal and judicial systems and the operative role of party autonomy as a prerequisite for this competition seem to be generally accepted.[5] Important studies dealing with the regulatory competition taking place in the field of civil procedure have been published by specialists of the EU civil procedure system.[6] The tremendous success of party autonomy and of jurisdiction clauses are part of a representation of the legal world as a world where regulatory competition

---

2 V. Redding (former Vice-President of the European Commission, EU Justice Commissioner), 'Justice Past, Justice Present and Justice Future – Three Messages to the European Council', Brussels, 20.06.2014 <http://europa.eu/rapid/press-release_SPEECH-14-481_en.htm>.

3 K. Geens (Belgian Minister of Justice), 'Creation of the Brussels International Business Court' (the translation is ours), Press Release 27.10.2017 <www.koengeens.be/fr/news/2017/10/27/creation-brussels-international-business-court>.

4 J. Dammann and H. Hansmann, 'Globalizing Commercial Litigation' [2008] *Cornell Law Review* 3.

5 W. Landes and R. Posner, 'Adjudication as a Private Good' [1979] *The Journal of Legal Studies* 235–84.

6 See among others (and the literature cited below): X. Krämer, 'Competitie in de Europese Civiele Rechtsruimte. Een spanningsveld in de grensoverschrijdende geschillenbeslechting?' [2014] 4 *Tijdschrift voor Privaatrecht (TPR)* 1745–806; G. Wagner, 'Dispute Resolution as a Product: Competition between Civil Justice Systems' in H. Eindenmüller, *Regulatory Competition in Contract Law and Dispute Resolution*, Hart 2013, 347–422. Both are citing a number of empirical studies.

does and should take place. The wide acceptance of such representation is however astonishing when considering that Landes and Posner's paper was published only seven years after the US Supreme Court eventually endorsed jurisdiction clauses in *Bremen v. Zapata*.[7]

The question of regulatory competition among judicial systems is thus not as irrelevant as it might seem at first sight. It is indeed deeply rooted into our imaginaries about the interaction of legal systems and takes particularly striking colours in the EU legal system.[8] This short contribution, rather than providing a fully-fledged study of the judicial regulatory competition in the EU, will first briefly introduce regulatory competition as a relevant concept for private international law and civil procedure (2), before turning to a few EU-specific examples. Current developments (such as the organisation of a system of competition via jurisdiction clauses and the creation of international business courts) illustrate the existence of a game of regulatory competition in the EU and beyond, but also raise questions as to the corresponding benefits, costs and externalities of this game (3). The conclusion will develop three propositions based on the findings of part 2 and 3.

2. REGULATORY COMPETITION AS A CONCEPT

2.1. A BRIEF PRESENTATION OF THE CONCEPT

The concept of regulatory competition was launched by Charles Tiebout in 1956.[9] Regarding a legal system and norms as products placed on a market in which customers can actively choose the most attractive product and on applying basic economic rules on supply and demand, it seems easy to conclude that the demand in favour of products A (Austria's legal system) or B (Belgium's legal system) will increase if the product matches customers' expectations. Following the virtuous curve of economics, legislators, like any other market actor, will adapt their legal system (their product) in order to attract customers.

Indeed, within economic reasoning, adjusting the product (in terms of content and price) to better suit customers' expectations is a positive development leading

---

7 On *Bremen v. Zapata* as 'an instance of "worldmaking"', i.e. a figure where a jurisdiction or judge imagines a 'particular kind of world and in doing so helps that world into being': J. Bomhoff, 'Back to The Bremen (1972): Forum Selection and Worldmaking' [2018] 6 *LSE Legal Studies Working Paper* <https://ssrn.com/abstract=3143982> or <http://dx.doi.org/10.2139/ssrn.3143982>; US Supreme Court, *The Bremen v. Zapata Off-Shore Co.*, 407 U.S. 1, 9 (1972).

8 Jacques Lacan developed the concept of the 'Imaginary' in his famous book: J. Lacan, *The Four Fundamental Concepts of Psycho-Analysis* (London 1994). The concept has later been used in other social sciences. For an introduction to the concept of 'Imaginary', see: A. Johnston, 'Jacques Lacan', E. N. Zalta (ed.), *The Stanford Encyclopedia of Philosophy*, 2013, revised 2018, https://plato.stanford.edu/entries/lacan/.

9 C. Tiebout, 'A Pure Theory of Local Expenditure' [1956] 64 (5) *Journal of Political Economy* 416–24.

to an increase in quality of the product (coined by the familiar expression: 'race to the top'). Regulatory competition should thus foster innovative, efficient and fair legal systems.

The idea of regulatory competition has largely been conceived and developed in federal systems: to put it short, in federal systems (and the literature on regulatory competition mainly comes from the US), regulatory competition is considered as a means to promote convergence of legal systems while respecting the principle of subsidiarity. Instead of enacting cumbersome federal rules, sometimes ill-informed of local realities, the federal power can let competition play among the federal entities.[10] The best legal system among them will attract businesses and consumers. Other legal systems are expected to adapt and therefore converge with the most attractive system. In the end, common standards should be enacted in the absence of top-down federal intervention.[11] Therefore, regulatory competition is often discussed in governance literature as an alternative to top-down regulation.[12]

The positive effects of regulatory competition (just like the positive effects of economic competition) rest on a series of prerequisites.[13] First, competition can only take place if the market is open and diverse. For legal products, an open market is a market where individuals can 'vote with their feet'.[14] Choosing among legal systems means that parties/consumers/businesses need to be able to (i) identify their best interest and (ii) 'delocalise', i.e. leave one legal system in favour of another system that is more attractive. Delocalisation can happen physically or virtually. In the EU for instance, individuals can indeed move from one legal system to the other and submit themselves to a new legal system when exercising their right to establishment, or circulation of citizens.[15] Parties can also

10 Showing that competition is used for 'discovering facts which, if procedure did not exist, would remain unknown or at least not be used' and that therefore 'competition can only be justified by our not knowing the essential circumstances that determine the behavior of the competitors': F.A. Hayek, 'Competition as a Discovery Procedure' [2002] 5 *The Quarterly Journal of Austrian Economics* 9–23 (spec. 9; translation of the famous lecture delivered by Hayek in 1968: 'Der Wettbewerb als Entdeckungsverfahren', Institut für Weltwirtschaft an der Universität Kiel, Kieler Vorträge N° 56).

11 A. Ogus, 'Competition between National Legal Systems: A Contribution of Economic Analysis to Comparative Law' [1999] 48 *The International and Comparative Law Quarterly* 405.

12 R. Van den Bergh, 'Regulatory Competition or Harmonization of Laws? Guidelines for the European Regulator' in A. Marciano and J.M. Josselin (eds), *The Economics of Harmonizing European Law*, Edward Elgar Publishing 2002, p. 27 (considering that a presumption in favour of regulatory competition derives from the EU principle of subsidiarity and trying to frame the conditions for a favourable functioning of normative competition).

13 On this point see: G. Rühl, 'Regulatory Competition in Contract law: Empirical Evidence and Normative Implications' [2013] 9 *European Review of Contract law* 61–89.

14 The expression is often attributed to Charles Tiebout. On this expression see: I. Somin, 'Foot Voting, Federalism, and Political Freedom' in J.E. Fleming and J.T. Levy (eds), *Federalism and Subsidiarity*, New York University Press 2014, pp. 83–119 (the author is using this expression in a different context and refers to the possibility to choose a political regime, more than a substantive law regime).

15 Art. 49 TFEU (establishment), Art. 21 TFEU (circulation of citizens).

choose to localise their litigation in front of the court of a Member State that has no or few contacts with the situation.[16] As private international law specialists know well, 'choosing' a legal system and placing a situation under the authority of a legal system can also happen virtually, without any geographical displacement by way of a choice of law clause.[17] Arbitration produces a delocalization that can be physical and virtual.

Second, regulatory competition takes actors who are willing to play the game. On the one hand, private parties should clearly identify the quality of legal systems as a strong incentive, justifying the delocalisation of their business or the choice of a particular system. On the other hand, legal systems should be willing to adapt in order to respond to the parties' expectations. The reunion of these two conditions (concerning the demand side and the supply side) need to be confirmed for a pure competition to occur. Many scholars doubt that they ever are.[18] For instance, the responsivity of States might depend on the field of law involved: where an incentive exists for adapting corporate law, nothing ensures that such incentive exists for States to adapt their contract law or even their procedural law.[19] In addition, the game can only happen as far as parties (i) are properly informed of the respective qualities of the various legal systems they wish to take into consideration and (ii) exercise a choice based on this criteria rather than on other considerations such as familiarity.[20] Information deficit is often a weak point of regulatory competition theories.

2.2. DIFFERENT FIGURES OF REGULATORY COMPETITION

The concept of regulatory competition is discussed under many different headings in the literature, which all play a role in the EU: competition can be described

16 Art. 25 Regulation 1215/2012 requires no connection with the Member State whose court has been chosen.

17 See among others G. Rühl, 'Party Autonomy in the Private International Law of Contracts: Transatlantic Convergence and Economic Efficiency' in E. Gottschalk, R. Michaels, G. Rühl and J. von Hein (eds), *Conflict of Laws in a Globalized World*, CUP 2007, pp. 153–83.

18 Warning against the simplicity of scholarly approach of normative competition, especially in regard of the fact that the prerequisites of a positive normative competition are never met in practice, see: J.P. Trachtman, 'Regulatory Competition and Regulatory Jurisdiction' [2000] 3 *Journal of International Economic Law* 331–48.

19 See G. Rühl, above n. 13, 71, explaining that States need an incentive to adapt their laws and that in the field of corporate law, such an incentive would be provided by franchise tax and registration fees, where in contract law, only the tax revenue resulting from local lawyers' work would provide a moderate incentive. See also the literature cited below n. 23.

20 Empirical studies tend to show that businesses actually choose the applicable law to their contract for mixed reasons relating to the quality and the familiarity of the chosen legal system. See the studies cited by: G. Rühl, above n. 13, 66–70. Among those studies, see in particular: S. Vogenauer and C. Hodges, 'Civil Justice Systems in Europe: Implications for Choice of Forum and Choice of Contract Law – A Business Survey' <www.fondation-droitcontinental.org/fr/wp-content/uploads/2013/12/oxford_civil_justice_survey_-_summary_of_results_final.pdf>.

as a positive or negative competition, regulatory competition is sometimes distinguished from regulatory arbitrage, and of course regulatory competition can take place at the substantive and/or procedural level.

The question whether regulatory competition fosters *race to the top* (positive effects) or *race to the bottom* (negative effects or the so-called Delaware effect) is debated and certainly deserves nuanced answers depending on the field of law and the region of the world involved. In theory (as in pure economic theory), competition necessarily increases the quality of products and the same is thought to be true for legal products. However, as the prerequisites of competition are rarely met and because the motivations to select a product or legal system do not systematically match the general interest, competition can also lead to deregulation. In any case, regulatory competition is regarded as creating *externalities*, i.e. costs supported by third parties or legal systems. The classical example is the following: one State, in order to attract businesses, lowers its environmental protection standards. Even if they do not adapt in a race to the bottom, neighbouring States (and their citizens) will endure costs and disadvantages due to the lower environmental standards of the first State.[21]

The latter example also enables us to identify the narrow distinction between *regulatory competition* and *regulatory arbitrage*. Regulatory competition can be said to take place when actors on both sides are playing the game: on the demand side, parties select legal systems according to their best interest and based on perfectly informed inquiries; on the supply side, States or legal systems respond to parties' expectations by adapting their legal apparatus (for better or for worse, since competition can be positive or negative). Thus, before the game actually generates competition between States or legal systems, the first part of the process is one of regulatory arbitrage where parties assess different legal systems and eventually decide to localise or delocalise their transactions or businesses in one of them in order to maximise their benefit.[22] Regulatory arbitrage could be described as the phase where parties put systems into competition. Regulatory arbitrage does not necessarily produce modifications of legal regimes when States (or legal systems) refuse to adapt. As illustrated by the example relating to environmental standards, the absence of response by legal systems or States does not imply that regulatory arbitrage is without consequence. Regulatory arbitrage can create externalities, because industries will localise on the territory of the State with lower standards, generating a loss of revenue for the State of their former localisation (loss of jobs and

---

21 On issues relating to the race to the top and to the bottom and externalities, see: H. Muir Watt, 'Aspects économiques du droit international privé – Réflexions sur l'impact de la globalisation économique sur les fondements des conflits de lois et des conflits de juridictions' [2004] 307 *Recueil des cours* 26.

22 The figure of regulatory arbitrage (a procedural and substantive form of forum shopping) is detailed by Annelise Riles for financial transactions: A. Riles, 'Managing Regulatory Arbitrage: A Conflict of Laws Approach' [2014] 47 *Cornell International Law Journal* 63–119.

tax revenues). Externalities can also be felt by the society at large because companies, due to their egoist, profit-driven choices, actually support policies contrary to the general interest.

Regulatory competition has mainly been addressed as a way to increase the quality of a legal system's *substantive* norms or political infrastructure. Posner and Landes' 1979 piece dealing with competition among judicial/procedural systems thus opened up new avenues. The two levels of regulatory competition can, to a certain extent, be distinguished. On the one hand, normative competition in regard to substantive law can take place in the absence of a regulatory competition as to procedural facilities. This would happen for instance if a State or federal entity were lowering the minimum capital for setting up a corporation. On the other hand, regulatory competition can focus exclusively on procedural facilities. This is illustrated by the new trend in continental Europe for setting up courts and procedures taking place in English. In practice however, the two forms of regulatory competition are often intertwined. For a start, regulatory competition in the field of civil procedure also needs an attractive legal system in terms of substantive law. For practical reasons (saving costs and time), parties may indeed tend to choose the *lex fori*. In addition, escaping from the legal system judged inefficient is often a choice made in respect of substantive law: delocalising a litigation to the court of another State is often a way to prevent the application of a specific substantive law, among other overriding mandatory rules. As a result, playing the regulatory competition game at the judicial/procedural level will probably foster regulatory competition at the substantial level. For these reasons, the second part of this chapter will not systematically distinguish between the two levels of regulatory competition.

To finalise this brief presentation, two features of regulatory competition need to be stressed. Firstly, the reality of regulatory competition and its extent, even in transnational settings, is debated.[23] Secondly, regulatory competition at a transnational level rests on a conflict of laws prerequisite: party autonomy in its choice of law and choice of forum dimension, allowing for regulatory arbitrage.[24] Conflict of laws literature has promptly identified the connection between party autonomy and regulatory competition.[25]

---

23 S. Vogenauer, 'Regulatory Competition through Choice of Contract Law and Choice of Forum in Europe: Theory and Evidence' [2013] 1 *European Review of Private Law* 13–78; see also J.P. Trachtman, above n. 18.

24 For a more detailed account and a critique, see: S. Francq, 'Party Autonomy and Regulation – Public Interests in Private International Law' [2016] 59 *Japanese Yearbook of International Law* 251–99.

25 Beyond the literature already cited, see for some of the major pieces in English and French: E. O'Hara and L. Ribstein, 'From Politics to Efficiency in Choice of Law' [2000] 67 *University of Chicago Law Review* 1151; A. Guzman, 'Choice of Law: New Foundations' [2002] 90 *Georgetown Law Journal* 883; G. Rühl, 'Methods and Approaches in Choice of Law: An Economic Perspective' [2007] 24 *Berkeley Journal of International Law* 801;

3. REGULATORY COMPETITION AS A REALITY

The debate concerning the reality of regulatory competition turns around whether the prerequisites of regulatory competition are ever fulfilled in practice. For instance, the proper information of the parties about various legal systems is often questioned. And obviously measuring and tracing the State responsivity to businesses' and individuals' potential expectations is a difficult task. Yet the quotes cited in the beginning of this paper reveal at least the existence of a discourse on regulatory competition affecting the judicial systems of EU Member States. It is therefore worth questioning whether the EU system does indeed offer the chances for judicial regulatory competition to take place and whether, and how, such competition actually takes place. I identify here two interrelated occurrences of regulatory competition concerning judicial systems of Member States, leaving other examples aside. The choice made among various manifestations of regulatory competition is dictated by recent events: the anniversary of the Brussels Convention and the system it put into place (3.1.) as much as its implications for Brexit (4); and the Belgian project for a business court working in English, the Brussels International Business Court (3.2.).

3.1. THE EU FURTHERS REGULATORY COMPETITION: A SYSTEM OF PARTY AUTONOMY ... AND DEREGULATION?

In some ways, the EU can be seen as having organised a system of regulatory competition among legal and judicial systems of the Member States or at least a system of regulatory arbitrage. In the area of civil justice, this is obviously related to the extensive use of party autonomy.[26] Party autonomy is regarded as one (if not *the*) cornerstone of the EU conflict of laws system.[27] The EU conflict of laws

J. Basedow and T. Kono (eds), *An Economic Analysis of Private International Law*, Mohr Siebeck 2006.

26 For considerations on regulatory competition in the internal market, see for instance: S. Deakin, 'Regulatory Competition after Laval' [2007–2008] 10 *Cambridge Yearbook of European Legal Studies* 581; 'Legal Diversity and Regulatory Competition: Which Model for Europe?' [2006] 12 *European Law Review* 440. See also: R. Van den Bergh, above n. 12.

27 See Recital 11 Regulation Rome I (Regulation 593/2008 of 17 June 2008 on the law applicable to contractual obligations [2008] OJ L177/6), Recital 19 Regulation Brussels I Recast (above n. 1). The EU conflict of laws system is of course larger than the Regulations on private international law and includes many conflict rules dispersed implicitly or explicitly in substantive secondary law, as well as ECJ case law. The importance of party autonomy differs depending on the type of act at stake. I simplify by referring only to EU Regulations on conflict of laws where party autonomy has taken a very important role, also in family matters (see for instance: Art. 4 and Recital 19 of Regulation 4/2009 of 18 December 2008 on jurisdiction, applicable law, recognition and enforcement of decisions and cooperation in matters relating to maintenance obligations [2009] OJ L7/1; Art. 5 and Recitals 15–20 of Regulation 1259/2010 implementing

discourse equates party autonomy and legal certainty or previsibility, an equation that can be questionable for several reasons, among which the fact that legal certainty and previsibility are very evasive notions.[28]

The situation of an exclusive dealer established in Belgium helps to easily grasp the system and its potential for regulatory competition at the judicial and substantive level. The classic case submitted to students in a PIL law course in Belgium is the following: an agreement of exclusive commercial concession is concluded with an exclusive dealer established in Belgium and later unilaterally terminated by the principal. The exclusive dealer wants to benefit from the generous provisions of the Belgian Code for Economic Law in terms of compensation.[29] The Code for Economic Law states that the exclusive dealer established in Belgium can in any case seize a Belgian tribunal which has to apply Belgian law.[30] To put things in a rather blunt light, the dealer is better off if the contract contains a jurisdiction clause in favour of third State courts rather than in favour of the court of another Member State.

If the choice of court designates for instance the courts of New York State and the principal is established in the US[31], the clause is probably not regulated by the EU system (i.e. Brussels I Recast) and not (yet) by the 2005 Hague Convention.[32] If the dealer seizes a Belgian tribunal and the principal opposes the jurisdiction clause, the choice of court will be assessed under Article 7 of the Belgian PIL Code. Confirming the long-standing case law of the Belgian Cour de Cassation, the provision submits the admissibility of the choice of court agreement to the *lex fori*.[33] Since the provisions of the Code for Economic law on unilateral termination

enhanced cooperation in the area of the law applicable to divorce and legal separation [2010] OJ L343/10). For an example of a case where party autonomy might result from case law in status matters see: ECJ, Case C-148/2, *Carlos Garcia Avello v. Belgian State*, ECLI:EU:C:2003:539.

28 On this point see: S. Francq, 'Le droit international privé européen, entre confiance mutuelle et sécurité juridique (les limites de l'imaginaire européen)' forthcoming in *Travaux du comité français de droit international privé 2017–2019*, Pédone.

29 See Title III, Art. X.35 and ff of the former law of 27 July 1961 on the unilateral termination of exclusive dealership agreement concluded for an undetermined duration, now inserted in the Code for Economic Law.

30 Art. X.39 of the Belgian Code for Economic Law.

31 Art. 25 Brussels I Recast applies to agreements in favour of the courts of a Member State. It is debated whether the Regulation applies to a situation where the choice of court provision designates the tribunal of a third State and the defendant is domiciled in the EU: on this point, comp. ECJ, Opinion 1/03, ECLI:EU:C:2006:81, para. 153 and ECJ, Case C-543/10, *Refcomp SA v. Axa*, ECLI:EU:C:2013:62, para. 17. On this controversy see: S. Francq, 'La refonte du Règlement Bruxelles I – Champ d'application et compétence' [2013] 5 *Revue de droit commercial belge* 307–33 and before the Recast, about the case *Owusu*: R. Fentiman, 'Civil Jurisdiction and Third States: *Owusu* and After' [2006] *Common Market Law Review (CMLR)* 705.

32 The Hague Convention of 30 June 2005 on Choice of Court Agreements has been signed by the United States but not ratified yet by this country. The Convention applies only to a jurisdiction clause in favour of the tribunal of a contracting State (Art. 3).

33 Under Art. 7 Belgian Code of PIL, the parties can formulate a choice of jurisdiction clause only in a matter where they freely dispose of their rights under Belgian law ('dans une matière où

of exclusive concessions apply to the situation and give the dealer the unconditional right to seize a Belgian tribunal, the jurisdiction clause will be set aside and the Belgian tribunal will accept its jurisdiction.[34] At the applicable law stage, if a choice of law clause designates the law of another country, the chosen law will be applied by the Belgian tribunal under Article 3 Regulation Rome I and the specific provision of the Belgian Code for Economic law will apply as overriding mandatory rules of the *lex fori* under Article 9(2) Regulation Rome I. The solution would in essence be the same if the parties had entered into an arbitration agreement.

In contrast, if the jurisdiction clause designates courts of another Member State, for instance London courts (still a Member State at the time of writing but not for long!), Article 25 Regulation Brussels I Recast applies and nothing enables the Belgian judge to set this clause aside as long as the basic conditions provided by Article 25 Regulation Brussels I Recast are fulfilled. The UK judge will duly respect the choice of law clause under Article 3 Regulation Rome I and will most probably apply a law other than Belgian law. In order to consider the application of the Belgian overriding mandatory rule, the UK court would have to use Article 9(3) Regulation Rome I. Even if Belgian law qualifies as the law of the place of performance of the contract, it is uncertain whether the Belgian law providing damages in case of unilateral termination of the contract renders the 'performance of the contract unlawful' according to the terms of Article 9(3) Regulation Rome I.[35]

EU law thus organises a system favourable to party autonomy based on the triangle formed by three provisions: Article 25 Brussels I Recast, Article 3 and Article 9(3) Regulation Rome I. These provisions, in their current formulation, render possible for the parties to circumvent national overriding mandatory rules.[36] Parties can 'delocalise' their relationship via jurisdiction and choice of law clauses and opt for a legal and judicial system with little or no contact to the situation. Doing so, they can opt out of important policies set in overriding mandatory rules of one Member State. The ability to opt out of a legal system and opt in favour of a legal system are topical prerequisites for regulatory competition.

---

elles disposent librement de leurs droits en vertu du droit belge'). The choice also needs to be validly concluded. The validity is assessed under the law applicable to the agreement, i.e. often the law applicable to the contract itself. See F. Rigaux and M. Fallon, *Droit international privé*, 3rd ed., Larcier 2005, pp. 777–81, no. 14.16–14.18.

34 This does not mean that in Belgium jurisdiction clauses designating third State tribunals and arbitration agreements are automatically set aside: this happens only when an overriding mandatory rule applies to the case and the chosen court or arbitration tribunal would not ensure an equivalent protection to the person protected by that law. See for more details: F. Rigaux and M. Fallon, above n. 33, p. 781, no. 14.18 and recently: Cass. (Belgium), 14 Octobre 2010, *Sebastian International*, N° RG C.08.0503.N; Cass. (Belgium), 3 Novembre 2011, *Air Transat*, N° RG C.10.0613.N.

35 One could argue that the specific termination modalities of the contract are invalid under Belgian law.

36 Part of the phenomenon is caused by the current formulation of Art. 9(3) Regulation Rome I as illustrated in the case *Nikiforidis*: ECJ, Case C-135/15, *Republik Griechenland v. Grigorios Nikifordis*, ECLI:EU:C:2016:774.

These prerequisites are materialised by the facilities regarding choice of jurisdiction and the recognition of judgement. Regulatory arbitrage can thus take place via the EU judicial system and has a direct impact on the effectiveness of substantive policies of Member States. One can therefore wonder whether such competition or regulatory arbitrage generates positive or negative effects.

To the knowledge of the author, no study has clearly demonstrated the existence of a Delaware effect (or race to the bottom) regarding commercial and contractual matters in the EU.[37] And indeed the Belgian legislator has maintained its protective policy in favour of exclusive dealers established in Belgium ever since it was first enacted in 1961. This constant policy could indicate that the 'supply side' is not playing the game of regulatory competition.

The system however generates some externalities, here in the form of regulatory gaps. Belgian law has a clear objective of protection of the weaker party supported by the economic rationality of a small country where more dealers are established than large companies or holders of world-wide brands. This policy is rendered ineffective by EU provisions relating to choice of court agreements designating Member State courts and provisions on choice of law and on overriding mandatory rules.[38] When the choice of court agreement designates the judicial system of a *third* State, the Belgian legislator is able to maintain the effectiveness of its protection system via Article 7 Code of PIL and Article X.39 Code for Economic Law. The externalities created by the regulatory competition established by the EU judicial system take place at two levels. First, the weaker party (here the dealer) is deprived of the protection intended by the Belgian legal system and will bear the costs generated by a unilateral termination of the contract where the Belgian system tends to place those costs on the shoulders of the principal. Second, in situations where the dealer is unable to face those costs and eventually becomes insolvent, suppliers and employees of the dealer, and eventually the Belgian social security system, will support extra costs. To sum up, two lessons can be learned from this example.

The first lesson is that the EU, as the system currently stands, does (involuntarily?) instigate regulatory competition or at least regulatory arbitrage at the judicial and substantive level, by offering the conditions for the parties to opt out of the legal system of one Member State and opt in favour of the legal system of another Member State, thereby circumventing overriding mandatory rules of the first State.

---

37 Nor is there evidence of a strong race to the top effect. In 2013, after reviewing all the important studies available, Stefan Vogenauer concluded: '... there is no indication whatsoever of European legislatures and courts actually improving their "products" ... There is no race to the top. The good news is that there is no race to the bottom either. In fact, there is no race at all.' (S. Vogenauer, above n. 23, 74, 75, see 35–74 for a review of studies and practice). The answer would need to be more nuanced in respect of tax or corporation law (*ibid.* n. 23, 16–26).

38 The phenomenon, rendered even more acute in France due to the case law of the Cour de Cassation (Cass. civ., 22 Octobre 2008, *Monster Cable*, n° 1003: considering that the existence of French overriding mandatory rules is not a valid reason for refusing to give effect to jurisdiction agreement designating a third State tribunal), has been coined as one of 'imperativité désactivée': D. Bureau and H. Muir Watt, 'L'impérativité désactivée' [2009] *Revue critique de droit international privé* 1–23.

The second lesson is that the benefit of such regulatory competition or regulatory arbitrage is unclear. Whether the Member States or the parties benefit from this situation seems doubtful. Indeed, in the chosen case, one party will benefit from the system at the cost of the other one. This observation points to one of the ambiguities of the game of regulatory competition in private law: the parties, identified as one player of the game (the demand side), do not have converging interests, where the theory of regulatory competition rests on the idea that the parties will select a system according to their best (common) interest.[39]

3.2. MEMBER STATES PLAY THE GAME OF REGULATORY COMPETITION… FOR UNCLEAR REASONS

3.2.1. *Regulatory competition at civil procedure level: costs and benefits*

In an excellent paper published in 2014, Xandra Krämer analyses how Member States actually engage in various forms of civil justice competition. After stressing that some Member States have no discussion about civil justice attractiveness (which includes Belgium), she describes how the Netherlands reformed its civil justice system to render it more attractive. She points in particular to several strategies such as: (i) the shortening of the duration of litigations; (ii) the possibility to deliver provisional measures with an extraterritorial effect (the famous 'kort geding' used in the 90s in patent litigation); (iii) the development, earlier than most other Member States, of specific legislation on collective redress ('Wet Collectieve Afwikkeling van Massaschade') which attracted important litigations in the Netherlands and the modernisation of the law on arbitration; and (iv) last but not least, the plan for an international commercial court functioning in English, the Netherlands Commercial Court. The latter project is now almost completed.[40] And of course, after Krämer's publication, Belgium joined the club of countries attempting to attract international litigations.[41]

---

39 F. Parisi and L. Ribstein, 'Choice of Law' in P. Newman (ed), *The New Palgrave Dictionary of Economics and the Law*, vol. I, Macmillan 1998, p. 236 (supporting the idea that parties will in fact choose the system that maximises their common welfare).

40 The law was adopted by the House of Representatives on 8.03.2018 and is now in the Senate (where the Minister of Justice has already answered the questions), <www.eerstekamer.nl/wetsvoorstel/34761_engelstalige_rechtspraak>.

41 See for Belgium the Draft Law on a Brussels International Business Court (submitted to the Chamber of Representatives on 15.05.2018; Doc. 54–3072/001, <www.lachambre.be/FLWB/PDF/54/3072/54K3072001.pdf>. See the comments of Geert Van Calster submitted to the parliament: <https://gavclaw.files.wordpress.com/2018/07/bibc-hoorzitting-parlement-10-juli-2018-geert-van-calster.pdf> and the thoughtful analysis of Marc Fallon ('L'argumentaire de flexibilité et de mobilité internationales dans les projets de lois sur la BIBC et le code des sociétes', forthcoming RDC/TBH 2019).

On whether the game is played with success in general, and in the Netherlands in particular, Krämer brings nuances. On the one hand, she underlines the existence of rankings or systems of assessment where the quality of justice is an important factor and stresses that efforts to render the justice system more efficient and coherent in the Netherlands have been successful.[42] In particular, the shortening of litigation duration seems to alleviate the justice costs for public finances. On the other hand, Krämer cites studies challenging the idea that the establishment of specific business courts actually attracts litigation and investments and underlines how the expediency of justice does not necessarily equate with the quality of justice.[43]

The article of Krämer points to one important aspect of civil justice competition: the issue of cost and benefit. The idea of competition among legal and justice systems is based on economic incentives. States are said to enter into competition in order to attract businesses and investors and benefit from the establishment of these new corporations in the form of taxes, new jobs and other economic benefits. Indeed, the local legal market (in short, the local bar) seems to benefit from the efforts developed by States in favour of civil justice competition and public finances gain from a cost reduction due to the shortening of procedures. But nothing actually proves that society generally speaking or the State itself receives the financial benefit from the game, especially when competition is played at the procedural level.[44] This problem has been tackled by Jens Dammann and Henry Hansmann.[45]

According to these scholars, international and domestic litigation between merchants should be entitled to forum shopping in order to select the most efficient judicial system and escape from incompetent or inefficient home courts. Interestingly, one of the core problems is to isolate the incentive that would motivate States and governments to open their (efficient) court system to foreign litigation (and sometimes to litigation which has no connection whatsoever with their territory).[46] They identify the creation of business for the local bar as one

---

42 X. Krämer, above n. 6, 20–21, 27–28. Among the 'ranking' systems, the EU Justice Scoreboard is the most directly related to the quality of justice and focused on the EU (the 2018 edition is available here: <https://ec.europa.eu/info/policies/justice-and-fundamental-rights/effective-justice/eu-justice-scoreboard_en>).

43 X. Krämer, above n. 6, 35 (citing a manifesto published by Dutch judges in 2012 worrying that the pressure to meet 'targets' would damage the quality of case law); X. Krämer (above n. 6, 30) is also citing an interesting study by J.F. Coyle: J.F. Coyle, 'Business Courts and Interstate Competition' [2012] 53 *William and Mary Law Review* 1915–1983 (the study has been conducted in a US context where the language is not a factor; the author concludes 'that business courts are unlikely to attract business to a jurisdiction under any circumstances and are unlikely, as currently comprised, to attract incorporation business. It also suggested that while these courts can attract – and have attracted – litigation business to the jurisdiction that creates them, there are limits on the potential scope of such diversion', p. 1983).

44 See J.F. Coyle, above n. 43. Comp. X. Krämer, above n. 6, 30, stressing the reduction of legal costs due to the shortening of litigation duration.

45 J. Dammann and H. Hansmann, above n. 4.

46 *Ibid.*, 56 and ff.

incentive, affected however by important drawbacks.[47] Forcing foreign litigants to use local lawyers, where they might desire to work with their usual lawyers, would diminish the attractiveness of the system, as well as deprive those systems of any incentive to open up the bar to foreign lawyers and invest in efficient infrastructure and technologies reducing the need for the parties to travel and for the lawyer to be physically present.[48] Besides, law firms established in competitive States would capture the development of expertise at the disadvantage of those practicing in less developed countries. To the points brought up by Dammann and Hansmann, one could add that the benefit attributed to the local bar and the corresponding tax revenue do not automatically cover the costs endured by the State for opening up its court system and rendering it competitive.

Dammann and Hansmann eventually propose another incentive for civil justice competition: according to them, States should simply increase court fees for foreign litigation in a way that would not only cover the cost of the litigation, but also 'generate a positive return for the State'.[49] The increase of court fees is, according to them, the only way to cover the extra costs endured by a State when deploying strategies in order to render its judicial systems attractive on an international scale.

In the EU (and as far as EU citizens are concerned), a discrimination in court fees on the basis of the origin of litigants would seem directly contrary to Article 18 TFEU when imposed on other EU citizens.[50] Higher court fees for specific types of procedure would a priori be acceptable only if applied as well to the citizens of the forum.

3.2.2. *The BIBC & co: some considerations from the point of view of regulatory competition theory*

The recently proposed law establishing the Brussels International Business Court (the so-called BIBC), and similar projects in other EU Member States, follow the trend of rendering the justice system attractive for international litigations, in an attempt to capture post-Brexit litigation or even to become the new Singapore or

47 *Ibid.*, 57.

48 *Ibid.*, 58.

49 *Ibid.*, 4, 59–61 (citation p. 61).

50 See by analogy the cases on the 'cautio judicatum solvi': ECJ, Case C43/95, *Data Delecta and Forsberg*, ECLI:EU:C:1996:357 paras. 17, 22; ECJ, Case C323/95, *Hayes*, ECLI:EU:C:1997:169, para. 19; ECJ, Case C-291/09, *Guarnieri*, ECLI:EU:C:2011:217, paras. 19–20 (a Monegasque company cannot claim the benefit of Art. 18 TFEU and can thus be submitted to the security). Dammann and Hansmann do not cite the case on 'cautio judicatum solvi' but cases on discriminatory fees for access to education. They conclude that higher court fees have few chances to be accepted by the ECJ and that the only way to implement them would be via federal (EU) legislation. This hypothesis seems unlikely: not only would EU competence for regulating court fees be questionable, but also such a measure would make little sense in regard of Art. 18 TFEU and in terms of support from the civil society.

London for international business.[51] The way in which States rival with superlatives to describe the efficiency of their justice system and their existing or potential business courts, with almost identical vocabulary describing the perfect location, the perfect infrastructure and the high quality of their world-class judges, indicate that they have identified (existing or chimeric) financial benefits into opening up their court system to foreign litigation.[52] In Belgium in particular, the constitution of the BIBC rests on a number of strategies considered apt to render the new Belgian court attractive, among which: the use of English for the entire procedure and the judgement, the specific procedure inspired by the UNCITRAL model law on international commercial arbitration[53], the absence of an appeal proceeding and the mixed composition of the court (regular judges and ad hoc judges).

The Belgian project deserves serious consideration in many respects. The creation of a court functioning in English certainly is the most natural development in a country with a multilingual tradition localized at the heart of Europe. From the point of view of regulatory competition, two points however seem critical.

First, regulatory competition (at the procedural or substantive level) is meant to improve the quality of a legal system. In the case of the BIBC, the general improvement of the legal system will be difficult to achieve. In order to justify in constitutional terms, the establishment of a tribunal working in a language different from the official languages recognised in the Belgian Constitution, the Belgian legislator needs to prove that the English language is imposed by 'the necessities of the service or the general interest'.[54] The Conseil d'Etat was very clear on the need to single out a specific category of litigation for which the use of

---

51 X. Krämer, 'The Domino Effect of International Commercial Courts in Europe – Who's Next?' [2018] *Conflict of Laws* <http://conflictoflaws.net/2018/the-domino-effect-of-international-commercial-courts-in-europe-whos-next/>. On the German situation, see M. Weller, 'The Justice Initiative Frankfurt am Main – Translation of the Position Paper of B. Hess, T. Pfeiffer, Ch. Duve and R. Poseck' [2017] *Conflict of Laws* <http://conflictoflaws.net/2017/the-justice-initiative-frankfurt-am-main-2017-law-made-in-frankfurt/>. On the Paris International Commercial Courts: <www.cours-appel.justice.fr/paris/presentation-des-chambres-commerciales-internationales-de-paris-ccip>. See previously on the 'battle of the brochures' (i.e. a series of brochures made by Ministries for Justice of several EU Member States advertising the quality of their legal system): G. Rühl, above n. 13, 71; S. Vogenauer, above n. 23, 30–35.

52 Compare the video made to describe the Singapore International Commercial Court <https://youtu.be/Ab2_iQrGvw8> and the webpage of the Netherlands Commercial Court <www.rechtspraak.nl/English/NCC>. About the battle of the brochures, Stefan Vogenauer rightly underlines: 'None of these brochures is notable for its subtlety and impartiality' (S. Vogenauer, above n. 23, 33).

53 Adopted on 21.06.1985, amended in 2006: <www.uncitral.org/pdf/english/texts/arbitration/ml-arb/07-86998_Ebook.pdf>.

54 The Conseil d'Etat had stressed that Belgian public authorities had to function in the Belgian official languages except where 'the necessities of the service or public interest imposed the use of another language' (the translation is ours). See Opinion of the Conseil d'Etat, N° 62.411/2/AG, 2.03.2018, paras. 17–21 (published together with the Draft Law, above n. 41, pp. 94 ff, pp. 107–08).

English could be objectively justified in front of a Belgian court.[55] Therefore, the competence of the future BIBC is limited to one category of situations for which the need to use English can be objectively established: international litigations between enterprises where objective elements show that a language different from the official languages of Belgium has been regularly used by the parties.[56] As this type of situation is regarded as specific and placed in a different category than other usual commercial relations, the drafters of the project consider that the procedural innovations put in place for the functioning of the BIBC should not be rendered available to litigations which have no access to the BIBC.[57] These two situations are, according to the drafters of the law, objectively different and should thus receive a different treatment. Confusing litigation pending in front of the usual Belgian commercial courts and those pending in front of the BIBC concerning procedural issues would, according to them, cancel out the only reason justifying the existence of the BIBC as a tribunal functioning in English.[58] The Conseil d'Etat in contrast had requested the procedural advantages available in front of the BIBC to be accessible in front of other Belgian commercial courts, at least where seized with international situations.[59] The debate between the Conseil d'Etat and the drafters of the project points at the difficulty of identifying a category of 'international commerce' in objective terms and justifying how far this category requires (objectively again) a specific treatment: should the specific treatment exist only in terms of language? Or also in respect of the procedure? Most importantly from a perspective of regulatory competition, the discussion reveals that the procedural innovations resulting from the competitive effort made by the Belgian government will probably not percolate beyond the BIBC, a jurisdiction reserved for parties able to pay much higher court fees.[60] In other

55 See Opinion of the Conseil d'Etat, above n. 54, paras. 22–27.

56 Art. 18 of the Draft Law on the BIBC. The current drafting of this provision raises several issues of interpretation. One issue is whether the provision actually reflects the observations of the Conseil d'Etat. The Conseil d'Etat required that 'enough objective elements' show that 'the *English* language' was used by the parties (Opinion of the Conseil d'Etat, above n. 54, para. 27, emphasis added), where the draft provision refers to 'another language than French, Dutch or German'. More generally, as it is currently formulated, Art. 18 of the BIBC project does not prevent parties to a purely internal situation, who chose a foreign law (as permitted under Art. 3 Rome I Regulation) and used English in their correspondence (as can be objectively convenient between Dutch-speaking and French-speaking parties) to have access to the BIBC. In contrast, the Conseil d'Etat had stressed the need to exclude purely domestic situations from the BIBC jurisdiction (Opinion of the Conseil d'Etat, above n. 54, para. 23).

57 See the General Explanatory Statement in the Draft Law, above n. 41, p. 7.

58 *Ibid.*, pp. 7–8.

59 Opinion of the Conseil d'Etat, above n. 54, paras. 30–31, considering that the procedural 'advantages' available in front of the BIBC should be rendered available in front of other commercial courts seized with international litigations.

60 This observation confirms the finding of J.F. Coyle, above n. 43. The Conseil d'Etat stresses that in international situations, the difference between litigation going to the BIBC and other international litigation submitted to the usual Belgian jurisdiction will result from financial considerations: Opinion of the Conseil d'Etat, above n. 54, para. 31.

words, where regulatory competition theory counts on the 'laboratory' effect for the development of modern, innovative and efficient legislation, the Belgian project of BIBC shows that these improvements can be restricted in scope and beyond the reach of a large part of the population. Here indeed, extending on the long run the benefit of the new procedural advantages to all commercial litigation could be perceived as contradicting the justification put forward by the government when it first proposed the creation of the BIBC.

Second, regulatory competition theory teaches us that States need financial incentives to foster attractive, yet costly, legal innovations. In the case of the BIBC, it is probably too early to identify and measure the *potential financial benefits*, beyond those expected for a portion of the local bar. The Explanatory Statement of the draft legislation submitted to the Parliament is not very clear on this point beyond a general statement about 'litigations escaping' from the Belgian court system for language reasons.[61] The official justification is formulated in terms relating more to the service provided to international business actors established in Belgium, than to the possibility to attract new investments.[62] In contrast, the *issue of the costs* endured by the Belgian State and the Belgian judicial system to create and support this new tribunal has been addressed up front. The costs relating to this new tribunal include an additional remuneration for the presidents (part of the judiciary) and the members of the Registry proving a good command of English, as well as travel costs, hotel costs and a flat rate remuneration per case for the ad hoc judges (experts in international commercial law and non-members of the judiciary).[63] The new tribunal should be self-supported.[64] Following Dammann and Hansmann's insight, the drafters of the law propose that parties willing to have access to the BIBC should pay high court fees to finance all the expenditure related to the tribunal.[65] The project would thus present no financial burden on the Belgian State and produce only a positive impact in terms of economic development.[66] Infrastructure costs however do not

61 See General Explanatory Statement in the Draft Law, above n. 41, p. 5 and the Executive Summary p. 2; the impact analysis inserted in the Draft Law, pp. 88–93 announces 'economic impacts' (p. 90).

62 *Ibid.* See p. 93 of the impact analysis announcing a positive impact for companies which will eventually have at disposal an adapted procedure and tribunal.

63 Art. 11, 12, 13 and 14 of the Draft Law, above n. 41, pp. 153–54 and the explanation of every provision, pp. 21–22.

64 See the General Explanatory Statement in the Draft Law, above n. 41, p. 12.

65 Art. 37 of the Draft Law, above n. 41, p. 162 and the specific explanation of the provisions, pp. 32–35. The drafters provide an estimation of the court fees for the total amount of EUR 20,000 per case covering all the costs (additional remuneration for the members of the Judiciary and of the Registry, remuneration of ad hoc judges – EUR 5,500 per case – , compensation for the Judiciary in regard of the unavailability of their members sitting in the BIBC, actual court fees etc., p. 34).

66 See the impact analysis inserted in the Draft Law, above n. 41, pp. 88–93; comp. Opinion of the Conseil d'Etat, above n. 54, para. 7, p. 99, fn. 7 mentioning that the Inspector of finances expressed doubt on the self-sustainability of the project.

seem to be put at the charge of the parties in the draft legislation, even though the project announces the need for an up-to-date infrastructure, including technological facilities.[67] The financial burden of infrastructure and facilities cannot suffer to be neglected in regard of the scarcity of resources allocated to justice. For instance, the Registry of the Tribunal of First Instance in Brussels closed down for several weeks for security and hygiene reasons.[68] The Belgian judiciary has pointed at other 'indirect' costs generated by such a project, such as work overload for the whole judicial system generated by the unavailability of some of its members, when the Belgian judiciary considers itself understaffed and underfinanced.[69] In other words, it is hard to identify at this point whether the court fees imposed to have access to the BIBC would cover all the costs relating to the BIBC, not to mention 'generate a positive return for the State', according to the terms of Dammann and Hansmann, i.e. a financial benefit beyond the mere cost coverage.[70]

At this stage, the existence of objective reasons for regulatory competition at the procedural level seem difficult to identify. As the Belgian example shows: (i) financial incentive for the creation of such a tribunal would deserve to be substantiated and more clearly demonstrated, beyond the interest of the local bar; (ii) the overall benefit of regulatory competition in terms of innovation and a better performing judicial system can also be doubted. Eventually, regulatory competition with regard to civil justice ironically raises financial concerns. Where most civil justice systems are subsidised by public finances, the correlation between the efforts deployed by States to render their courts attractive and the resources they can gain from this beauty contest is not clearly demonstrated.

4. CONCLUSION: THREE HYPOTHESES

When terminating this brief overview of the concept of regulatory competition at the procedural level and of some of its practical aspects in the EU, three hypotheses can probably be formulated.

1. *Regulatory competition at the civil procedure level could generate high costs for unclear benefits.* Where their real incentives to engage into the regulatory competition game at the procedural level are difficult to detect, Member States

67 General Explanatory Statement in the Draft Law, above n. 41, p. 12.

68 RTBF Info, 'Le greffe du Palais de Justice de Bruxelles est fermé pour des raisons de sécurité', press article and videos: <www.rtbf.be/info/societe/detail_le-greffe-du-palais-de-justice-de-bruxelles-vient-de-fermer-pour-des-raisons-de-securite?id=9731445>. According to Stefan Vogenauer, the UK Ministry of Justice spent GBP 300 million for the construction of an '11-storey court complex opened in October 2011' (above n. 23, p. 71).

69 Open Letter of the judges of the Brussels Court of Appeal, 2.12.2017 <http://o0.llb.be/file/5a218368cd7095d1cd315c1b.pdf>.

70 J. Dammann and H. Hansmann, above n. 4, 61.

seem to engage (at least) in competitive discourses in an attempt to capture post-Brexit litigation, thanks to the establishment of business courts functioning in English (as planned in the Netherlands, France, Germany and Belgium). However, the benefit to be expected from such courts is unclear. In contrast, the costs are identified and probably go beyond the mere expenditures for setting up new tribunals. If States really intend to be competitive in procedural terms, the Dutch or the UK experience tend to show that they need to invest massively to increase the quality of justice, for instance in order to shorten the duration of civil procedures in ways that are compatible with due process. This goal might generate massive costs for instance in order to appoint more judges or develop up-to-date infrastructure.

2. *The EU civil justice system fosters regulatory competition, but can also mitigate it.* The EU, as noted earlier in this paper, has a role to play in the civil justice regulatory game. The EU can instigate regulatory competition and does so via the triangle formed by Article 25 Brussel I Recast, Article 3 and Article 9 Rome I Regulation. However, in other instances the EU has also mitigated regulatory competition. This is the case, for instance, of the Directive on the posting of workers. This Directive intends to prevent a deregulatory game benefiting companies established (sometimes artificially) in Member States with low protection standards for workers, which are posting their workers in other Member States. Companies benefit from the application of the law of the place where they are established, because this will most often also be the place where the work is habitually carried out (designated by Art. 8, §2 Regulation Rome I). Thus, by selecting the place of their establishment, they can also 'manipulate' the designation of the law applicable to their workers' contracts. They can later post their workers in other Member States and still apply the law of the place where the work is *habitually* carried out. The Directive entitles the host Member State to apply its overriding mandatory rules to posted workers temporarily present on its territory and also enables workers to seize the courts of the host State in order to claim the application of its laws.[71] Thereby, the Directive derogates to the normal provision of Brussels I Recast (according to which the litigation should take place in the Member State where the worker habitually performs his/her work, Art. 21, §1 Brussels I Recast) and combines a jurisdiction rule and a conflict of laws rule to curtail the existing regulatory competition between Member States with low and high standards of workers' protection. The EU can thus decide to create the conditions for regulatory competition or regulatory arbitrage at the substantive or procedural level, to limit such competition to fields where competition has been proven to produce positive results or to prevent competition even in an open market. In each case, the PIL methods (allocation of jurisdiction and allocation of normative competence) will be

---

71 Art. 3 and 6 Directive 96/71/EC of 16 December 1996 concerning the posting of workers in the framework of the provision of services, as completed by Directive 2014/67.

used. This observation highlights the need for conceptualizing more clearly the potential regulatory impact of PIL tools used in PIL Regulations.

3. *Drafting a post-Brexit specific agreement with the UK requires to take into consideration regulatory competition issues and the potential externalities of such an agreement.* Brexit seems to constitute a catalyst for regulatory competition at the judicial level. Beyond the potentially successful attempts of Member States to capture litigations currently attracted to London, Brexit has another story of regulatory competition to tell us. Already in the realm of the EU, under Regulation Brussels I Recast and Regulation Rome I, we have identified a space for parties to escape from important policies of Member States by using the procedural facilities regarding choice of court and recognition of judgement, while benefiting from the possibility to opt out of the overriding mandatory laws. If the same procedural facilities are simply offered to the UK once it will be a third State, parties could easily designate UK courts and find there an opportunity to evade Member States overriding mandatory laws by choosing the law of a third State and even circumvent the application of EU – overriding – mandatory laws (which will no longer be mandatory for UK judges as part of the *lex fori* once the UK becomes a third State). If UK judgements are recognised according to the same facilities as before Brexit, a judgement obtained in the UK in contradiction with an EU mandatory rule might have to be recognised in the EU. Therefore, the 'cut and paste' technique for a special agreement with the UK, according to which the text of Brussels I Recast and Rome I Regulation should be copied in a special agreement with the UK, may pave the way for the worst aspects of regulatory competition. In order to prevent regulatory gaps, due to negative civil justice competition, the EU negotiator of Brexit should organise a robust post-Brexit recognition system of UK decisions in the EU and maybe… read Article 7 of the Belgian code of PIL.

THE APPLICATION OF THE BRUSSELS *IBIS* REGULATION IN THE EU MEMBER STATES

Burkhard Hess
Professor Max Planck Institute Luxembourg

1. INNOVATIONS OF THE BRUSSELS *IBIS* REGULATION

1.1. THE TRANSITIONAL REGIME

Since 10 January 2015, the recast Brussels I Regulation (Brussels *Ibis*) has applied in all EU Member States (Article 80 Brussels *Ibis*)[1] for proceedings initiated after that date. In practice, however, this date has not marked any major changes. One reason is found in the transitional regime of Article 66 Brussels *Ibis*. According to its first paragraph, the new Regulation only applies to proceedings which are initiated after this date. The more important provision is found in the 2nd paragraph which states that the new enforcement regime of Articles 36 ff. of the Recast only applies to enforceable titles which were obtained in proceedings under the new Recast.[2] This provision protracts the application of the new regime considerably – enforcement cases under the new regime have not yet reached the courts in Member States where Articles 36 ff. of the old Brussels I Regulation are still being applied. Therefore, my contribution in this volume has a limited scope. It cannot address the new – and problematic – direct enforcement regime of the Recast because while practice in the EU Member States is now well underway, case-law interpreting the new Regulation has not yet reached us in earnest.[3] Even so, the direct enforcement regime is arguably the most important change of the recast Regulation.

---

1 Regulation 1215/2012 of 12 December 2012, OJ 2012 L 351/1 ff.; in Denmark, the Recast applies via the Bilateral Agreement of 19 October 2005, [2007] OJ L94/70, Magnus, in: Magnus & Mankowski, *Brussels Ibis Regulation (2016), Introduction*, para 54.

2 Schlosser/Hess, *Article 66 EuGVVO (Commentary)*, 4th ed. 2015, para 3.

3 The first cases are expected to occur soon. The only enforcement case I am aware of related to the enforcement of a Dutch provisional measure in Belgium under Articles 41 and 43 Brussels *Ibis*. See the database hosted by the Asser Institute for updates on case-law: www.asser.nl/brusselsibis/, last consulted 5 September 2018.

In the meantime, the German Federal Civil Court (Bundesgerichtshof/BGH) has sent a first preliminary reference to the Court of Justice of the EU (CJEU) which addresses direct enforcement under the Recast. The BGH referred several practical questions on the form in Annex I, to the CJEU, which demonstrate that the (complicated) German law on provisional enforceability is difficult to reconcile with the categories of the form.[4] However, the preliminary reference demonstrates the practical difficulties of direct enforcement under the Brussels I*bis* Regulation. Under the former regime, recognition proceedings permitted the adaptation of a foreign judgment to the specificities of the enforcement laws of the Member State of enforcement.[5] Under the Recast, the form (Article 53 Brussels I*bis* Recast) replaces the (individual) adaptation of a foreign judgment in exequatur proceedings. It remains to be seen whether the form in Annex I will be sufficiently sophisticated to replace the adaptation process.

1.2. MAJOR CHANGES IN REGULATION 1215/2012

Against this background, my paper addresses judicial practice under the Recast regarding its scope, the jurisdictional regime and the new rules on pendency as well as on related actions. In these areas, first decisions from the EU Member States and – especially – the Court of Justice have been published and I will highlight some of them here. Before exploring them, I would like to briefly summarize the major changes of the Recast in these areas.[6]

The Recast implemented only minor corrections. It added a new head of jurisdiction on the return of cultural property, clarified the applicable law and the effects of jurisdiction clauses and enlarged the jurisdiction for consumer contracts, insurances and employees to defendants in third States. Larger and more ambitious proposals regarding the delineation to arbitration[7], the inclusion of third State situations[8] and provisional measures[9] were not endorsed. All in all, there is a structural continuity between the Brussels I Regulation and its recast and a strong similarity between the two instruments.[10] This continuity is highlighted by Recitals 1, 7 and 8 and 34 of the Recast Regulation.

---

4 BGH, 25.1.2018, ECLI:DE:BGH:2018:250118BIXZB89.16.0.

5 Hess, *Europäisches Zivilprozessrecht* (2010), §6, para 222.

6 For an assessment cf. Domej, ‚Die Neufassung der EuGVVO – Quantensprünge im europäischen Zivilprozessrecht', *RabelsZ* 98 (2014), 508 ff.

7 Hess, in: Hess, Pfeiffer & Schlosser, *The Heidelberg Report* (2008), paras 105 ff.

8 Nuyts, Study JLS/C4/2005/07-30-CE)0040309/00-37 On residual jurisdiction in the Regulations Brussel I and Brussels II*bis*, 2007.

9 Hess, in: Hess, Pfeiffer & Schlosser, *The Heidelberg Report* (2008), paras 619 ff.

10 Nuyts, La réforme du Règlement Bruxelles I, Rev. crit. 2013, 1 ss; Pfeiffer, Die Fortentwicklung des Europäischen Prozessrechts durch die neue EuGVO, ZZP 127 (2014), 409 ff.

2. THE PRACTICE IN THE EU MEMBER STATES AND THE FIRST CASE-LAW OF THE CJEU

2.1. THE SCOPE OF THE REGULATION

According to Article 1 (1), Regulation Brussels *Ibis* applies to civil and commercial matters. In this respect, the wording of the Recast remains unchanged (although the exception of so-called *acta jure imperii* was included after the *Lechouritou* judgment of the CJEU[11]). However, the concept is not entirely clear and some recent judgments of the CJEU have been criticized in the literature.[12]

In this context, *Pula Parking* was the most important decision.[13] The facts of this case were simple. In 2010, a German resident had parked his car in a public parking space in Pula, Croatia while visiting the town as a tourist. He failed to pay for the parking. Five years later, the publicly-owned company Pula Parking, entrusted with administration of parking space in Pula (and with the power to collect outstanding debts), requested a Croatian public notary to issue a writ of enforcement against the German defendant for the amount of 100 HRK (appr. € 13.15). The writ was sent to the addressee by (ordinary) mail. Eventually, the defendant challenged the writ in the Croatian court and argued that the matter did not fall within the scope of 'civil and commercial matters'. In line with the applicable national procedure, the case was transferred to the Pula Municipal Court which referred to the CJEU the question of whether Regulation (EU) No 1215/2012 was applicable in the present case.

The CJEU confirmed the necessity to interpret Article 1 (1) of the Regulation in an autonomous way, independently from the specific approach in the Member State concerned (Croatia). When assessing the legal quality of the claim, the Court of Justice emphasised that the 'parking debt' was not coupled with a fine and, rather, it was a 'mere compensation for the services rendered', i.e. the 'provision' of a parking space to the German tourist.[14] Following the conclusions of AG Bobek[15], the Court characterised the underlying legal relationship as a contractual one. In the next step, the contractual relationship between the parties was classified as a 'private one' and, finally, assimilated to a civil and commercial matter.[16]

---

11 CJEU, 15.2.2007, case C-292/05, *Lechouritou,* EU:C:2007:102.

12 Hess, The Private-Public Divide in International Dispute Resolution, RdC 388 (2018), paras 55 ff.

13 CJEU, 9.3.2017, case C-551/15, *Pula Parking,* EU:C:2017:193 – this judgment was the first case where the CJEU addressed the (recast) Regulation 1215/2012 in substance.

14 CJEU, 9.3.2017, case C-551/15, *Pula Parking,* EU:C:2017:193, paras 34–36. In this respect, the CJEU did not explain why a 'contractual relationship' existed between the municipal authorities of Pula and the tourist or between the parking authority and the tourist. The simple parking of a car in a public street does not amount to the conclusion of a contract.

15 Conclusions AG Bobek, 27.10.2016, case C-551/15, *Pula Parking,* EU:C:2016:825, para 49.

16 CJEU, 3/9/2017, case C-551/15, *Pula Parking,* EU:C:2017:193, para 38.

This legal reasoning is not convincing. The Court characterised the parties' underlying relationship as contractual although no explicit contract was actually concluded. To the contrary, the mere parking of a car in a public space cannot amount to the conclusion of a lease contract – the streets in Pula are subject to a public law regime – similar to highways and regional streets.[17] Of course, the local administration may change the regime by gating the streets and requesting a payment for utilisation. However, as far as public streets are concerned there is at least a presumption that their use is subject to public regulation. Assuming the conclusion of a contract without any intentional act of concluding it is too far-reaching.[18] Moreover, the fictitious contract was used by the Court as the main ground for the assumption of a private law relationship. Again, this reasoning is unconvincing: the mere existence of a contract between a public authority and a private individual does not signify the existence of a private law relationship.[19]

Consequently, the CJEU has opened the door for public authorities to 'privatize' debt collection in cross-border settings. As a result, public authorities may now freely choose in which way to proceed. In domestic settings, they may prefer to directly collect outstanding debts by means of administrative acts. In cross-border situations, they may adopt a private law approach by stressing the 'services' rendered to the foreign tourists. Yet, one might wonder whether public authorities are really free (like subjects of private law) to decide how they impose fees on citizens and to what extent they may depart from the framework of public law (confining their 'freedom' of activity).[20]

Besides, it should be noted that the broad approach of the CJEU to the concept of 'civil matters' has already encouraged private debt collectors to offer their 'services' to public local authorities in the EU Member States in order to 'collect' administrative fines (or, better framed: to collect private service fees from EU citizens at high prices).[21] As a result, respect for local laws (on paying parking fees) might be improved although the frustration of EU citizens about a Union which is encouraging 'free enforcement riders imposing unreasonable fees' will certainly

---

17 Hess, 'Factual Contracts in European Law? Critical Reflections on the Conclusions of AG Bobek of October 27', 2016 in case C-551/15, post on conflict of laws, 22 November 2016, http://conflictoflaws.net/2016/factual-contracts-in-european-law-critical-reflections-on-the-conclusions-of-ag-bobek-of-october-27–2016-in-case-c-55115-pula-parking-tederahn-2/.

18 In addition, for the user of parking space, it remains entirely unclear with whom the 'contract' is concluded: the local administration, the authority/entity monitoring the street, the local police?

19 This demonstrates the French doctrine of the public law contract (contrat public ou administratif), see Audit & Schill, Introduction, in: Audit & Schill (ed.), *Transnational Law of Public Contracts* (2016), pp. 3, 5.

20 One must mention here the Framework Decision of 24.5.2005, [2005] OJ L76/16 which permits the cross-border enforcement of fines regarding traffic infringements.

21 Example: (exorbitant) entry fees for cars in London might be enforced Europe-wide by private debt collectors. Corresponding services are already promoted on specialized websites. Usually, the 'collecting fees' are 3 to 5 times higher than the underlying public law claim.

increase.[22] This side effect of the *Pula* case seems to be rather unwelcome – and it has already become a business practice in Europe.[23]

Visible changes to the text of the Regulation are found in Article 1 (2) which refers to new instruments in civil matters, especially the Maintenance[24] and the Successions[25] Regulations. This enlarged list demonstrates the growing development and communitarization of European procedural law and the changed function of Article 1 (2). Today, this provision usually delineates the scope of the different EU instruments *inter se*,[26] it no longer demarcates the autonomous procedural laws of the EU Member States from the scope of the Brussels Regulation.[27]

However, there is one exception: arbitration, Article 1(2) lit d) of the Brussels *Ibis* Regulation. Here, the text of Article 1 (2)(d) has literally remained unchanged, but Recital 12 to the Brussels *Ibis* Regulation tries to clarify the relationship between arbitration and the Brussels I regime. Still, one has to acknowledge that Recital 12 has not clarified the relationship between arbitration and the Recast Regulation.[28] In one of the first cases after the enactment of the Recast – *Gazprom* – AG Wathelet tried to change fundamentally the relationship between the Regulation and investment arbitration by proposing a priority of arbitration over the dispute settlement regime of the Regulation. He tried to make an argument out of Recital 12 of the Brussels *Ibis* Regulation.[29] The Grand Chamber of the CJEU did not take up this pro-arbitration stance and (simply) decided the case under the 2001 Brussel I Regulation. It correctly held that the relationship between the Regulation and arbitration had not been changed.[30]

---

22 Under the present circumstances, this does not appear to be a viable solution for strengthening the trust of citizens in the achievements of EU law.

23 Nordmeier, ‚Privates Inkasso nach Verkehrsverstößen im Ausland, Vortrag vor dem Goslaer Verkehrsgerichtstag' (to be published in *Deutsches Autorecht* 2018).

24 So far, the CJEU has given 9 decisions dealing with Regulation 4/2009; 'recently' 16.1.2018, case 604/17, *PM*, EU:C:2018:10, on the delineation between the Brussels II*bis* and the Maintenance Regulation.

25 Regulation 650/2012 – here the CJEU was involved in the most disputed issues from the very beginning, see Hess, 'Die Europäische Erbrechtsverordnung (EuErbVO) in der Rechtsprechung des Europäischen Gerichtshofs und Deutscher Gerichte', '*Seminario de Derecho y Jurisprudencia*', Madrid (2017).

26 Ex.: CJEU, 20.12.2017, case C-649/16, *Valach and Others*, EU:C:2017:986, delineation of Regulation 1215/2012 and 1348/2000 in the case of an action for liability in tort against a creditors' committee for which there was a rejected restructuring plan in insolvency proceedings.

27 There are still some cases which address the delineation between the Regulation and national law, cf. CJEU, 14.6.2017, case C-67/17, *Todor Iliev*, EU:C:2017:459 (matrimonial dispute, Bulgarian family law was applicable).

28 Hess, Schiedsgerichtsbarkeit und Europäisches Zivilprozessrecht, JZ 2014, 538 ff.

29 Opinion AG Wathelet, 4.12.2014, case C-536/13, *Gazprom*, EU:C:2014:2414, paras 112 ff.; on Recital 12 of the Brussels *Ibis* Regulation, cf. *Hess*, JZ 2014, 538, 540 ff.

30 CJEU, 13.5.2015, case C-536/13, *Gazprom*, EU:C:2015:316.

2.2. JURISDICTION

With regard to the heads of jurisdiction, the Recast does not introduce fundamental changes. It maintains – for good reasons – the distinction between general and specific heads of jurisdiction and it does not enlarge the concept of the specific heads of jurisdictions. Accordingly, the CJEU has not changed its case-law in this area of law – the continuity between Regulation 44/2001 and the Recast Regulation 1215/2012 is predominant.[31] Typical examples in this respect are the decisions in *Schrems*[32] where the Court was asked about the application of Articles 15 and 16 of the former Brussels I Regulation on collective actions of assigned claims brought by consumers and political activists.[33] Here, the Court following the conclusions of AG Bobek[34], took a cautious approach by leaving the decision to enlarge the Regulation to collective actions to the EU law-maker.

There are some decisions of the Court relating to jurisdiction under the Recast which closely follow the established case-law on Article 5 (1) and (3) of the former Brussels I Regulation – a typical example is case C-216/16 *Kareda*[35] where the Court determined the place of performance of a credit agreement and the competent court for the action of recourse between joint and separate debtors under Article 7 (1) (b) of the Regulations Brussels *Ibis* on the basis of its former case-law.[36] Another example is *Saey Home & Garden*[37] about the place of performance of a distribution agreement – in the case at hand it was Spain, because the agreement related to this Member State.

The most prominent case in this context is *Bolagsupplysningen*[38] where the CJEU had to decide about an action on the infringement of personality rights. The plaintiff, an Estonian company, requested from the Swedish defendant (an employer association) the rectification of allegedly incorrect information published on the defendant's website, the deletion of negative and aggressive comments on a discussion forum on that website and compensation for harm suffered. Extending its judgment in *eDate*[39], the CJEU ruled that Article 7 (2) of Regulation (EU)

---

31 Cf. Recital 34 of the Brussels *Ibis* Regulation which is usually quoted by the CJEU, ex. CJEU, 14.6.2017, case C-67/17, *Todor Iliev*, EU:C:2017:459, para 23.

32 CJEU, 25.1.2018, case C-498/16, *Schrems*, EU:C:2018:37.

33 The same result was reached in CJEU, 31.1.2018, case C-106/17, *Paweł Hofsoe*, EU:C:2018:50, where an insurance claim had been assigned to a third party. The Court – correctly – stated that Article 11 of the Brussels *Ibis* Regulation providing for a specific protective head of jurisdiction for a weaker party, does not apply to the claim filed by an assignee.

34 Opinion AG Bobek, 14.11.2017, case C-498/16, *Schrems*, EU:C:2017:863.

35 CJEU, 15.6.2017, case C-249/16, *Kareda*, EU:C:2017:472, paras 40 ff.; same opinion CJEU, 8.3.2018, case C-64/17, *Saey Home & Garden*, EU:C:2018:173, para 33 ff. (on Article 7 no 1 b) of the Brussels *Ibis* Regulation).

36 Another example is CJEU, 16.11.2016, case C-417/15 *Wolfgang Schmidt*, EU:C:2017:881 (on Articles 7 no 1 and 24 no 1 of the Brussels *Ibis* Regulation).

37 CJEU, 8.3.2018, case C-64/17, *Saey Home & Garden*, EU:C:2018:173, see fn. 35.

38 CJEU, 17.10.2017, case C-194/16; *Bolagsupplysningen and Ilsjan*, EU:C:2017:766.

39 CJEU, 25.10.2011, cases C-509/09 and C-161/10, *eDate Advertising and Martinez*, EU:C:2011:685.

No 1215/2012 must be interpreted as meaning that an action for the infringement of personality rights over the Internet may be brought before the courts of the Member State in which its centre of interests is located. In the case at hand, the plaintiff's main interests were located in Sweden where the plaintiff operated his business activities and not in Estonia where it was registered. The Court specified in this case that, when the plaintiff is a legal person which carries out the main part of its activities in a different Member State from the one in which its registered office is located[40], that person may sue the alleged perpetrator in that other Member State by virtue of it being where the damage occurred. The Court departed from the 'mosaic principle'[41] and held that the same provision must be interpreted as meaning that an action for rectification of that information and removal of comments allegedly infringing one's personality rights cannot be brought before the courts of each Member State in which the information published on the Internet is or was accessible. What counts is the centre of main interests (or of the business activities) of the targeted person. This case-law can be seen as a continuation and refinement of former developments in the protection of personality rights by the CJEU.

These examples demonstrate how much the case-law of the Court is dominated by continuity of the practice under the Brussels I Regulation and under the Recast. This continuity is easy to achieve as the Recast does not change the basic structure or the underlying principles of the Regulation. For legal practice, this continuity facilitates the application of the Regulation as the most important instrument of European civil procedural law.[42]

2.3. PENDENCY AND RELATED ACTIONS

However, in the area of pendency, a major change was implemented with regard to jurisdiction clauses. According to Article 31 (2) and (4) Regulation Brussels *Ibis*, a court designated by an exclusive arbitration agreement shall decide on its jurisdiction regardless of whether this court was seized first[43] or second. Once the court designated in the agreement has established its jurisdiction, any other court shall decline jurisdiction in favour of that court. By this exception from the priority rule in Article 29 (1), the Recast considerably reinforces the effectiveness of choice of court agreements.[44]

40 In the instant case one of the alleged victims was a legal person established under Estonian law which carried out its business activities in Sweden.

41 As established by CJEU, 7.3.1995, case C-68/93, *Shevill*, EU:C:1995:61, paras 32 and 33; cf. Hess, in: Hess & Mariottini (ed.), *The Protection of Privacy* (2014), p. 81 ff.

42 Cf. Wilke, 'The impact of the Brussels I Recast on important "Brussels" case law', *JPInt'l L* 11 (2015), 128 ff.

43 This is the basic rule in Article 29 (1) of the Brussels *Ibis* Regulation.

44 More critical Wilke, *JPInt'l L* 11 (2015), 128, 131.

The new rule has not, as yet, been tested in practice. There is, however, a multitude of cases where the new regime applies: these cases belong to the Volkswagen shareholder litigation in the so-called diesel litigation. Here, the statutes of the company contain a clause[45] which states that disputes between shareholders and the company, including disputes arising out of the capital markets, shall be exclusively brought before the Braunschweig District Court.[46] In Austria, several lawsuits were brought by Austrian shareholders under Articles 17 and 18 of the Brussels *Ibis* Regulation against Volkswagen AG in the local courts at the shareholders' domicile. In the end, the Austrian Supreme Court (OGH) declined contractual jurisdiction of the Austrian courts under Articles 18 and 7 (1) of the Regulation as the shares had not been bought from the defendant company but from local banks.[47] However, the OGH expressed some doubts whether the scope of the jurisdiction clause included all claims related to the capital markets. Article 29 and 31 of the Recast were not tested as the shareholders had only invoked Austrian courts.[48]

3. AU DÉLÀ DE BRUSSELS *IBIS*: THE CURRENT CRISIS OF THE EUROPEAN UNION IN THE RECENT PRACTICE OF THE CJEU

3.1. THE WIDER PERSPECTIVE: STRENGTHENING THE RULE OF LAW

Addressing the practice of the CJEU regarding Brussels *Ibis* would be incomplete without looking at the neighbouring EU instruments of the Regulation. Here, several developments are worth mentioning. On the one hand, there is a growing and expanding case-law of the CJEU regarding the interpretation of the procedural instruments of the second generation such as the Regulation on

---

45 The clause is based on the case-law of the CJEU, 10.3.1992, case C-214/89, *Powell Duffryn*, EU:C:1992:115, para 19, where the Court had held that a shareholder may consent to a jurisdiction clause by acquiring shares of a company.

46 This clause in the statutes reads as follows: '§29 Place of jurisdiction: The sole place of jurisdiction for all disputes between shareholders and of the beneficiaries or obligors of financial instruments relating to the Company's shares on the one hand, and the Company on the other, shall be the Company's domicile unless mandatory statutory provisions require otherwise. This also applies to disputes relating to compensation claimed for damage caused by false or misleading public capital market information, or the failure to provide such information. Foreign courts shall not have jurisdiction over such disputes.'

47 OGH, 7.7.2017, IPRax 2018, 96 (annotated by Heindler, *IPRax* 2018, 103).

48 The case at hand demonstrates an inherent weakness of Article 31 (2) Brussels *Ibis* Regulation: The underlying concept should not only apply when concurring law-suits are filed but also in constellations where the defendant contests the jurisdiction of the court (under the Regulation) by invoking a jurisdiction clause. It would make sense for the chosen court to decide on its jurisdiction. On the other hand, Volkswagen did not file any action (for a negative declaration) against the Austrian defendants in the Higher Regional Court of Braunschweig.

Uncontested Claims[49], the Payment Order Regulation[50] and the Small Claims Regulation.[51] These instruments are based on the principle of direct enforcement of judgments (without any review in the requested Member State) and backed by so-called procedural minimum standards which shall protect the right of defence, especially the defendant's right to be heard.[52]

In this area of law, the Court of Justice has developed a remarkable jurisprudence. In several judgments, the Court highlighted the need for a strict application of the procedural guarantees of the Regulations. The following examples demonstrate this attitude. In the case of *Collect Inkasso OÜ*[53], a court in Estonia had rendered several default judgments against individual debtors (obviously customers) which were conveyed to them by personal and substituted service. Later, the creditor applied for a certification of these judgments as a European Enforcement Order (EEO). However, the court became aware that the default judgment did not exactly indicate the name and the address of the court where the debtor could challenge the default judgment. As Articles 17 and 18 of the EEO Regulation provide for the correction of procedural deficiencies, the Estonian court asked the CJEU whether the EEO could be issued in the pending cases. The CJEU held that information for the defendant about the address of the institution with which a challenge must be lodged is a mandatory minimum requirement in order to protect the right of defence. Therefore, the Court concluded that a judgment which was delivered without informing the defendant properly cannot be certified as an EEO.[54] In a judgment of 9 March 2017, *Zulfikarpašić*[55], the Court stated that payment orders given by Croatian notaries cannot be issued as an EEO as the notaries cannot be considered as courts in the sense of Regulation 805/2004.[56]

---

49 Regulation 805/2004, [2004] OJ L143/15.

50 Regulation (EU) 1896/2006, [2006] OJ L399 as amended.

51 Regulation (EU) 861/2007, [2007] OJ L199 as amended.

52 Hess, *Europäisches Zivilprozessrecht* (2nd ed. to be published in 2019), §11, para 2 ff.

53 CJEU, 28.2.2018, case C-289/17, *Collect Inkasso OÜ*, EU:C:2018:133.

54 The Court stated: 'The minimum standards set out in Chapter III of Regulation No 805/2004 express the EU legislature's intention to ensure that procedures leading to the adoption of judgments concerning uncontested debts offer adequate guarantees of respect for the rights of the defence in the Member State of origin, taking account of the fact that, in principle, there is no review thereof in the Member State of enforcement. (37) Indeed, as follows from the case-law of the Court, those minimum standards, which include indication of the address of the institution concerned, seek to ensure, in accordance with recital 12 of Regulation No 805/2004, that the debtor is informed, firstly, about the court action against him, the requirements for his active participation in the proceedings to contest the claim at issue and, secondly, the consequences of his non-participation in sufficient time and in such a way as to enable him to arrange for his defence. In the specific case of a decision delivered in default, for the purposes of Article 3(1)(b) of Regulation No 805/2004, those minimum procedural standards thus seek to ensure the existence of adequate guarantees of respect for the rights of the defence (see, to that effect, judgment of 16 June 2016, *Pebros Servizi*, C511/14, EU:C:2016:448, paragraph 44).'

55 CJEU, 9.3.2017, case C484/15, *Zulfikarpašić*, EU:C:2017:199, para 48.

56 In *Pula Parking*, given on the same day, the CJEU held that payment orders given by Croatian notaries do not qualify as 'decisions' under the Brussels *Ibis* Regulation, CJEU, 9.3.2017, case C-551/15, *Pula Parking*, EU:C:2017:193, paras 44 ff.

From a scholarly point of view, these decisions are not very compelling. However, they demonstrate the firm intention of the Court of Justice to reinforce the right of defence by strictly applying the standards guaranteed by these instruments. It seems that the CJEU is aware of the imminent dangers of these regulations which permit the direct cross-border enforcement of judgments without any exequatur proceedings. Yet, in return, these procedures provide for a residual control in the EU Member State of origin.[57] Therefore, the Court of Justice has reinforced the judicial control of the proceedings and of the substantial claim in the Member State of origin where the enforceable title is rendered. This corresponds to the underlying design of these instruments but the CJEU also clearly reinforced the procedural guarantees of these instruments.

3.2. MUTUAL TRUST AS A CORNERSTONE OF JUDICIAL COOPERATION

Finally, the direct link between the rule of law and mutual trust as a cornerstone of judicial cooperation in civil matters becomes evident. The direct enforcement of decisions coming from one EU Member State in other EU Member States presupposes that the procedural rights of the defendant have been fully respected and that the proceedings in the Member State of origin were given in front of a judge (or in proceedings permitting the full review of the title obtained by a judge).[58]

Here, the pertinent case-law of the Court of Justice is directly linked to its general case-law on mutual trust. This principle is not limited to civil cooperation.[59] The most important developments regarding mutual trust are found in criminal cooperation. Here, the court has cautiously developed a case-law which does not impose blind trust: the recognition of judgments coming from other EU Member States requires that the Member State of origin respects fundamental rights standards. In this respect, trust must be 'earned' by the Member State of origin and can – in exceptional cases – be reviewed by the requested court.[60] In its Opinion on the Accession of the Union to the ECHR, the full Court of Justice held:

> ...it should be noted that the principle of mutual trust between the Member States is of fundamental importance in EU law, given that it allows an area without internal borders to be created and maintained. That principle requires, particularly with regard to the area of freedom, security and justice, each of those States, save in exceptional circumstances, to consider all the other Member States to be complying with EU law and particularly with the fundamental rights recognised by EU law.[61]

57 Hess, *Europäisches Zivilprozessrecht*, §11, paras 2 ff.
58 CJEU, 9.3.2017, case C-551/15, *Pula Parking*, EU:C:2017:193, paras 54 f.
59 Prechal, 'Mutual Trust Before the Court of Justice of the European Union', *European Papers* 2 (2017), 75 ff.
60 For an explicit statement in this respect cf. Lenaerts, 'La vie après l'avis: exploring the principle of mutual (but not blind) trust', *CMLR* 54 (2017), 805, 807 ff.
61 CJEU, 18.12.2015, avis 2/13, *Accession to the ECHR*, para 191.

In this paragraph, the Court sets a direct link between mutual trust and the respect of fundamental rights. Furthermore, the Court recognizes that non-respect of fundamental rights may entail that in exceptional and severe circumstances, mutual trust and automatic recognition are suspended among the EU Member States. Recent case-law of the CJEU demonstrates that this situation has already occurred in asylum cases[62] and in criminal matters[63]. Therefore, according to recent case-law of the CJEU, mutual trust is limited by an inherent public policy exception.[64] The recent case-law on the procedural minimum standards in EU instruments on direct enforcement must be read against the background of this case-law of the Court. Mutual trust does not only entail automatic recognition but is directly connected with respect for fundamental rights and the rule of law.[65] This connection was highlighted in the latest judgment of the CJEU on this subject, on 6 March 2018 in *Achmea* (addressing investment arbitration).[66] On 23 March 2018, the Irish High Court sent a preliminary reference to the CJEU asking whether infringement proceedings under Article 7 of the Treaty of the European Union against Poland (for non-compliance with fundamental EU values: the independence of the judiciary) entail that a European Arrest Warrant cannot be executed when the request comes from Poland.[67] At the centre of this preliminary reference is the principle of mutual trust and its inherent limits.[68]

4. FURTHER PERSPECTIVES: EUROPEAN PROCEDURAL LAW BETWEEN STABILIZATION, ADAPTATION AND FURTHER LEGISLATIVE AMBITIONS

If one looks at the present state of European law of civil procedure, several diverging trends can be identified. On the one hand, rapid law-making in this area has come to an end. Far-reaching and ambitious projects in European procedural law are not in the pipeline – this area of law is currently influenced by

62 CJEU, 21.12.2011, joined cases C-411/10 and C-493/10, *N.S.*, EU:C:2011:865, paras 98 and 101; CJEU, 10.12.2013, case C-394/12, *Abdullahi*, EU:C:2013:813.

63 CJEU, 5.4.2016, cases C-404/15 and C-659/15 PPU, *Aranyosi and Căldăraru*, EU:C:2016:198.

64 Lenaerts, *CMLR* 54 (2017), 805, 807 – a couple of years ago, this limitation was considered as contrary to EU law, Hess, Europäisches Zivilprozessrecht (2010).

65 Lenaerts, *CMLR* 54 (2017), 805, 837 f. (stressing the importance of the CFR).

66 CJEU, 6.3.2018, case C-284/16, *Slovak Republic v. Achmea BV*, EU:C:2018:158, cf. Hess, The fate of Investment Dispute Resolution after the Achmea decision of the European Court of Justice (2018), MPILux Research Paper Series 2018 (3), https://papers.ssrn.com/sol3/papers.cfm?abstract_id=3152972.

67 *The Minister for Justice and Equality v. Artur Celmer*, High Court of Ireland, Record No 2017 EXT 291.

68 The case is dealt within the CJEU under the urgent preliminary ruling procedure, case no. C-216/18 PPU – *Minister for Justice and Equality (Défaillances du système judiciaire)*.

neighbouring areas on data protection and consumer protection.[69] However, these developments do not exclude procedural law from playing a major role in these fields which are based on the concept of 'private enforcement'. With regard to existing instruments of European private international law, the current legislative activities are aimed at evaluating their application in the Member States and at improving them in an evolving way.

As far as the case-law of the CJEU is concerned, the general trend goes further. On the one hand, the Court of Justice pursues the development of the existing instruments through consistent case-law. On the other hand, the Court is engaged in a general trend of reinforcing European fundamental values, of strengthening institutional structures and of preserving its legitimacy by increasing the constitutional and foundational values of European law in general, including European procedural law. In this sensitive political development, civil procedural law is certainly not at the forefront. However, it has to play its role within a general trend of strengthening procedural provisions and procedural fundamental rights. In this respect, the recent case-law of the CJEU on the procedural protection of the rights of defence is important. And at the moment, we do not know to what extent the principle of mutual trust will be preserved or transformed by the current developments.[70]

Finally – and this is an aspect which I have not addressed so far – European legal scholarship is engaged in far-reaching projects on the codification of civil procedure. The European Parliament is currently pursuing a project on 'procedural minimum standards' to be adopted in a European instrument. So far, only a resolution of Parliament has been adopted.[71] The more ambitious project is currently being prepared by the European Law Institute and Unidroit in cooperation with a group of specialists in procedural law.[72] This project aims at developing a comprehensive set of rules (or better: a codification) of civil procedure to be applied in all EU Member States. It remains to be seen whether this model law will influence the legislative process at the European and national levels. Nevertheless, it demonstrates the ongoing ambitions of scholars to improve European integration in procedural law.

---

69 See the Proposal for a directive of the European Parliament and of the Council on representative actions for the protection of the collective interests of consumers, and repealing Directive 2009/22/EC, Brussels, 11.4.2018, COM(2018) 184 final.

70 In this respect, the preliminary reference of the Irish High Court is of great significance.

71 Resolution of 4.7.2017, P8_TA (2017) 282.

72 For a brief description, cf. Stadler, 'Harmonisierung des Europäischen Zivilprozessrechts – Mindeststandards oder Modellregeln?', *JZ* 2017, 693, 698.

BRUSSELS CALLING. THE EXTRA-EU EFFECT OF EUROPEAN PRIVATE INTERNATIONAL LAW

Thalia KRUGER
University of Antwerp and
Honorary Research Associate, University of Cape Town

1. INTRODUCTION: BRUSSELS CALLING

During the nineteen-sixties the European Economic Community (EEC) was a regional organisation with only six Member States[1], all adhering to the continental European civil law legal tradition. They were only at the start of a long process to incorporate their markets. Already at this early stage, it became apparent that in order to ensure the proper functioning of an internal market and to avoid abuses (debtors quickly and easily moving their assets), a regime of the recognition and enforcement of judgments within the EEC was necessary.

From an outside (sometimes referred to as 'third State') perspective, two elements of this early choice are significant. First, the focus was on the recognition and enforcement within the EEC: this was an internal initiative serving an internal goal. Its aims were different from the initiatives undertaken by the Hague Conference on Private International Law[2], which were more global in their nature.

Second, the Member States of the EEC opted for a double convention (sometimes called a 'mixed convention'), i.e. a convention including provisions not only on recognition and enforcement, but also on jurisdiction. This choice has had a vital impact outside the Member States.

The purpose of this contribution is to examine the effect of the Brussels *Ibis* Regulation outside its natural place of functioning, namely the EU. Many transactions today are concluded and/or executed partly in the EU and partly elsewhere. This extra-EU effect was not a major concern for the drafters of the previous editions of

1 Belgium, France, Germany, Italy, Luxembourg and the Netherlands.
2 See the Chapter by Marta Pertegás in this volume, p. 67.

the Brussels Convention[3] or the Brussels I Regulation (2001 version)[4]. At the time of the drafting of the Brussels I*bis* Regulation, the EU institutions did consider the issue of its global effect. However, only small changes were made. These include a broadened scope for the benefit of certain forum agreements and of EU consumers dealing with companies outside the EU. Important improvements in Brussels I*bis* include the limited possibility to decline jurisdiction in favour of courts outside the EU and a yielding to the Hague Choice of Court Convention. All considered, the current calls by Brussels to the world are still insufficient in a global context.

2. HISTORICAL CONTEXT: BRUSSELS AWAKENING

In the nineteen-sixties the idea of a double convention was quite novel. Most international instruments (bilateral and multilateral) focused on the recognition and enforcement of judgments without imposing direct rules of jurisdiction. At most they had only what is called "indirect" rules of jurisdiction. Thus, some of these conventions contained acceptable bases of jurisdiction upon which recognition and enforcement would be possible. These bases of jurisdiction were indirect in the sense that a court considering enforcement would test whether the court issuing the judgment complied with them. Thus, the conventions did not oblige courts to abide by these jurisdiction rules, but if they did not, there was a risk that the resulting judgment would not be capable of being enforced. On the other hand, in the case of a double convention the Contracting States commit to use only the direct jurisdiction rules agreed in the convention. The enforcing court will be able to assume that the court that issued the judgment respected these rules. Therefore, enforcement will be easier. The Hague Conference on Private International Law later attempted this approach of a double convention on a global level, but the endeavours failed.[5]

The goal for the Brussels Convention, since its first version, was to include direct jurisdiction rules in a convention which ultimately had the purpose to facilitate the recognition and enforcement of judgments. The thinking was that if all members of the club agreed to the same jurisdiction rules for international disputes, there would be less difficulty to enforce the resulting judgments.

---

3 Brussels Convention on jurisdiction and the enforcement of judgments in civil and commercial matters of 27 September 1968, [1972] OJ L299/32 of 9 October 1978, *[1978] OJ L304/1* of 25 October 1982, *[1982] OJ L388/1* of 26 May 1989, *[1989] OJ L285/1* of 29 November 1996, consolidated version *[1998] OJ C27/1*.

4 Council Regulation (EC) No 44/2001 of 22 December 2000 on jurisdiction and the recognition and enforcement of judgments in civil and commercial matters, *[2001] OJ L12/1*.

5 See Interim Text – Summary of the Outcome of the Discussion in Commission II of the First Part of the Diplomatic Conference (6–22 June 2001), prepared by the Permanent Bureau and the Co-reporters, available at https://www.hcch.net/en/publications-and-studies/details4/?pid=3499&dtid=35 (consulted 30 May 2018).

The problem, though, was that the double nature of the Convention was incomplete.[6] The Convention's jurisdiction rules were not (and are still not) universal: they are not always applicable, but only subject to certain rules of personal scope (see below). However, the recognition and enforcement rules apply to all judgments from Member State courts. At the time of enforcement, the enforcing court will not (bar in the case of exclusive jurisdiction and protective bases of jurisdiction) test the basis of jurisdiction used by the court issuing the judgment. All judgments emanating from Member State courts are included in the recognition and enforcement regime, irrespective of whether the jurisdiction was originally based on the Convention or not.

An example explains the problem: a dispute between a French buyer and a Chinese seller of plastic toys falls outside the personal scope of the Convention if the French buyer is the plaintiff and the Chinese seller the defendant. A French court would therefore not have to apply the Convention's bases of jurisdiction but can use French domestic law. The French court can take jurisdiction on the basis that the plaintiff is a French national.[7] This ground of jurisdiction is considered exorbitant and is not permitted when the Convention applies.[8] However, at the stage of enforcement, the Convention does apply to this case: it regulates the enforcement in all Member States of judgments issued in other Member States.

This incomplete duality disadvantages litigating parties resident outside the EU (the Chinese seller in the example above). In fact, the position under the Convention is worse for them than it was prior to the creation of the Brussels Convention: at that time, the French court would still have taken jurisdiction, but enforcement in other States would have been more difficult. The incomplete duality of the Convention thus amplifies the negative effect of exorbitant bases of jurisdiction. Scholars from outside the EEC (as it then was) were quick to pick up this negative effect of the Brussels Convention. In particular, American authors heavily criticised the negative effect on their residents.[9] The almost abolition of exequatur in Brussels I*bis* further amplifies this negative effect on these residents.

---

6 Discussed extensively in T. Kruger, *Civil jurisdiction rules of the EU and their impact on third States*, Oxford, Oxford University Press 2008. See also the discussion of the problem by P. Franzina, 'L'universalisation partielle du régime européen de la compétence en matière civile et commerciale dans le règlement Bruxelles I*bis*: une mise en perspective' in E. Guinchard, *Le nouveau règlement Bruxelles I bis*, Brussels, Bruylant 2014, pp. 39–82, esp. at pp. 59–63.

7 Art. 14 French *code civil*.

8 Such exorbitant bases of jurisdiction can vary, but can be divided into three main categories: those related to the nationality of the plaintiff, those related to the presence or activities of the defendant and those related to the presence of property belonging to the defendant (sometimes of insignificant value and unrelated to the dispute). See the discussion by the European Group of Private International Law (GEDIP): See the report of its Seventeenth meeting, held in Hamburg in 2007, M. Fallon, P. Kinch and C. Kohler (eds), *Building European Private International Law*, Cambridge, Intersentia 2011, 651–699, at p. 666, also available at https://www.gedip-egpil.eu/reunionstravail/gedip-reunions-17t-fr.html.

9 K.H. Nadelmann, 'Jurisdictionally improper fora in treaties on recognition and enforcement of judgments. The Common Market Draft' *Columbia Law Review* 1967, 995–1023; K.H.

3. FROM THREE TO FOUR SCOPE RULES

Despite the criticism that existed from the first version of the Brussels Convention, the personal scope remained the same throughout the various versions until the 2012 version, which brought only a slight change.

The Conventions and Regulation (2001 version) apply if one of three scope rules is adhered to.[10] The first is where the defendant is domiciled in a Member State. The second arises where an exclusive basis of jurisdiction leads to jurisdiction of a Member State court. These bases of jurisdiction concern matters such as immovable property, and the registration and validity of intellectual property.[11] The third scope rule is if the parties, one of which is domiciled in a Member State, agree on a forum in the EU.[12] If none of these three scope rules points to a Member State, the courts are free to use their domestic rules of jurisdiction.

The Brussels I*bis* Regulation brought a slight change to this matter. However, the slight change was preceded by an extended study and ambitious plans.

The Commission had ordered a large study on the matter before making the proposal. This study was finalised in 2007.[13] It gave an extensive explanation of the issues and the interaction between the bases of jurisdiction in the Brussels I Regulation and the residual bases of jurisdiction in national law. After an overview of the reasons why the original Brussels Convention only included jurisdiction rules for the selected situations, the authors considered the viability of extending the personal scope of the Regulation. The authors examined five possible ways of extending this scope[14]:

a) Application when a dispute is intra-Community, not only when the defendant is domiciled in the EU;
b) Application as soon as either the plaintiff or the defendant is domiciled in the EU;
c) Application to Community disputes, defined by referring to the geographical scope of EU law;

Nadelmann and A.T. von Mehren, 'Equivalences in treaties in the conflicts field' *American Journal of Comparative Law* 1966–1967, 195–203.

10 Art. 4 Brussels Conventions and Brussels I Regulation (2001 version).

11 Art. 16 Brussels Conventions; Art. 22 Brussels I Regulation (2001 version).

12 Art. 17 Brussels Conventions; Art. 23 Brussels I Regulation (2001 version).

13 A. Nuyts and K. Szychowska, 'Study on Residual Jurisdiction (Review of the Member States' Rules concerning the "Residual Jurisdiction" of their courts in Civil and Commercial Matters pursuant to the Brussels I and II Regulations)', Study for the European Commission, 2007.

14 *Ibid*, p. 105–117.

d) Extending the scope to claims against non-EU defendants on the basis of specific connecting factors;
e) Extending the scope to all situations, irrespective of the domicile of the defendants. This would mean harmonising the so-called residual bases of jurisdiction, which now fall under domestic law (such as that of France, discussed above[15]).

The Commission, in its Proposal of 2010, chose the fifth option.[16] It considered the personal scope as one of the four main shortcomings of the Regulation, stating in the Explanatory Memorandum:

> Access to justice in the EU is overall unsatisfactory in disputes involving defendants from outside the EU. With some exceptions, the current Regulation only applies where the defendant is domiciled inside the EU. Otherwise jurisdiction is governed by national law. The diversity of national law leads to unequal access to justice for EU companies in transactions with partners from third countries: some can easily litigate in the EU, others cannot, even in situations where no other court guaranteeing a fair trial is competent. In addition, where national legislation does not grant access to court in disputes with parties outside the EU, the enforcement of mandatory EU law protecting e.g. consumers, employees or commercial agents is not guaranteed.[17]

The Commission thus took the bold step of proposing to extend the bases of jurisdiction to all defendants.[18] This would mean that the exorbitant bases that still exist in national legislation would be entirely deleted for all civil and commercial matters that fall within the material scope of the Regulation. The Regulation would thus have a universal application.

This step should have been possible in light of the fact that another Regulation in the area of civil jurisdiction, the Maintenance Regulation[19], already followed this approach. Other Regulations that followed Brussels I*bis* also took this approach:

---

15 Art. 14 French *code civil:* see §6 above. Since the entry into force of the Belgian Code on Private International Law (Act of 16 July 2014), Belgium has no exorbitant bases of jurisdiction. The remaining bases are to a large extent similar to those in the Brussels I Regulation (such as Art. 96 on jurisdiction for contract and tort disputes). For the bases of jurisdiction of other Member States, see the comprehensive study by NUYTS and SZYCHOWSKA (n. 13 above).

16 Proposal for a Regulation of the European Parliament and of the Council on jurisdiction and the recognition and enforcement of judgments in civil and commercial matters (Recast), 14 December 2010, COM (2010) 748. See also R. LUZZATTO, 'On the proposed application of jurisdictional criteria of Brussels I Regulation to non-domiciled defendants' in F. POCAR, I. VIARENGO and F.C. VILLATA, *Recasting Brussels I*, Cedam, Liman 2012, pp. 111–116.

17 *Ibid.* p. 3.

18 This was in line with the recommendations by the GEDIP (see n. 8 above).

19 Council Regulation (EC) No 4/2009 of 18 December 2008 on jurisdiction, applicable law, recognition and enforcement of decisions and cooperation in matters relating to maintenance obligations, *[2009] OJ L7/1.*

the Succession Regulation[20], the Matrimonial Property Regulation[21] and the Regulation on the Property Consequences of Registered Partnerships.[22] However, the step was bold in the sense that this would have been one of the most significant changes to the general structure of the Brussels regime since its inception.

The new approach required amendments to various provisions. First of all the recitals requiring a link with the territory of an EU Member State were deleted and replaced by an explanation that the Regulation would establish a 'complete set of rules on international jurisdiction of the courts in the Member States'[23] and would require a flexible mechanism allowing Member State courts to take account of proceedings pending in third States.[24]

The Proposal maintained the existing bases of jurisdiction, but allowed them to be used also against defendants from third States. For these defendants, two extra provisions were added, encompassing the residual jurisdiction that was previously governed by domestic law. The first new provision concerned subsidiary jurisdiction based on the location of the property of the defendant, on the condition that the value of the property is not disproportionate to the value of the claim and that the dispute had a sufficient link with the court seised.[25] The second provision is *forum necessitatis*, providing access to a Member State court if i) proceedings could not reasonably be brought in a third State or a third court judgment would not be capable of recognition in the Member State of the court seised and ii) the dispute has a sufficient link with the State of the court seised.[26]

Lastly, the Proposal allowed Member State courts to decline jurisdiction in favour of third State courts (see below).[27]

The European Parliament considered that the time was not ripe for such extension, stating that 'the question whether the rules of the Regulation should be extended in this way requires wide-ranging consultation and political debate.'[28]

---

20 Regulation (EU) No 650/2012 of the European Parliament and of the Council of 4 July 2012 on jurisdiction, applicable law, recognition and enforcement of decisions and acceptance and enforcement of authentic instruments in matters of succession and on the creation of a European Certificate of Succession, *[2012] OJ L201/107.*

21 Council Regulation (EU) 2016/1103 of 24 June 2016 implementing enhanced cooperation in the area of jurisdiction, applicable law and the recognition and enforcement of decisions in matters of matrimonial property regimes, *[2016] OJ L183/1.*

22 Council Regulation (EU) 2016/1104 of 24 June 2016 implementing enhanced cooperation in the area of jurisdiction, applicable law and the recognition and enforcement of decisions in matters of the property consequences of registered partnerships, *[2016] OJ L183/30.*

23 Recital 17 of the Commission's Proposal.

24 Recital 21 of the Commission's Proposal.

25 Art. 25 of the Commission's Proposal.

26 Art. 26 of the Commission's Proposal.

27 Art. 34 of the Commission's Proposal.

28 See the Explanatory Statement by the European Parliament accompanying its Resolution of 20 November 2012 on the adoption of the Regulation, P7_TA(2012)0412.

The Parliament had indeed already taken this stance in 2010 in reaction to the Commission's Green Paper and before the publication of its Proposal.[29] The Council followed this point of view.

Only three elements of the ambitious plan of the Commission remained in the final version of the Brussels *Ibis* Regulation. The first concerns the second scope rule discussed above: if parties choose a forum, their domicile is irrelevant for purposes of the application of the Regulation. This means that if a buyer from Andorra and a seller from Macao agree to the jurisdiction of the French courts, Brussels *Ibis* will apply. This amendment has to be seen in the light of the Hague Choice of Court Convention.[30] This Convention aims at the global respecting of choice-of-court agreements, but as it covers a matter already covered by Brussels I, a complex disconnection rule was introduced (see below).

The second element that survived is the extension of the Regulation to consumers and employees domiciled in the EU, litigating against defendants domiciled outside the EU.[31] Brussels *Ibis* applies to these cases while they fall outside the scope of Brussels I. This extension enhances the protection of consumers in the EU. However, in certain countries (such as Belgium) this change is only a regulatory one: the rules in domestic law are virtually the same as those in Brussels I.[32] The litigants will now rely directly on the Regulation and not on domestic law, but in the end the same court will have jurisdiction.

The third is the rule on declining jurisdiction, which is the subject of the next chapter.

4. DECLINING JURISDICTION

One of the major issues concerning the extra-EU effect of Brussels I is whether a court in the EU can decline jurisdiction in favour of a court outside the EU. If jurisdiction is based on domestic law (e.g. because the defendant is domiciled outside the EU), national rules of declining jurisdiction come into play. These rules can be diverse in nature and include *forum non conveniens*.

On the other hand, when jurisdiction is based on Brussels I, Member State courts may not use their domestic rules to decline jurisdiction. The Court of Justice

---

29 See the European Parliament resolution of 7 September 2010 on the implementation and review of Council Regulation (EC) No 44/2001 on jurisdiction and the recognition and enforcement of judgments in civil and commercial matters (2009/2140(INI)). See also A. Borrás, 'The application of the Brussels I Regulation to defendants domiciled in third States: from the EGPIL to the Commission Proposal' in E. Lein (ed), *The Brussels I Review Proposal Uncovered*, British Institute of International and Comparative Law, London, 2012, 57–74.

30 Hague Convention of 30 June 2005 on Choice of Court Agreements.

31 Art. 6 Brussels *Ibis* Regulation (recast), which now refers also to Arts. 18(1) and 21(1).

32 See Art. 97 Belgian Code on Private International Law.

of the EU explained in *Owusu v Jackson* that the Brussels system (Convention as it was at the time) contains common rules and that national law should not be permitted to derogate from them.[33]

Before this case, there was uncertainty about the possibility to decline jurisdiction. Even after the case, some debate has remained, specifically with respect to situations of forum clauses in favour of third State courts and *lis pendens*.[34]

The *Owusu* case concerned a claim for damages against one defendant domiciled in England and various others domiciled in Jamaica, for an accident that took place in Jamaica. The basis of jurisdiction of the Jamaican courts was not linked to immovable property or a similar connection that would have led to exclusive jurisdiction in accordance with Brussels I.

The Court of Appeal of England and Wales, which referred the question to the Court of Justice, phrased its second question broadly, seeking certainty about when declining of jurisdiction would be permissible. However, the Court of Justice refrained from answering this question, as it was not connected to the facts of the case before the Court of Appeal and thus hypothetical. The Court therefore considered the question outside the ambit of the preliminary reference procedure.[35] The silence by the Court of Justice has prolonged the uncertainty.

The issue landed on the table of the judges in Luxembourg once more in the form of the *Lugano Opinion*.[36] This concerned a dispute between the European Commission and the EU Member States on whether the negotiation and signing of the Lugano Convention[37] was a shared competence or one belonging exclusively to the European Community (as it then was). The Court's decision analysed in detail the extra-EU impact of the Regulation. As part of this analysis, the Court explained the extra-EU effect as follows: the provisions of the Lugano Convention enables the 'selection as the appropriate forum of a court of a non-member country which is a party to that [Lugano] Convention, where the defendant is domiciled in a Member State.' It states that 'in the absence of the Convention, that

33 CJEU C-281/02 *Owusu v Jackson*, 1 March 2005, ECLI:EU:C:2005:120.

34 See e.g. R. Fentiman, 'National Law and the European Jurisdiction Regime' in A. Nuyts and N. Watté (eds), *International Civil Litigation in Europe and Relations with Third States*, Brussels, Bruylant, 2005, 83–128.

35 Art. 234 EC Treaty as it then was; now Art. 267 TFEU.

36 Opinion 1/03 of 7 February 2006, ECLI:EU:C:2006:81.

37 Convention on jurisdiction and the recognition and enforcement of judgments in civil and commercial matters, first version concluded in Lugano on 16 September 1988 is in force in the EU Member States and in Iceland, Norway and Switzerland. It was updated various times after an amendment of the Brussels Convention/Regulation to keep the two instruments parallel. At the update subsequent to the enactment of the Brussels I Regulation (2001), the question of competence arose.

latter State would be the appropriate forum, whereas under the Convention it is the non-member country.'[38] Here the Court of Justice clearly indicates that there is no possibility to decline jurisdiction that is based on the Regulation.

Brussels I*bis* introduced a limited possibility to decline jurisdiction in favour of courts in third States. As explained above, this is a remnant of the more ambitious plans by the European Commission.

This limited possibility exists when a case is pending in a court in a third State before it is brought before a court in the EU.[39] In such situations the Regulation now authorises the Member State court to decline its (Regulation-based) jurisdiction if such jurisdiction is based on a general or specific jurisdiction rule, but not when it is based on an exclusive ground of jurisdiction, a forum clause, or a protective rule for employees, consumers or insured parties. It can only decline jurisdiction if the proceedings in the third State court were brought first. The provision takes the same approach as that for *lis pendens* between Member State courts: the court should first stay its proceedings and only when it becomes clear that the other court would issue a judgment, dismiss them. For parallel proceedings with third States, the requirements are that the foreign judgment will be capable of recognition and enforcement and that the stay is necessary for the proper administration of justice.

This limited amendment to Brussels I has to a certain extent kept the uncertainty alive. On one hand, the argument is that the issue is simply not addressed. On the other hand, if the legislator addressed part of the issue, *a contrario* declining jurisdiction in other situations is not permitted. There is not much national case law about this matter.[40]

5. CHOICE OF FORUM

In line with the discussion above, the Regulation is silent on the situation when parties agree to a choice of forum in favour of a court in a third State while a court in a Member State would have jurisdiction on the basis of the Regulation. This situation concerns for instance a Bulgarian and a Turkish party agreeing to the jurisdiction of a court in Turkey and then disrespecting this choice when the plaintiff institutes proceedings.

---

38 Para 153 of Opinion 1/03 of 7 February 2006, ECLI:EU:C:2006:81.

39 Art. 33 Brussels I*bis*.

40 See the analysis by Nuyts and Szychowska (n. 13 above), p. 82. The authors obtained information from all the Member States and found that there was not much application on this particular issue.

One of two distinct scenarios can arise: first, the plaintiff can be the Bulgarian party. This means that the defendant (Turkish party) is domiciled outside the EU and domestic bases of jurisdiction arise. The Bulgarian court would therefore have to examine its jurisdiction on the basis of Bulgarian law. It seems that this should include not only the bases of jurisdiction under Bulgarian law, but also the grounds to decline jurisdiction under Bulgarian law. National courts decline their jurisdiction in these situations.[41] Whether this is on the basis of national law or on the basis of the so-called 'reflexive effect' of the Regulation itself, is still subject to debate. Due to space limitations, I will not enter into that debate here.[42]

Second, the plaintiff can be the Turkish party and the defendant the Bulgarian party. This situation is theoretically harder, but also less likely to arise in practice, because it concerns the third State party preferring a court other than its home forum. The Regulation is silent on the matter which can be interpreted either way, as stated above.

There is some alleviation for choice-of-court agreements in favour of third State courts in the form of the Choice-of-Court Convention.[43] This Convention imposes on courts in Contracting States the duty of respecting such agreements. The EU has ratified the Convention and it is in force in the Member States.[44] Denmark is not bound by the EU's ratification, but has ratified the Convention separately.[45] When a court in a Contracting State that is outside the EU is chosen, the choice will be safeguarded by this Convention.[46] The effect of this Convention is as yet limited: besides the EU, it is in force only in two States.[47]

The fact that the Regulation is silent on other choice-of-court agreements does not seem to be an oversight by the EU legislators, which have clearly consciously engaged with these issues. Possibly the lack of a mechanism to decline jurisdiction in the case of a choice for a foreign court is meant as support for the Hague Convention: if States want EU Member States to respect such agreements in favour of their courts, they should ratify the Convention.

---

41 *Ibid* p. 73.

42 For a discussion, see A. Nuyts, "La théorie de l'effet reflèxe" in M. Storme and G. de Leval (eds), *Le Droit Processuel & Judiciaire Européen*, Bruges, la Charte 2003, pp. 73–89; T. Kruger (above n. 6) 234–245; A. Layton, "The Brussels I Regulation in the international legal order: some reflections on reflectiveness" in E. Lein (ed), *The Brussels I Review Proposal Uncovered*, London, British Institute of International and Comparative Law 2012, pp. 75–81.

43 Hague Convention of 30 June 2005 on Choice of Court Agreements.

44 See the status table at https://www.hcch.net/en/instruments/conventions/status-table/?cid=98.

45 On 30 May 2018, which means that it will be in force there as of 1 September 2018.

46 See the complicated disconnection clause in Art. 26 of the Convention; see also Art. 71 Brussels I*bis*.

47 Mexico and Singapore. It has also been signed but not yet ratified by China, Montenegro, Ukraine and the US; see full states table at https://www.hcch.net/en/instruments/conventions/status-table/?cid=98.

6. CONCLUSION: BRUSSELS ENTICING

This overview has shown the evolution in the relation between the Brussels regime and the outside world over the past fifty years. In the first forty years, the basic approach did not change. Since the *Owusu* judgment and the *Lugano Opinion* by the Court of Justice of the EU, the question has received more attention. It was one of the central matters during the Recast process. The Commission was prepared to make big changes, but the other institutions did not follow. The Regulation does contain some changes. The most positive is the introduction of a possibility for Member State courts to decline jurisdiction in favour of a court in a third State that was seised first. Unfortunately, there is not a broad possibility to decline jurisdiction in the case of a choice-of-court agreement in favour of a third State court when the Member State court has jurisdiction on another basis. The Hague Choice-of-Court Convention can offer a solution for these cases, but outside the application of that Convention it seems that there is no possibility to decline jurisdiction.

The more fundamental problem is that, despite the advances made, the dual nature of the Regulation remains incomplete. There is not yet radical consistency. This is a pity because such consistency has proved possible in other regulations in the same legal sphere (such as the Maintenance and Succession Regulations). There will be future amendments and improvements to the Brussels I regime. Undoubtedly this matter will be back on the legislator's table and hopefully significant progress will be made.

THE (NOT SO SYMBIOTIC?) RELATION BETWEEN THE INSOLVENCY AND THE BRUSSELS I REGIMES

Arie VAN HOE
Solicitor NautaDutilh
Affiliated researcher University of Antwerp

1. INTRODUCTION

The purpose of this paper is to examine the relation between the Insolvency (Recast) Regulation and the Brussels I (Recast) Regulation. This relation is notoriously unclear ('*einen der umstrittensten und schwierigsten Komplexe des Internationalen Insolvenzrechts*'[1]). In order to shed some light on the matter, the boundary[2] between both regulations will be examined.

A complicating factor in this respect, is the evolving and particular nature of insolvency proceedings. The *evolving* nature of insolvency proceedings is illustrated by a clear shift from liquidation to reorganization.[3] Modern insolvency proceedings are no longer (solely) focused on the liquidation of (the assets of) the debtor.[4] Instead, across the European Union a trend can be witnessed whereby insolvency proceedings are used to reorganize (the enterprise of) the debtor.[5] This shift has led to the introduction of all kinds of new insolvency proceedings, with

1 P. MANKOWSKI, M. F. MÜLLER and J. SCHMIDT, *Europäische Insolvenzverordnung 2015*, München, Verlag C. H. Beck 2016, p. 159.

2 See, D. ROBINE, 'Les actions connexes' in F. JAULT-SESEKE and D. ROBINE, *Le nouveau règlement insolvabilité: quelles évolutions?*, Paris, Joly éditions 2015, (61) p. 61, nr. 1: '*Les actions connexes soulèvent une question de "frontière". Il s'agit plus précisément d'évoquer la frontière entre la règlement insolvabilité et le (…) règlement Bruxelles I révisé.*'

3 K. WIMMER, A. BORNEMANN and M. D. LIENAU, *Die Neufassung der EuInsoVO*, Köln, Luchterhand Verlag 2016, p. 9, nr. 31.

4 See, Recital 10 Insolvency (Recast) Regulation: '*The scope of this Regulation should extend to proceedings which promote the rescue of economically viable but distressed businesses and which give a second chance to entrepreneurs.*'

5 R. BORK and R. MANGANO, *European Cross-Border Insolvency Law*, Oxford, Oxford University Press 2016, p. 18, nr. 1.38.

different characteristics than traditional insolvency proceedings.[6] The *particular* nature of insolvency[7] proceedings relates to creditors (but also creditors between themselves[8]) and debtors trying to resolve a financial and/or economic problem. The outcome of this process affects other stakeholders (in particular employees). This is the core of insolvency proceedings.[9] Related to this core are a multitude of 'related' proceedings, which in principle exist autonomously from insolvency proceedings, but frequently arise in the context thereof.[10]

In order to understand the present, it is good to understand the past. Therefore, the structure of this paper is chronological. Three stages are distinguished. First, I briefly look at the situation before the Insolvency Regulation and the Brussels I Regulation. Secondly, I consider the relationship between the Brussels I Regulation and the Insolvency Regulation. Lastly, I examine the current situation.

2. PHASE 1: THE BRUSSELS CONVENTION

It is well-known that the 1968 Brussels Convention did not apply to 'bankruptcy, proceedings relating to the winding-up of insolvent companies or other legal persons, judicial arrangements, compositions and analogous proceedings'. These proceedings were not excluded from the scope of application because they were considered irrelevant for international business. Instead, the idea was to cover

---

6 L. Sautonie-Laguionie, 'Introduction' in A. Cottiga-Raccah and L. Sautonie-Laguionie, *Le nouveau droit européen des faillites internationales*, Brussels, Larcier 2018, (1) 10: *'(...) le droit doit offrir d'autres solutions sous peine d'être un droit en échec. Il doit permettre aussi, et le plus souvent possible, de faire redémarrer une activité car ce n'est qu'en ce cas que nombre de créanciers pourront être payés, que des emplois seront sauvés et que l'économie pourra prospérer en préservant ses acteurs. De nouvelles procédures ont dont été créées, centrées davantage sur le sauvetage des entreprises que sur la liquidation de leur patrimoine.'*

7 See, R. Bork, *Principles of Cross-Border Insolvency Law*, Antwerp, Intersentia 2017, p. 17, nr. 1.30; E. Dirix, 'Het insolventierecht anno 2014' in H. Braeckmans (ed.), *Curatoren en vereffenaars: actuele ontwikkelingen III*, Antwerp, Intersentia 2014, (3) p. 28, nr. 30.

8 Insolvency law provides a solution for the common pool problem which arises if a debtor is unable to pay his creditors. It aims to replace the first come, first served situation with a compulsory legal regime that coordinates the different interest involved, R. Bork and R. Mangano, *European Cross-Border Insolvency Law*, Oxford, Oxford University Press 2016, p. 11, nr. 1.03.

9 G. van Calster, *European Private International Law*, Oxford, Hart Publishing 2016, p. 42, nr. 2.2.2.10.1: *'The subject of insolvency proceedings by its nature almost always involves a multitude of stakeholders, and the subject-matter of the multitude of claims is much more varied than in the average private international law scenario.'*

10 Y. Brulard and J. Materne, 'Les actions annexes' in Y. Brulard (ed.), *L'insolvabilité nationale, européenne et internationale*, Limal, Anthemis 2017, (123) p. 123, nr. 1: *'Les droit nationaux prévoient différentes actions qui peuvent être introduites en raison de l'existence d'une procédure d'insolvabilité soit contre le débiteur lui-même et/ou soit contre des tiers du débiteur lui-même, ses dirigeant ou contre certains de ses créanciers ou tiers en lien contractuel ou non avec le débiteur, actions qui ont une conséquence sur la poursuite des activités du débiteur ou sur le dividende que percevront les créanciers.'*

them with a separate instrument, taking into account the special nature of the matter and the profound differences between the Contracting States of the Brussels Convention[11], in particular with respect to the question of what actions or disputes fall within the jurisdiction of the court opening the insolvency proceedings.[12] It is an equally well-known fact that the Insolvency Convention was a (very) long time in the making (and in fact never became reality).[13]

The seminal judgment (precedent *avant la lettre*)[14] with respect to the 'bankruptcy exception' is the *Gourdain* judgment.[15] In this judgment (dealing with the French *action en comblement de passif*), the Court of Justice held that a decision ordering the *de facto* manager of a legal person to pay a sum into the assets of the company must be considered as falling within the bankruptcy exception. More generally, the Court of Justice ruled that an action is related to bankruptcy only if it derives directly from the bankruptcy *and* it is closely linked to proceedings for realising the assets or judicial supervision.[16] These criteria will remain relevant up to and including the Insolvency (Recast) Regulation.

3. PHASE 2: INSOLVENCY REGULATION – BRUSSELS I REGULATION

3.1 ABSENCE OF CLEAR RULES

The Brussels I Regulation, just like the 1968 Brussels Convention, did not apply to bankruptcy, proceedings relating to the winding-up of insolvent companies or other legal persons, judicial arrangements, compositions and analogous proceedings. Regretfully, the Insolvency Regulation did not contain clear rules on

11 G. VAN CALSTER, *European Private International Law*, Oxford, Hart Publishing 2016, p. 40, nr. 2.2.2.10.

12 M. VIRGOS and F. GARCIMARTIN, *The European Insolvency Regulation: Law and Practice*, The Hague, Kluwer Law International, 2004, p. 55, nr. 74: '*(…) national laws adopt very different solutions on the extent of that jurisdiction, in particular on the question of whether it is confined to the core procedure itself or extends to other ancillary actions related to insolvency.*'

13 For useful background, see, R. BORK and R. MANGANO, *European Cross-Border Insolvency Law*, Oxford, Oxford University Press 2016, 13–24; K. VAN ZWIETEN, 'An introduction to the European Regulation, as made and as recast' in R. BORK and K. VAN ZWIETEN (eds.), *Commentary on the European Insolvency Regulation*, Oxford, Oxford University Press 2016, (1) 9–22.

14 R. BORK and R. MANGANO, *European Cross-Border Insolvency Law*, Oxford, Oxford University Press 2016, p. 108, nr. 3.70.

15 *Gourdain*, C-133/78, ECLI:EU:C:1979:49.

16 See, W. G.-RINGE, 'Jurisdiction for actions which derive directly from the insolvency proceedings and are closely linked with them' in R. BORK and K. VAN ZWIETEN (eds.), *Commentary on the European Insolvency Regulation*, Oxford, Oxford University Press 2016, (201) p. 203, nr. 606: '*This decision is commonly understood as the birth hour of a European 'vis attractiva concursus', according to which the insolvency court takes on for itself the (often exclusive) jurisdiction for related disputes.*'

its relationship with the Brussels I Regulation.[17] There was no clear rule regarding jurisdiction for actions deriving directly from insolvency.[18] Only with respect to recognition, did the Insolvency Regulation explicitly refer to judgments deriving directly from the insolvency proceedings and which are closely linked with them (art. 25. 1 Insolvency Regulation).[19]

3.2 CASE-LAW OF THE COURT OF JUSTICE

In the absence of clear rules in the Insolvency Regulation, it was up to the Court of Justice to determine the boundaries between both regimes in its case-law.[20] A couple of guiding principles can be derived from this case-law. In *Seagon*, the Court of Justice held that article 3(1) of the Insolvency Regulation must be interpreted as meaning that it also confers international jurisdiction on the Member State within the territory of which insolvency proceedings were opened in order to hear and determine actions which derive directly from those proceedings and which are closely connected to them.[21] Concentrating all the actions directly related to the insolvency of an undertaking before the courts of the Member State with jurisdiction to open the insolvency proceedings appears consistent with the objective of improving the effectiveness and efficiency of insolvency proceedings having cross-border effects.[22] In later judgments, the Court of Justice made clear that *Seagon* (also) applies in situations whereby the place of residence or registered office of the person against whom an action to have a transaction set aside is in a third country.[23] The Court of Justice furthermore confirmed that also

---

17 P. Mankowski, M. F. Müller and J. Schmidt, *Europäische Insolvenzverordnung 2015*, München, Verlag C. H. Beck 2016, p. 160, nr. 2; M. Vanmeenen, 'De herziening van de Insolventieverordening' in B. Allemeersch en T. Kruger (eds.), *Handboek Europees burgerlijk procesrecht*, Antwerpen, Intersentia 2015, (327) p. 354, nr. 24.

18 Recital 6 of the Insolvency Regulation did however refer to jurisdiction for 'judgments which are delivered directly on the basis of the insolvency proceedings and are closely connected with such proceedings'. Recital are however not binding, R. Bork and R. Mangano, *European Cross-Border Insolvency Law*, Oxford, Oxford University Press 2016, p. 107, fn. 103.

19 D. Robine, 'Les actions connexes' in F. Jault-Seseke and D. Robine, *Le nouveau règlement insolvabilité: quelles évolutions?*, Paris, Joly éditions 2015, (61) p. 63, nr. 4: '*L'article 25 du règlement du 29 mai 2000 n'évoque toutefois que la reconnaissance des décisions. On pouvait certes y voir une référence implicite à la compétence juridictionnelle, mais il n'en est pas directement question.*' See also, P. Mankowski, M. F. Müller and J. Schmidt, *Europäische Insolvenzverordnung 2015*, München, Verlag C. H. Beck 2016, p. 160, nr. 2.

20 On the interpretation of the Insolvency Regulation and the role of the Court of Justice, see, R. Bork and R. Mangano, *European Cross-Border Insolvency Law*, Oxford, Oxford University Press 2016, 30–38.

21 *Seagon*, C-339/07, ECLI:EU:C:2009:83, para 21.

22 *Seagon*, C-339/07, ECLI:EU:C:2009:83, para 22. See also, W. G.-Ringe, "Jurisdiction for actions which derive directly from the insolvency proceedings and are closely linked with them" in R. Bork and K. van Zwieten (eds.), *Commentary on the European Insolvency Regulation*, Oxford, Oxford University Press 2016, (201) pp. 204–205.

23 *Schmid*, C-328/12, EU:C:2014:6, para 39; *H*, C-295/13, ECLI:EU:C:2014:2410, 33.

the courts of the Member State in which secondary insolvency proceedings have been opened have jurisdiction to rule on a related action, concurrently with the courts of the Member State in which the main proceedings have been opened.[24]

The Court of Justice also further clarified the Gourdain criteria. In order to determine whether an action derives directly from insolvency proceedings (first Gourdain criterion), the decisive criterion adopted by the Court to identify the area within which an action falls is not the procedural context of which that action is part, but the legal basis thereof. According to that approach it must be determined whether the right or the obligation which forms the basis of the action has its source in the ordinary rules of civil and commercial law or in derogating rules specific to insolvency proceedings.[25] The mere fact that an insolvency practitioner is a party to the proceedings is not sufficient to classify the proceedings as proceedings deriving directly from the insolvency and being closely linked to these proceedings.[26] As to the second Gourdain criterion, the closeness of the link between a court action and the insolvency proceedings is considered to be decisive.[27]

Finally, according to the Court of Justice the intention of the EU legislature was to adopt a broad definition of the concept of 'civil and commercial matters' in Article 1(1) of the Brussels I Regulation and, consequently, to provide that the article should be broad in its scope. By contrast, the scope of the Insolvency Regulation should not be given a broad interpretation.[28]

4. PHASE 3: INSOLVENCY RECAST REGULATION – BRUSSELS I RECAST REGULATION

4.1 DOUBLE (NOT: FATAL) ATTRACTION

The Insolvency (Recast) Regulation contains specific rules regarding jurisdiction for actions deriving directly from insolvency. A distinction can be made in this respect between an attraction to insolvency proceedings on the one hand and an

24 *Comité d'entreprise de Nortel Networks and Others*, C-649/13, ECLI:EU:C:2015:384, 46.

25 *Valach and Others*, C649/16, ECLI:EU:C:2017:986, para 29; *Tünkers France and Tünkers Maschinenbau*, C641/16, EU:C:2017:847, para 22; *Nickel & Goeldner Spedition*, C-157/13, ECLI:EU:C:2014:2145, 27.

26 *German Graphics Graphische Maschinen*, C-292/08, ECLI:EU:C:2009:544, para 33.

27 *Valach and Others*, C649/16, ECLI:EU:C:2017:986, para 37; *Tünkers France and Tünkers Maschinenbau*, C641/16, EU:C:2017:847, para 282.

28 *Valach and Others*, C649/16, ECLI:EU:C:2017:986, para 25; *Tünkers France and Tünkers Maschinenbau*, C641/16, EU:C:2017:847, para 18; *German Graphics Graphische Maschinen*, C-292/08, ECLI:EU:C:2009:544, para 25; *Nickel & Goeldner Spedition*, C-157/13, ECLI:EU:C: 2014:2145, 22.

attraction to an(other) action in civil and commercial matters on the other hand.[29] The relevant Recitals and articles, which are discussed below, are the following:

Recital 6:
This Regulation should include provisions governing jurisdiction for opening insolvency proceedings and actions which are directly derived from insolvency proceedings and are closely linked with them. This Regulation should also contain provisions regarding the recognition and enforcement of judgments issued in such proceedings, and provisions regarding the law applicable to insolvency proceedings. (…)

Recital 35:
The courts of the Member State within the territory of which insolvency proceedings have been opened should also have jurisdiction for actions which derive directly from the insolvency proceedings and are closely linked with them. Such actions should include avoidance actions against defendants in other Member States and actions concerning obligations that arise in the course of the insolvency proceedings, such as advance payment for costs of the proceedings. In contrast, actions for the performance of the obligations under a contract concluded by the debtor prior to the opening of proceedings do not derive directly from the proceedings. Where such an action is related to another action based on general civil and commercial law, the insolvency practitioner should be able to bring both actions in the courts of the defendant's domicile if he considers it more efficient to bring the action in that forum. This could, for example, be the case where the insolvency practitioner wishes to combine an action for director's liability on the basis of insolvency law with an action based on company law or general tort law.

Article 6 Insolvency (Jurisdiction for actions deriving directly from insolvency proceedings and closely linked with them):
1. The courts of the Member State within the territory of which insolvency proceedings have been opened in accordance with Article 3 shall have jurisdiction for any action which derives directly from the insolvency proceedings and is closely linked with them, such as avoidance actions.
2. Where an action referred to in paragraph 1 is related to an action in civil and commercial matters against the same defendant, the insolvency practitioner may bring both actions before the courts of the Member State within the territory of which the defendant is domiciled, or, where the action is brought against several defendants, before the courts of the Member State within the territory of which any of them is domiciled, provided that those courts have jurisdiction pursuant to Regulation (EU) No 1215/2012.
The first subparagraph shall apply to the debtor in possession, provided that national law allows the debtor in possession to bring actions on behalf of the insolvency estate.
3. For the purpose of paragraph 2, actions are deemed to be related where they are so closely connected that it is expedient to hear and determine them together to avoid the risk of irreconcilable judgments resulting from separate proceedings.

---

29 D. Robine, 'Les actions connexes' in F. Jault-Seseke and D. Robine, *Le nouveau règlement insolvabilité: quelles évolutions?*, Paris, Joly éditions 2015, (61) p. 64, nr. 7: '*Il y a donc consolidation de la connexité inclusive dans le champ d'application du règlement insolvabilité (…) et création d'une connexité extractive de ce champ d'application.*'

4.1.1 *Attraction to insolvency proceedings*

Unlike its predecessor, the Insolvency (Recast) Regulation contains an express rule with respect to actions deriving directly from insolvency proceedings and closely linked with them. Such actions shall[30] be brought before the courts of the Member State (whereby it is up to the national law to decide whether this is the same court which has opened the insolvency proceedings[31]) within the territory of which insolvency proceedings have been opened in accordance with Article 3 Insolvency (Recast) Regulation.[32] The principle applies both to main and secondary insolvency proceedings, in line with the existing case law of the Court of Justice.[33] Efficiency considerations justify a deviation from the principle *actor forum rei sequitur.*[34]

No formal definition of such actions which derive directly from insolvency proceedings and are closely linked with them is provided (other than the examples and exclusion in recital 35).[35] The absence of more precise criteria is criticized.[36]

---

30 The use of 'shall' indicates an exclusive forum, Y. Brulard and J. Materne, 'Les actions annexes' in Y. Brulard (ed.), *L'insolvabilité nationale, européenne et internationale*, Limal, Anthemis 2017, (123) p. 127, nr. 12; R. Bork and R. Mangano, *European Cross-Border Insolvency Law*, Oxford, Oxford University Press 2016, p. 111, nr. 3.75. See also, D. Robine, 'Les actions connexes' in F. Jault-Seseke and D. Robine, *Le nouveau règlement insolvabilité: quelles évolutions?*, Paris, Joly éditions 2015, (61) p. 66, nr. 12. See however, W. G.-Ringe, 'Jurisdiction for actions which derive directly from the insolvency proceedings and are closely linked with them' in R. Bork and K. van Zwieten (eds.), *Commentary on the European Insolvency Regulation*, Oxford, Oxford University Press 2016, (201) pp. 210–212 (optional jurisdiction).

31 P. Mankowski, M. F. Müller and J. Schmidt, *Europäische Insolvenzverordnung 2015*, München, Verlag C. H. Beck 2016, p. 172, nr. 30; W. G.-Ringe, 'Jurisdiction for actions which derive directly from the insolvency proceedings and are closely linked with them' in R. Bork and K. van Zwieten (eds.), *Commentary on the European Insolvency Regulation*, Oxford, Oxford University Press 2016, (201) p. 210, nr. 6.32; D. Robine, "Les actions connexes" in F. Jault-Seseke and D. Robine, *Le nouveau règlement insolvabilité: quelles évolutions?*, Paris, Joly éditions 2015, (61) p. 66, nr. 11.

32 R. Bork and R. Mangano, *European Cross-Border Insolvency Law*, Oxford, Oxford University Press 2016, p. 106, nr. 3.66: '*This regime consist in enlarging the scope of the EIR, derogating from the rules on jurisdiction in civil and commercial matters laid down by the Brussels Ia Regulation, and concentrating litigation in the forum concursus. It is a form of accessorial jurisdiction.*'

33 R. Bork and R. Mangano, *European Cross-Border Insolvency Law*, Oxford, Oxford University Press 2016, p. 112, nr. 3.81; D. Robine, 'Les actions connexes' in F. Jault-Seseke and D. Robine, *Le nouveau règlement insolvabilité: quelles évolutions?*, Paris, Joly éditions 2015, (61) p. 68, nr. 15.

34 C. G. Paulus, *Europäische Insolvenzverordnung*, Frankfurt am Main, Deutscher Fachverlag 2017, p. 218, nr. 1.

35 M. Vanmeenen, 'De herziening van de Insolventieverordening' in B. Allemeersch en T. Kruger (eds.), *Handboek Europees burgerlijk procesrecht*, Antwerpen, Intersentia 2015, (327) p. 357, nr. 26. In its resolution form February 2014, the European Parliament proposed the following definition: '*action directly deriving from insolvency proceedings and closely linked with them means an action directed at obtaining a judgment that, by virtue of its substance, cannot be, or could not have been, obtained outside of, or independently from, insolvency proceedings, and that is exclusively admissible where insolvency proceedings are pending*' (European Parliament legislative resolution of 5 February 2014 on the proposal for a regulation of the European Parliament and of the Council amending Council Regulation (EC) No 1346/2000 on insolvency proceedings (COM(2012)0744 – C7-0413/2012 – 2012/0360(COD), am. 22.).

36 P. Mankowski, M. F. Müller and J. Schmidt, *Europäische Insolvenzverordnung 2015*, München, Verlag C. H. Beck 2016, p. 160, nr. 3.

In general, it can be argued that Article 6.1. has to be interpreted in line with the case-law of the Court of Justice, in the sense that the insolvency proceeding has to be considered as a *condicio sine qua non* of that action.[37] Among the criteria for the delimitation between an action grounded in civil/commercial law and an action connected to insolvency proceedings are whether the claim can be brought by anyone or just the insolvency practitioner; whether the claim is brought in the interest of all creditors and whether the rule in question derogates from the general rules of civil/commercial law with a goal of improving insolvency proceedings.[38]

4.1.2 Attraction to an(other) action in civil and commercial matters

Sometimes it is more efficient for an insolvency practitioner not to consolidate actions in the Member State within the territory of which an insolvency proceedings has been opened but, instead, to consolidate actions in the Member State where another action against the same defendant is pending.[39] For such related actions, the European legislator has made it possible[40] to bring both actions before the courts of the Member State within the territory of which the defendant is domiciled (or, where the action is brought against several defendants, before the courts of the Member State within the territory of which any of them is domiciled) provided that those courts have jurisdiction pursuant to the Brussels I (Recast) Regulation.[41] Article 6.2 Insolvency (Recast) Regulation presupposes the existence of a related action in civil and commercial matters.[42] Actions are

---

37 R. Bork and R. Mangano, *European Cross-Border Insolvency Law*, Oxford, Oxford University Press 2016, p. 110, nr. 3.73. See also, C. G. Paulus, *Europäische Insolvenzverordnung*, Frankfurt am Main, Deutscher Fachverlag 2017, p. 219, nr. 3: '*Vereinfacht ausgedrückt, müssen derartige Klagen also gerade ihren Entstehungsgrund in einem Insolvenzverfahren bzw. im Insolvenzrecht haben and dürfen mithin nicht einfach nur anlässlich eines Insolvenzverfahrens geltend gemacht werden.*'; P. Mankowski, M. F. Müller and J. Schmidt, *Europäische Insolvenzverordnung 2015*, München, Verlag C. H. Beck 2016, p. 163, nr. 9: '*Einzelstreitverfahren sind dann insolvenzrechtlich "infiziert", wenn sie ein Großes Näheverhältnis zu Insolvenzverfahren aufweisen.*'

38 W. G.-Ringe, 'Jurisdiction for actions which derive directly from the insolvency proceedings and are closely linked with them' in R. Bork and K. van Zwieten (eds.), *Commentary on the European Insolvency Regulation*, Oxford, Oxford University Press 2016, (201) p. 206, nr. 618.

39 D. Robine, 'Les actions connexes' in F. Jault-Seseke and D. Robine, *Le nouveau règlement insolvabilité: quelles évolutions?*, Paris, Joly éditions 2015, (61) p. 70, nr. 17.

40 The use of 'may' indicates an selective forum, R. Bork and R. Mangano, *European Cross-Border Insolvency Law*, Oxford, Oxford University Press 2016, p. 112, nr. 3.80.

41 R. Bork and R. Mangano, *European Cross-Border Insolvency Law*, Oxford, Oxford University Press 2016, p. 112, nr. 3.78: '*Art. 6(2) is a specific application of the doctrine concerning the jurisdiction of concurrent actions, and complies with a commonly accepted observation according to which the exclusivity of the forum for related actions could frustrate the effectiveness of insolvency proceedings when the IP bases his assertion on two concurrent actions of which one should be attracted to the forum concursus and the other should follow the rules laid down by the Brussels Ia Regulation.*'.

42 P. Mankowski, M. F. Müller and J. Schmidt, *Europäische Insolvenzverordnung 2015*, München, Verlag C. H. Beck 2016, p. 174, nr. 34: '*Abs. 2 greift nur bei kombinierten Klagen, nicht bei zwei isolierten Klagen.*'; D. Robine, 'Les actions connexes' in F. Jault-Seseke and D.

deemed to be related where they are so closely connected that it is expedient to hear and determine them together to avoid the risk of irreconcilable judgments resulting from separate proceedings.[43] A typical example is the combination of an action for director's liability on the basis of insolvency law with an action based on company law or general tort law.

4.2. MECE PRINCIPLE?

Does the Insolvency (Recast) Regulation dovetail with the Brussels I (Recast) Regulation? Put differently, do both regulations comply with the MECE principle (Mutually Exclusive and Collectively Exhaustive)? In the best of worlds, one should indeed expect all (insolvency) proceedings to find a place in one regulation, thereby avoiding a regulatory gap or regulatory overlap.[44] Recital 7 of the Insolvency (Recast) Regulation however indicates otherwise:

> Bankruptcy, proceedings relating to the winding-up of insolvent companies or other legal persons, judicial arrangements, compositions and analogous proceedings and actions related to such proceedings are excluded from the scope of Regulation (EU) No 1215/2012 of the European Parliament and of the Council (4). Those proceedings should be covered by this Regulation. The interpretation of this Regulation should as much as possible avoid regulatory loopholes between the two instruments. However, the mere fact that a national procedure is not listed in Annex A to this Regulation should not imply that it is covered by Regulation (EU) No 1215/2012.

The fact that not all (insolvency) proceedings are covered by either the Insolvency (Recast) Regulation or the Brussels I (Recast) Regulation can be illustrated with the example of the English schemes of arrangement. These 'proceedings', which are frequently used by continental companies to restructure their debt, are excluded from the Insolvency (Recast) Regulation (as they are not mentioned in Annex A, which is exhaustive[45]). The question whether they are covered by the Brussels I (Recast) Regulation is up for debate (with the answer probably being

Robine, *Le nouveau règlement insolvabilité: quelles évolutions?*, Paris, Joly éditions 2015, (61) p. 70, nr. 18: '*(...) faute d'existence d'une autre action en matière civile ou commerciale, il n'y a pas d'option pour le praticien d'insolvabilité ou le débiteur non dessaisi.*'

43 See also Article 30 of the Brussels I (Recast) Regulation, with respect to related actions, P. Mankowski, M. F. Müller and J. Schmidt, *Europäische Insolvenzverordnung 2015*, München, Verlag C. H. Beck 2016, p. 176, nr. 43; D. Robine, «Les actions connexes» in F. Jault-Seseke and D. Robine, *Le nouveau règlement insolvabilité: quelles évolutions?*, Paris, Joly éditions 2015, (61) p. 71, nr. 20.

44 In this respect, the Court of Justice previously held that the Brussels I (Recast) Regulation and the Insolvency Regulation must be interpreted in such a way as to avoid any overlap between the rules of law that those instruments lay down and any legal vacuum (*Valach and Others*, ECLI:EU:C:2017:986, para 24).

45 Recital 9 Insolvency (Recast) Regulation.

no).[46] Recital 7 of Insolvency (Recast) Regulation in any event makes clear that the exclusion from the Insolvency (Recast) Regulation does not automatically entail inclusion in the Brussels I (Recast) Regulation.[47]

5. CONCLUSION

The relation between the Insolvency and the Brussels I regimes has always been a complicated one. The Insolvency (Recast) Regulation can be considered as a step in the good direction. The rules on double attraction make it possible to concentrate actions in the Member State where the insolvency proceedings are opened, while maintaining some flexibility for insolvency practitioners. The absence of clear criteria with respect to annex proceedings however will surely generate further uncertainty and thus case-law on national and European level.

---

46 See, L. Kortmann and M. Veder, 'The Uneasy Case for Schemes of Arrangement under English Law in Relation to non-UK Companies in Financial Distress: Pushing the Envelope?', *Nottingham Insolvency and Business Law e-Journal* 2015, 239–261.

47 R. Bork and R. Mangano, *European Cross-Border Insolvency Law*, Oxford, Oxford University Press 2016, p. 8, nr. 1.15: '*This specification is crucial to prevent the interpreter from automatically considering some English and Welsh procedures, which are not listed in Annex A, as included in the scope of the Brussels Ia Regulation.*'

BRUSSELS I RECAST AND THE HAGUE JUDGMENTS PROJECT

Marta PERTEGÁS
University of Antwerp and Maastricht University

1. INTRODUCTION

This chapter considers the ongoing negotiations of a Convention on the Recognition and Enforcement of Judgments in Civil and Commercial Matters (hereafter, 'the Judgments Project') at the Hague Conference on Private International Law (hereafter, 'the HCCH') from the perspective of its complementarity to the Brussels I Recast Regulation, which today still stands as the main pillar of the 50 year-old (or young) European Private International Law.

Euphemistically put, the Judgments Project has known its ups and downs since it was proposed as a new item for intergovernmental negotiations to the HCCH in 1992.[1] It is, at the time of writing, still uncertain what the outcome of the final negotiations will be. For the purposes of this paper, however, we will base ourselves on the 2018 Draft Convention, leaving the discussions about open issues aside. This paper aims instead at situating the Judgments Project, from the perspective of the EU, as a component of the construction of the EU Civil Justice legal framework. For that purpose, it provides a succinct overview of the scope and main features of the draft Convention that will hopefully emerge as the new offspring of the Judgments Project. To illustrate some of the draft Convention's main features, four different scenarios (based on real cases) are discussed. Finally, some predictions about the road ahead are made, based on the author's personal conviction that it is essential, for the international legal community as a whole and thus for the EU and the European citizens in particular, that the Judgments Project is crowned with success.

1 See the extensive bibliography kept by the Permanent Bureau of the HCCH, available at hcch.net (under Judgments Project Section).

2. THE JUDGMENTS PROJECT AS A COMPONENT OF THE EU CIVIL JUSTICE POLICY

Prima facie, the Judgments Project may appear to be peripheral to the primary objectives of the EU in the area of private international law. The 'judicial cooperation in civil matters' (or 'private international law' in more standard terms) that the EU progressively develops pursuant to Article 81 TFEU (and its predecessors), has principally generated Regulations, Directives and other EU legislation directed to the proper functioning of the internal market. Given that one of that internal market's main goals is the free movement of goods, services and economically active persons within the territory of the EU, the internal dimension of the Civil Justice policy has received priority attention in the initial decades of its development. It therefore comes as no surprise that, for the progressive creation and consolidation of the EU area of freedom, security and justice, the focus has been and still very much remains the movement of persons and a high level of protection to citizens *within the area itself*. The Judgments Project, being an intergovernmental initiative with EU involvement but global reach, has until recently attracted relatively minor attention in the EU, particularly if compared with the interest generated in other regions of the world, such as the Asia Pacific or Latin America.

At present, as EU PIL reaches half a century of existence with a consolidated and relatively dense normative framework, the 'EU involvement in efforts to unify the rules of private international law' surfaces as one of the priority action areas for the EU legislature. Attention is progressively shifting to a broader dimension of EU Civil Justice, which is instrumental to universal objectives of access to justice and respect for human rights, and where there is united attention on the 'internal' and the 'external' dimension. In this context, it is questionable whether traditional notions in EU PIL as 'third States' or 'external action' still resonate or, instead, should rather be abandoned as they depict an inward-looking or EU-centric policy. While the EU presently makes every effort to position itself as a pivotal actor in international relations, language that reflects a vision of 'the EU and the rest of the world' or 'fortress Europe' may not be adequate. Instead, neutral or comprehensive concepts (such as 'EU and non-EU States' or 'joining up internal and external policies') appear to be more appropriate to reflect the position that the EU attributes to itself in international relations and global governance.

It is actually not only a matter of semantics: there is the underlying policy question of which approach EU Civil Justice should take in this broader context. The merits of unilateral EU legislative action, in particular to ensure a more consistent treatment of non-EU litigants in EU PIL, have been put forward. In particular, with regard to the recognition and enforcement of judgments from non-EU Member States, many commentators see merit in the development of EU rules on recognition and enforcement of foreign judgments, irrespective of the fate of the Judgments Project.[2] For the time being, the European Commission has prioritised the multilateral approach and shown leadership in the ongoing Hague multilateral work with the endorsement of the negotiation mandate given by the Council.[3] Meanwhile, the European Parliament has commissioned an important study on the future Judgments Convention.[4] The open and dynamic approach kept by the EU institutions so far is to be praised and maximises the chances of the Judgments Project in its current objective of international standard-setting for the recognition and enforcement of foreign judgments.

From the perspective of the further construction of a global EU policy on judicial cooperation in civil matters, the Judgments Project is a priority project. Admittedly, multilateral action pursued on the basis of diplomatic negotiations, the conclusion of an international treaty and all necessary efforts for the subsequent ratification both by the EU and by its strategically important partners may take a considerable amount of time, certainly longer than the unilateral EU action that has been proposed by influential observers.[5] Still, I think that the EU is rightly setting the priority on multilateral action, in line with its own objective of strengthening a 'rules-based multilateral order' and the widening of 'the reach of international norms and institutions'.[6] The commitment shown by the EU has definitely been one of the key factors for the progress of the Judgments Project since its relaunch in 2011 and it undoubtedly maximises the chances of a successful completion of the draft Convention. In addition, as discussed below, the completion of the Judgments Project may benefit other essential EU policies, such as trade and international relations, more generally. As discussed below, raising awareness about the relevance of the Judgments Project for the advancement of other connected EU objectives, for example relating to the EU international and trade agenda, is important.

---

2 See, among others, M. Fallon and T. Kruger, 'The Spatial Scope of the EU's Rules on Jurisdiction and Enforcement of Judgments', *Yearbook of Private International Law*, Vol. 14 (2012/2013), 1–35; T. Domej, 'Das Verhältnis nach 'außen'. Europäische v. Drittstaatensachverhalte', *in* J. von Hein and G. Rühl, *Kohärenz im Internationalen Privat- und Verfahrensrecht der Europäischen Union*, Tübingen, Mohr Siebeck 2016, 90–109; A. Bonomi, 'European Private International Law and Third States', *IPRax* 2017, 184–193. See also the conclusions reached by the authors of the Study referred to below in footnote 4.

3 Council of the European Union, JUSTCIV 84, 8 June 2017 (partial declassification of document 8324/16), available at data.consilium.europa.eu.

4 P. De Miguel Asensio *et al*, Study requested by the JURI Committee of the European Parliament, PE 604.954, April 2018, available at www.europarl.europa.eu. The authors of this Study recommend the adoption of unilateral rules on recognition and enforcement of judgments from non-EU States, in parallel to the continuation of the efforts for the completion of the draft Convention.

5 See the valuable recommendations of the GEDIP on the revision of the Brussels I Regulation with regard to external situations, as consolidated in 2010 and available at www.gedip-egpil.eu and, more specifically, the recommendations of the Study referred to in the previous footnote.

6 See 'A Global Strategy for the European Union's Foreign and Security Policy', adopted in 2017, at http://europa.eu/globalstrategy/en.

2.1. THE RELEVANCE OF THE JUDGMENTS PROJECT FOR THE EXTERNAL TRADE POLICY

Empirical research may still be in its infancy when it comes to evidencing the correlation between trade agreements and judicial cooperation, but it seems irrebuttable that appropriate access to justice, including the cross-border effects of judgments, contributes to the creation of a stable legal framework and thus to more incentives for foreign trade and investment. However, at the EU level, there appears to be no common or coordinated approach between trade and judicial cooperation. It has even been stated that 'judicial cooperation is simply out of sight for DG Trade'.[7] Moreover, the slow pace at which judicial cooperation has progressed, compared with the vigorous creation and functioning of trade schemes between EU and non-EU Member States, is remarkable.[8]

The EU is 'deeply integrated into global markets' and ranks as one of the main trading partners for the biggest economies of the world.[9] In addition, the EU is the number one trading partner for developing countries.[10] Trade outside the EU is the exclusive competence of the EU and the common commercial policy has been a stable component of EU policy since its early ages.

In contrast, it is only relatively recently that Article 3(2) TFEU confirms that the EU has exclusive competence for:

> the conclusion of an international agreement when its conclusion is provided for in a legislative act of the Union or is necessary to enable the Union to exercise its internal competence, or in so far may affect common rules or alter their scope.

While the matter of the external competence of the EU in the area of judicial cooperation appears to be settled at last, it undoubtedly generated considerable debate and commentary over the past decades. This possibly gave rise to hesitations in the development of the non-EU dimension of the judicial cooperation policy[11], and may partially explain the slow and hesitant progress of such area, and its disconnection with EU trade policy.

---

7 See M. Weller, 'Judicial Cooperation of the EU in Civil Matters in Its Relations with non-EU States – A Blind Spot?', in A. Uzelac and R. van Rhee (eds.), *Public and Private Justice: The Transformation of Civil Justice*, Springer 2018 (forthcoming), available at: SSRN.com.

8 *Ibid.*

9 According to the latest data available on the EUROSTAT website of the EU (http://ec.europa.eu/eurostat/statistics-explained/index.php/International_trade_in_goods_for_the_EU_-_an_overview, March 2018).

10 Ibid. See also the publication by the High Commissioner '60 years of EU in the world' available at https://europa.eu/globalstrategy.

11 For an extensive overview and bibliography, see P. Mankowski and O. Knöfel, 'Verhältnis zu Drittstaaten', *in* S. Leible and J.P. Terhechte (eds), *Europäisches Rechtsschutz- und Verfaherensrecht,* Volume 3 of *Enzyklopädie Europarecht*, Baden-Baden, Nomos 2014, 1085–1133 or P. Franzina (ed.), *The External Dimension of EU Private International Law after Opinion 1/13*, Antwerp-Portland, Intersentia 2017.

Be this as it may, the gradually accepted understanding that legal certainty and predictability are magnets to attract investment and trade connects the two (EU) policies. The consolidation of judicial cooperation in a worldwide perspective should contribute to the objectives and goals that the EU has set in the trade area and, in that regard, the completion of a Judgments Convention is an essential factor. The draft Preliminary Report of the future Convention rightly recalls the benefits of the draft Convention for 'international trade, investment and mobility through enhanced judicial co-operation'.[12]

2.2. THE GEOPOLITICAL RELEVANCE OF THE JUDGMENTS PROJECT (FROM AN EU PERSPECTIVE)

The Judgments Project can also be linked to the EU's foreign policy. Article 21 TEU sets out what the EU attempts to achieve in the international arena:

> The Union's action on the international scene shall be guided by the principles which have inspired its own creation, development and enlargement, and which it seeks to advance in the wider world: democracy, the rule of law, the universality and indivisibility of human rights and fundamental freedoms, respect for human dignity, the principles of equality and solidarity, and respect for the principles of the United Nations Charter and international law.

It is remarkable that judicial cooperation in civil and commercial matters is not mentioned in the EU Global Strategy for the EU's foreign and security policy.[13] While it will not resolve the most pressing global problems of our world, judicial cooperation in civil and commercial matters facilitates international transactions and exchanges, fosters human and family relationships, and protects weaker parties and vulnerable persons, and thus assists with the implementation of human rights and the respect for the rule of law. The link between judicial cooperation in civil and commercial matters and the foreign and security policy is visible in the context of specific actions and programmes of the EU foreign affairs and international relations agenda (such as the 2017 Joint Declaration of the Eastern Partnership Summit[14] or the 2017–2020 Association Agenda EU-Georgia[15], to name a few recent examples). It is recommended that these

---

12 See the Draft Explanatory Report by Rapporteurs F. Garcimartín and G. Saumier, Prel. Doc. Nr. 10 of May 2018, para. 5.

13 See *supra* footnote nr. 6 and, in particular, https://europa.eu/globalstrategy/en/global-strategy-promote-citizens-interests.

14 Joint Declaration of the Eastern Partnership Summit, Brussels, 24 November 2017, para. 10, available at www.consilium.europa.eu.

15 Association Agenda between the European Union and Georgia 2017–2020, para 2.4, available at https://eeas.europa.eu.

punctual linkages evolve into a more systematic connection between the two EU policies.

3. THE HAGUE JUDGMENTS PROJECT – STATE OF AFFAIRS AND SOME KEY FEATURES OF THE SCHEME UNDER DEVELOPMENT

Having situated the Judgments Project in the broader context of the EU's policy on judicial cooperation, this section will refer to the Project's current state of affairs. It also highlights some of the salient features of the recognition and enforcement scheme under development, when compared to the (for an EU audience) more familiar scheme on recognition and enforcement of foreign judgments of the Brussels I Recast Regulation.[16]

3.1. CURRENT STATE OF PLAY

The 2018 Draft Convention is the most recent publicly available text produced by the Judgments Special Commission at the time of proof-reading of the last proofs.[17] The Special Commission agreed on this text during its final meeting in May 2018, setting the scene for discussions at the last negotiating stage, the Diplomatic Session, which is expected to conclude a new Hague Convention on recognition and enforcement of foreign judgments (in short, the Judgments Convention) in mid-2019.[18] Such achievement would undoubtedly represent the successful culmination of a project that dates back almost thirty years. However, the Project may still continue thereafter, as the Judgments Project's Expert Group is expected to meet 'shortly after the conclusion of the Diplomatic Session' to address matters relating to international jurisdiction.[19]

---

16 The Brussels I Recast Regulation is Regulation (EU) No 1215/2012 of the European Parliament and of the Council of 12 December 2012 on jurisdiction and the recognition and enforcement of judgments in civil and commercial matters (recast).

17 Https://www.hcch.net/en/projects/legislative-projects/judgments/special-commission.

18 Conclusions and Recommendations adopted by the Council on General Affairs and Policy of the HCC at its most recent annual meeting (13 to 15 March 2018), paras. 3–5.

19 This remains to be confirmed by the Council on General Affairs and Policy of the HCCH. In earlier years, the Council on General Affairs and Policy of the HCCH had mandated the relaunch of the Expert Group's activities on international jurisdiction 'soon after the Special Commission has drawn up a draft Convention' (a mandate that was completed at the 4th meeting of the Special Commission in May 2018). See, in particular, the 2016 Council Conclusions and Recommendations, para 13, available at https://assets.hcch.net/docs/679bd42c-f974-461a-8e1a-31e1b51eda10.pdf). The plans for further work on international jurisdiction are thus postponed, but not abandoned. This may in turn have consequences for a future revision of the Brussels I Recast Regulation, with regard in particular to 'the possible need for a further extension of the rules on jurisdiction to defendants not domiciled in a Member State, taking

3.2. MAIN FEATURES (FROM AN EU PERSPECTIVE)

It goes without saying that many features of recognition and enforcement schemes, which are common to both the HCCH Conventions on recognition and enforcement (such as the 1971 Enforcement Convention or the relevant chapter of the 2007 Child Support Convention) and the 'Brussels *acquis*'[20], have found their way into the 2018 Draft Convention. I will revert to some of those commonalities when analysing a few scenarios later on. I will first refer to the issues where the 2018 Draft Convention clearly diverges from the EU norm.

3.2.1. No abolition of exequatur

First and foremost, the abolition of *exequatur* that the Brussels I Recast Regulation extended to (most) civil and commercial matters was never considered a realistic policy option for the future Hague Convention. Instead, recognition and enforcement under the 2018 Draft Convention is subject to both a review based on a jurisdictional control, as well as the operation of the grounds for denial of recognition and enforcement. The latter is not new when compared to the Brussels I Recast Regulation. The former, on the other hand, is an unfamiliar additional test for the EU practice, according to which the requested court reviews the connection of the court of origin with the original dispute. This jurisdictional test is absent in the Brussels I Recast Regulation: as a complete double instrument, the Regulation not only deals with the circulation of foreign judgments but also incorporates a system of common rules of international jurisdiction, based on a high degree of mutual trust, making a review on jurisdictional grounds practically redundant.[21]

A possible comparison could still be drawn with the review of jurisdiction that the requested court performs, under the Brussels I Recast Regulation, when the judgment conflicts with the exclusive rules of jurisdiction (Section 6 of Chapter II) or when a judgment is rendered against weaker parties under the Regulation and that judgment conflicts with Sections 3, 4 or 5 of Chapter II). This comparison is adequate as far as the operation of Article 6 of the 2018 Draft Convention is concerned (see below). The operation of its Article 5, on the other hand, has no

---

into account the operation of this Regulation *and possible developments at international level*' (Article 79 Brussels I Recast Regulation, emphasis added).

20 The 'Brussels *acquis*' refers to the Brussels I Recast Regulation as well as to its predecessors, i.e., Council Regulation (EC) No 44/2001 of 22 December on jurisdiction and the recognition and enforcement of judgments in civil and commercial matters (Brussels I) and the Convention on jurisdiction and the enforcement of judgments in civil and commercial matters (Brussels Convention).

21 It is noteworthy, however, that like the Brussels I Recast Regulation, the November 2017 Draft Convention excludes a review of the law applied by the court of origin.

equivalent under the EU scheme. I will illustrate the operation of Article 5 of the 2018 Draft Convention using a few scenarios below.

Turning to the grounds for denial of recognition and enforcement first, the policy foundations of the grounds for denial in the Brussels I Recast Regulation (i.e., a manifest incompatibility with public policy, insufficient notice of process or a prior conflicting judgment) are also found in the 2018 Draft Convention. However, the list of grounds envisaged for the future Convention goes further to include specific denial grounds for judgments obtained by fraud or judgments rendered in breach of a choice of court agreement or a court designation in a trust document.[22] It follows that the recognition and enforcement of judgments rendered by a court other than the one that was determined in a choice of court agreement or a trust designation may be stricter under the Draft Convention provisions than under the Regulation provisions.

Even for the similar grounds for denial (i.e., a manifest incompatibility with public policy, insufficient notice of process or a prior conflicting judgment), it is very much the question whether the application criteria developed by European courts in the context of EU Regulations will be extended to the application of international Conventions. As some doctrinal writings made clear, it seems unrealistic that the very strict application of such grounds to judgments between the EU Member States is systematically extended to judgments originating in non-EU Contracting States.[23] This eventually is a matter that should be left to the discretion of the courts in the future Contracting States. They may draw inspiration from the future Explanatory Report as well as from the interpretation of analogous provisions in other HCCH Conventions containing recognition and enforcement schemes.

3.2.2. *Recognition without procedure*

Article 4 of the November 2017 Draft Convention notably refers to the *recognition* of a foreign judgment and, as such, appears to require the intervention of a local court for such recognition. Is the 'Brussels' principle of 'automatic' recognition (without 'any special procedure being required' or in other words, without review by the courts of the State where recognition is sought) then possible under the Convention? The answer is not uniformly provided by the Convention and depends on the law of the requested State.[24]

---

22 See Article 7 of the 2018 Draft Convention (leaving intellectual property judgments aside as these are still subject to further negotiations) and compare with Article 45 of the Brussels I Recast Regulation.

23 See A. Bonomi, *supra* nr. 2, p. 192.

24 See Article 4 of the 2018 Draft Convention and compare with Article 36 Brussels I Recast Regulation. See the Draft Explanatory Report by Rapporteurs F. Garcimartín and G. Saumier, *op. cit. supra* nr. 12, para. 317 (with regard to Article 14).

3.2.3. *No 'mandatory' application*

The demarcation between EU and national rules on recognition and enforcement is relatively straightforward: when a case falls under the scope of the Brussels I Recast Regulation, recognition and enforcement cannot be left to national law. The mandatory application of the Regulation is uncontested.

The relationship between the future Convention and national law is different, as the recognition or enforcement of judgments under national law remains a possibility except for the matters referred to in Article 6 (i.e. exclusive bases of jurisdiction for judgments on rights in rem in immovable property; on long-term tenancies of immovable property and, as the draft currently stands, on certain intellectual property cases). For other cases, the national scheme on recognition and enforcement of the requested State will co-exist with the Convention. The Convention should thus be seen as generally creating a floor, and not a ceiling, for recognition and enforcement. As such, Article 16 of the 2018 Draft Convention is based on the premise that the application of national rules works *favor recognitionis*, that is, it allows for recognition and enforcement in cases where the Convention would not.[25]

3.2.4. *Narrower material scope of application?*

Despite a common reference to 'civil' and/or 'commercial' matters in the title of both the 2018 Draft Convention and the Brussels I Recast Regulation, there appears to be little doubt that the material scope of application of the future Convention will be narrower than that of the Brussels I Recast Regulation. Firstly, some specifically excluded matters only feature in the text of the future Convention, such as certain maritime claims and defamation.[26] At the time of writing, it is still unclear whether significant other portions of civil and commercial litigation may be excluded from scope. This refers to the possible exclusions of 'privacy (with the fate of privacy-related contractual claims still to be determined)' and 'intellectual property (and analogous matters)'.[27] Carving out judgments pertaining to these areas of intangible property would drastically lower the practical interest of the future Convention, in particular with the ever increasing number of judgments connected to the use of digital technologies (including the use of the Internet). At the same time, discussions have reflected very significant policy differences

25 See the Draft Explanatory Report by Rapporteurs F. Garcimartín and G. Saumier, *op. cit. supra* nr. 12, paras. 328–330.

26 See Article 2(1) (g) and (k) of the 2018 Draft Convention.

27 See the bracketed Article 2(1) (l) and (m) of the 2018 Draft Convention, among other possible exclusions. Another source of future asymmetry is available through the provisions on Declarations (see Articles 18, 19 and the bracketed Article 20 which may exclude judgments pertaining to governments).

so that the achievement of consensus in these areas is far from certain and will probably be left for the final Diplomatic Conference.

3.2.5. Envisaged operation: a few scenarios

Leaving such uncertainties aside, this section attempts to provide a few illustrations of the operation of the 2018 Draft Convention. Using a sample of judgments rendered in cross-border cases in different jurisdictions, the operation of the draft Convention is further illustrated.

3.2.5.1. A judgment rendered by a court other than the one designated in a choice of court agreement

In 2011, the Higher Regional Court of Hamburg[28] was requested to enforce a judgment rendered in Japan concerning a motor vehicle purchase contract against a German buyer. The judgment ordered the payment of the purchase price to the seller residing in Japan. In the German enforcement proceedings, the defendant argued that the Japanese judgment had been rendered by a court other than the one designated in a choice of court agreement between the parties (a German court). The judgment was rendered by a non-chosen court so it falls outside the scope of application of the rules on recognition and enforcement of the 2005 Choice of Court Convention (even if Japan were a Contracting State to that Convention). The Hamburg Court ruled that, in the given circumstances, the enforcement of the Japanese judgment would be contrary to public policy in Germany.

Under the 2018 Draft Convention, this judgment may pass the jurisdictional test of Article 5 provided the parties have stipulated that the payment of the purchase price is to take place in Japan (and subject to the possible defence that the payment of the price in Japan 'clearly did not constitute a purposeful and substantial connection to that State').[29] However, the question remains whether the grounds of refusal in Article 7 apply. Article 7 (1)(d) provides as ground of refusal that the proceedings in the court of origin were 'contrary to an agreement (…) under which the dispute in question was to be determined in a court other than the court of origin'. The German court may thus refuse recognition and enforcement if it considers the judgment to be contrary to the parties' stipulation in favour of the German court. The Explanatory Report states that 'the law of the requested State, including its private international law rules' will provide further guidance as to

28 OLG Hamburg, 18 April 2011, 6 U 15/11, available at https://openjur.de.

29 See Article 5 (1) (g). This formulation is to a large extent a US 'export' and as such should rely on its primary sources, at least until courts around the world have had the opportunity of developing an autonomous interpretation of this qualifier. See, for further information, R. Brand and C. Mariottini, 'Note on the concept of 'purposeful and substantial connection' in Article 5(1)(g) and 5(1)(n)(ii)', Prel. Doc. No 6 of September 2017, available on www.hcch.net.

the validity and effectiveness of the agreement. For Germany, as well as for other EU Member States, this seems to refer to the law of the chosen court (i.e. German law) on the basis of Article 25 (1) of the Brussels I Recast Regulation.

3.2.5.2. Medical malpractice

This illustration stems from a 2006 judgment rendered by the Israel Supreme Court in the Marsika v. Dolens case.[30] At the time of the issues giving rise to the dispute, Professor Dolens was a Slovenian brain surgeon who lived and practiced in Slovenia (occasionally in other EU Member States as well). He was alleged to have committed medical malpractice when treating an Israeli patient in Slovenia. The patient sued Dolens in Israel and summons were served on Dolens while he was visiting Israel. The Israeli courts (including the Supreme Court) accepted transient jurisdiction and awarded the plaintiff approximately 2 million euro as damages.

Should recognition and enforcement be sought in Slovenia or any other EU Member State under the November 2017 Draft Convention, this judgment would be interesting from several angles. Firstly, it is a helpful illustration of the scope of application of the draft Convention. Alleged medical malpractice is included under the general term of 'judgments relating to civil or commercial matters' in Article 1 (1). Secondly, it is doubtful that the narrow jurisdictional test for tort judgements (Article 5 (1) (j)) would apply to this case, as the harmful event occurred in Slovenia. Thirdly, the circulation of the judgment under the Convention may also be refused under the ground of refusal in Article 7(1)(a)(ii), provided transient summons as performed in the current case would be considered to be incompatible with the fundamental principles of Slovenia concerning service of documents (should Slovenia be the requested State). Lastly, the amount of the damages awarded by the court of origin may be reduced pursuant to Article 10 in case the requested court considers it necessary to reduce non-compensatory damages (in case the Israeli judgment awarded exemplary or punitive damages).

3.2.5.3. Opt-out class action

The third illustration is based on a very interesting judgment of 23 March 2017 of the Court of Appeal of Ghent.[31] This judgment indirectly relates to the intricacies of the bankruptcy of a Belgian company (Lernout & Hauspie) with worldwide

30 I came across a summary of this judgment in K. Siehr, 'Global Jurisdiction of Local Courts and Recognition of their Judgments Abroad', *in Festschrift für Ulrich Magnus*, Munich, Sellier 2014, 515–529, at p. 519–520.

31 Court of Appeal of Ghent, 23 March 2017, (*Lernout & Hauspie, re Dexia and KPMG*), available at www.conflictoflaws.net. This case is pending before the Belgian Supreme Court at the time of writing.

operations. It stems from the US decisions approving class action settlements in the United States between the duped shareholders of Lernout & Hauspie and, respectively, the Belgium-based bank and Belgium-based auditor of the bankrupt company. The recognition of such US decisions was accepted by the Ghent Court of Appeal and considered to be compatible with Belgium's international public policy on the basis of Article 25 (1) (1) of the Belgian Code of Private International Law.

Would the outcome be similar if a future Convention would apply to the circulation of judgments between the US and Belgium (or other EU Member States)? The first important element to keep in mind is Article 16 of the Convention, according to which the national rules on recognition co-exist (in case they are more favourable) with the Convention rules. It follows that Belgian courts may continue to apply their liberal treatment of foreign class action settlements. However, as far as the current negotiations go, it is not entirely clear whether class action settlements fall within the scope of the 2018 Draft Convention. It remains to be seen whether the specific nature of (opt-out) class actions will be further considered in the final stage of negotiations. It might have been preferable to consider class actions in the last round of 'technical' negotiations of the Special Commission (i.e., at its May 2018 meeting) than leaving the matter to the Diplomatic Session. Finally, it is also interesting to note that the US judgment only indirectly concerns an insolvency and, as such, is not excluded from the Convention pursuant to Article 2 (1) (e) ('on insolvency (...) and analogous matters').

3.2.5.4. The Convention's greatest potential: contributing to the circulation of outgoing EU judgments

All previous illustrations are related to incoming judgments (i.e., judgments rendered by non-EU courts whose recognition and enforcement is requested in EU Member States). What about the reverse direction? Will the future Convention facilitate the recognition and enforcement of EU judgments internationally? This actually seems to me the greatest asset of the Judgments Project from an EU perspective. Although a thorough analysis remains beyond the remits of this contribution, I may for instance, refer to the attractiveness and reliability of court adjudication in the EU, as well as the solid reputation of a number of EU-based courts for the resolution of international commercial disputes. EU courts, if compared to those in other regions of the world, are generally well prepared to deal with cross-border cases. Moreover, the establishment of a number of tailormade international commercial courts in the European continent may restore the international weight of EU-based court adjudication in the post-Brexit time. Following the developments in, for instance, Paris and Frankfurt, the (Amsterdam-based) Netherlands Commercial Court is set to be operational in late 2018 and the Brussels International Commercial Court may follow soon after. Needless to say, the operations of all these courts will be greatly assisted by the reassurance that their judgments are enforceable at the international level (or, at least, in the Contracting States of either the 2005 Choice of Court Convention or the future Convention).[32]

Looking more particularly to the EU's main trading partners, would the application of the future Convention contribute to more predictable cross-border transactions? Admittedly, there are several (at this stage still unpredictable) factors to take into account, including the position that the US and China will take on the ratification of a future HCCH Judgments Convention.[33] Assuming, however, that several of the main trade actors (USA, China, Japan, the EU, etc.) are bound as Contracting States/Parties, the Convention scheme offers more legal certainty and predictability than the ones currently applicable to outgoing EU judgments in the other two biggest jurisdictions.

The recognition and enforcement of EU judgments in China (leaving the special regimes of Taiwan, Hong Kong and Macao aside) is subject to the principle of reciprocity. This means that, in the absence of (bilateral) treaties, recognition and enforcement of a foreign judgment in China is only possible if there is proof that, in the reverse situation, a Chinese judgment would be recognised and enforced in the judgment's country of origin.[34] Reciprocity is thus very much dependant on the existence of a reverse precedent and presupposes an adequate access to foreign law (while it is not always easy to trace back the outcome of Chinese judgments in foreign States where recognition and enforcement is sought). Compared to this reciprocity test, the mere existence of a multilateral scheme under HCCH auspices would

---

32 See, for recommendations from a post-Brexit perspective, G. Rühl, 'Judicial Cooperation in Civil and Commercial Matters after Brexit: Which Way Forward?', *ICLQ* 2017, vol. 67, 99–128, esp. 128 ('both the UK and the EU are well advised to apply a more global strategy and to foster the conclusion of international treaties in the framework of the HCCH').

33 An optimistic assessment could be based on the ongoing work that both States conduct towards the ratification of the other Convention that was concluded in the context of the Judgments Project, i.e. the 2005 Choice of Court Convention. A more pessimistic prospect could indeed rely on the low number of HCCH Conventions both the USA and China have ratified so far, despite their long-standing and strong presence in the development of the HCCH agenda. As J. Basedow rightly puts it, some States that recently acceded to the HCCH have a better track record than the USA (or China) when it comes to the ratification of Conventions. See J. Basedow, 'EU-Kollisionsrecht und Haager Konferenz – Ein schwieriges Verhältnis', *IPRax* 2017, 195.

34 See, for instance, W. Zhang, *Recognition and Enforcement of Foreign Judgments in China*, Alphen aan de Rijn, Wolters Kluwer 2014, 365 p.; B. Elbalti, 'Reciprocity and the recognition and enforcement of foreign judgments: a lot of bark but not much bite', *Journal of Private International Law*, 2017, 184–218, esp. 201; Y. Guo, 'China' in A Chung (ed.), *Recognition and Enforcement of Judgments in Asia*, Asian Business Law Institute 2017, available at http://abli.asia/LinkClick.aspx?fileticket=I0rTeJ0yljw%3d&portalid=0; Y. Wang, 'A turning point of reciprocity in China's recognition and enforcement of foreign judgments: a study of the *Kolmar* case', *Nederlands Internationaal Privaatrecht* 2017, Vol. 4, 772–789.

constitute a significant step forward. Practically speaking, it would mean a single more predictable gateway to China for judgments in provenance of the EU, thus ensuring the equal treatment of judgments irrespective of their EU State of origin.

As to the US, it is generally considered that US courts take a liberal approach to recognizing and enforcing foreign money judgments, while non-money judgments have hardly been considered. This may be an oversimplification for a multi-layered system with a federal core and 'significant substantive law differences from state to state'.[35] Indeed, it seems hardly possible to cast a global assessment of such a plurality of state regimes, combined with the use of the Full Faith and Credit Clause that appear to facilitate forum shopping for the lowest recognition law threshold. It can be presumed, however, that a uniform multilateral scheme under the future Convention will offer more certainty and foreseeability than the current multi-state scheme for EU litigants in quest of recognition and enforcement of their judgments in the US.

4. SOME CONCLUDING REMARKS: THE JUDGMENTS PROJECT AS A PRIORITY (EU) OBJECTIVE

It is hoped that the current efforts in the context of the Judgments Project will crystallise in a new Convention on recognition and enforcement of judgments. The whole HCCH community, and the EU in particular, will be reinvigorated by such a major international accomplishment.

From a global perspective, the new Convention would fulfil a long-standing aspiration of the international legal community which, for decades and in a series of sequential efforts, has pursued the conclusion of a multilateral scheme on recognition and enforcement of foreign judgments in civil and commercial matters. If concluded, it is hoped that the Convention can provide a widely acceptable and reliable international framework on the basis of which certain foreign judgments can circulate and other judgments are confined to the territory of their country of origin. This in turn may discourage excessive and costly litigation strategies in cross-border cases and provide a higher level of certainty, simplicity and effectiveness in access to justice. After all, the creation and consolidation of such an international scheme is not an exercise in isolation, but rather a contribution of the private international law community to the enhancement of the rule of law in the world and thus to the achievement of the UN Sustainable Development Goals (UN SDG). UN SDG 16.3 specifically encourages the international community to

35 See, for instance, R. Brand, 'Evolution of U.S. Judgments Recognition Law', *Columbia Journal of Transnational Law* 2017, Vol. 55, 277–342.

'promote the rule of law at the national and international levels and ensure equal access to justice for all'.

Specifically for the EU, the Judgments Project is an important project to demonstrate leadership and commitment as international actor in the area of judicial cooperation in civil and commercial matters. This paper has attempted to demonstrate that the Judgments Project deserves to be considered a valuable component of the current EU agenda in this area, as well as a factor to be taken into account for further developments with regard to the Brussels I Recast Regulation (Article 79). In a broader assessment, the successful completion of a future Judgments Convention may boost the position of the EU as a solid and active actor in the international arena, not only with regard to civil justice, but also politically and economically speaking, provided the links between such EU policies and judicial cooperation in civil and commercial matters are gradually accepted.

CROSS-BORDER PROVISIONAL MEASURES: STEPPING BACKWARDS IN THE BRUSSELS I RECAST[1]

Arnaud Nuyts
Professor at the Université Libre de Bruxelles (ULB)
Attorney, Member of the Bar of Brussels

1. INTRODUCTION

At first glance, it would seem that fifty years have passed and that the regime of provisional and protective measures[2] has remained entirely unchanged in European law. The central provision on this matter in the Brussels I Regulation Recast[3] (Article 35) is drafted in nearly identical terms as the corresponding provision of the 2001 Regulation[4] (Article 31), which itself borrowed from the 1968 Brussels Convention[5] (Article 24).[6] It is a very short provision which gives the power to the courts of any Member State to grant provisional measures under their own law *'even if the courts of another Member State have jurisdiction as to the substance of the matter'*. On its terms, the provision appears to be a very straightforward rule of delegation to domestic law for anything related to the granting of provisional measures.

Yet, beyond this appearance of simplicity lies one of the most complex matters of the Brussels regime, which is the subject of a very rich jurisprudence and of a

---

1 This paper was presented at the Jura Falconis 2018 *Conference on European Private International Law at 50* at the KU Leuven on 23 March 2018. The paper draws from earlier writing on the matter, including A Nuyts, 'Les mesures provisoires dans le Règlement Bruxelles *Ibis*'[2013] *Revue de droit commercial belge* 301; 'Article 2' and 'Article 35', in A Dickinson and E Lein (eds) *The Brussels I Regulation Recast*, OUP 2015, p. 97–105 and 357–372.

2 Hereafter, 'provisional measures'.

3 Regulation (EU) No 1215/2012 of 12 December 2012 on jurisdiction and the recognition and enforcement of judgments in civil and commercial matters (the 'Recast Regulation').

4 Regulation No 44/2001 of 22 December 2000 on jurisdiction and the recognition and enforcement of judgments in civil and commercial matters (the '2001 Regulation').

5 Convention of 27 September 1996 on jurisdiction and the recognition and enforcement of judgments in civil and commercial matters (the 'Brussels Convention').

6 The only minor difference is that the words 'under this Regulation' have been deleted. The reason for, and meaning of, this change are discussed below.

sophisticated legal system which has evolved over time, including in the Recast Regulation.[7]

There are three main factors that have elevated the strategic importance of this matter over time. Firstly, in modern commercial litigation, provisional measures have often an important practical impact on the parties and their dispute. When at the outset of a commercial contract dispute, a party obtains an asset freezing injunction, or the provisional attachment of assets, this may place the other party in an impossible practical situation which may force a settlement. Likewise, when the party alleging an IP infringement is able to obtain an interim injunction preventing the marketing of products which are alleged to be infringing the IP rights, this will give this party the upper hand throughout the process. Provisional measures are often outcome determinative.

Secondly, there has been a development in the practice of several Member States to grant *cross-border* provisional measures, namely measures that affect persons and assets situated in the territory of other States. The English courts have played an active role in the development of these types of measures, starting with world-wide freezing injunctions and moving over the years to other cross-border *in personam* measures, such as disclosure orders, receivership orders and search orders. The courts of other Member States have followed suit with the development of similar or other techniques, such as EU wide interim injunctions precluding the marketing of products.[8]

Thirdly, provisional measures have the potential to disrupt the entire jurisdictional framework of the Brussels regime. The Regulation establishes a very well-thought out allocation of jurisdiction as between the courts of the Member States, based on a hierarchical system. Article 35 has the potential to undermine this entire system by allowing the courts of a Member State not having jurisdiction under the uniform rules to grant provisional measures based on their own domestic law.

---

7 Legal writing on the subject is quite abundant. See e.g. F Garcimartin, 'Provisional and Protective Measures in the Brussels I Regulation Recast' [2014/2015] *Yearbook of Private International* Law 57 (hereafter 'Garcimartin'); I Pretelli, 'Provisional and Protective Measures in the European Civil Procedure of the Brussels I System', V Lazic and S Stuij (eds.), *Brussels Ibis Regulation*, 2017, p. 97 s. (hereafter 'Pretelli'); J-F Van Drooghenbroeck and C De Boe, 'Les mesures provisoires et conservatoires dans le règlement Bruxelles *Ibis*', in E Guinchard (ed.), *Le nouveau règlement Bruxelles Ibis*, Bruylant, p. 167 s. (hereafter 'Van Drooghenbroeck and De Boe'); T Hartley, *Civil Jurisdiction and Judgments in Europe*, OUP 2017, Chapter 22, Provisional, Including Protective, Measures (hereafter 'Hartley'); A Dickinson, 'Provisional Measures in the 'Brussels I' Review: Disturbing the Status Quo?' [2010] *J Priv Int L* 519 (hereafter 'Dickinson'); C Heinze, 'Choice of Court Agreements, Coordination of Proceedings and Provisional Measures in the Reform of the Brussels I Regulation' [2010] *Rabels Z* 581 (hereafter, 'Heinze'); C Honorati, 'Provisional Measures and the Recast of Brussels I Regulation: A Missed Opportunity for a Better Ruling' [2012] *Rivista di diritto internazionale privato e processuale* 525 (hereafter 'Honorati'); M Nioche, 'Décision provisoire et autorité de la chose jugée'[2012] *Rev. crit. DIP* 277.

8 For a brief description of the domestic practice in various Member States in the matter of provisional measures, see the Report of B. Hess, T. Pfeiffer and P. Schlosser, *The Brussels I Regulation 44/2001 – Application and Enforcement in the European Union*, C.H. Beck 2008.

Taking into account these three features, the Court of Justice of the European Union ('the Court of Justice'), and more recently the European legislator, have introduced various limitations to the use of cross-border provisional measures. These limitations affect both the stage of the *granting* of provisional measures, and the *effect* of provisional measures once they have been granted. The first stage relates to the jurisdiction of the court to order provisional measures, and the second stage to the recognition and enforcement of provisional measures in other Member States.

The purpose of this contribution is to review these limitations. In this respect, a fundamental distinction must be established between two options, depending on the basis of the jurisdiction of the court that is being requested to issue a provisional measure. This fundamental distinction has been articulated in 1998 in *Van Uden*[9], where the Court of Justice highlighted the difference between the case where the measures are granted by a court having jurisdiction as to the substance of the matter and by a court which does not have jurisdiction over the substance. There is a so-called 'two track system'[10], and the legal regime of provisional measures is entirely different depending on the track that is pursued by the claimant.

2. FIRST OPTION: THE COURT HAS JURISDICTION OVER THE SUBSTANCE OF THE CASE

When the court has jurisdiction over the substance of the case under the Regulation, there is no limitation to the jurisdiction of the court to grant provisional measures (2.1), and the provisional measures must be recognized and enforced in the other Member States provided that they are not made on an *ex parte* basis (2.2).

2.1. UNLIMITED JURISDICTION TO GRANT PROVISIONAL MEASURES

When the court has jurisdiction over the substance of the matter – for instance, the request to grant provisional measures is brought before the court of the domicile of the defendant – then Article 35 is not engaged. The court having jurisdiction as to the substance also has *inherent jurisdiction* to issue provisional measures, without any of the restrictions that derive from the application of Article 35 (these restrictions are reviewed below). As was held in *Van Uden*:

> 'the court having jurisdiction as to the substance of a case under one of the heads of jurisdiction laid down in the [Regulation] also has jurisdiction to order any provisional and protective measures, without that jurisdiction being subject to any further conditions'[11]

9 Case C-391/95 *Van Uden* [1998] ECR I-1709 para 22.

10 Garcimartin, p. 59.

11 Case C-391/95 *Van Uden* [1998] ECR I-1709 para 22. See case C-99/96 *Hans-Hermann Mietz v Intership Yachting Sneek BV* [1999] ECR I-2277 para 41.

Thus, the *Van Uden* ruling, whose precedential value is not affected on this point by the Recast Regulation, implies that the court having jurisdiction as to the substance is empowered to issue provisional measures without any limitations. There is no need to enquire whether the measures that are granted by the court meet the conditions to be considered as 'provisional'. Furthermore, it is not necessary to establish any kind of territorial or other connection with that court. The assumption is that the territorial ambit of the jurisdictional power derived from Articles 4 and 7 to 26 of the Regulation, is unlimited. The jurisdictional bases laid down in these provisions are assumed to be sound and in accordance with procedural justice, and can therefore be extended to any kind of decision taken by the court.

The only outer limit to the power of the court having jurisdiction as to the substance to issue provisional measures derives from public international law: the court of a Member State cannot issue a provisional measure that encroaches on the sovereignty of another State. Following the traditional *Lotus* jurisprudence[12], courts cannot exercise their execution power on the territory of another Member State. The issue of whether and when the attachment or freezing of assets may involve such encroachment is subject to discussion.[13] These discussions do not, as such, concern the functioning of the Brussels regime.

The fundamental condition to be satisfied, under the Regulation, for the court to have unlimited jurisdiction to grant provisional measures is therefore that the court has *jurisdiction as to the substance of the case*. In *Van Uden*, the Court stated that this means that the court must have jurisdiction '*under one of the heads of jurisdiction laid down in [the Regulation]*'[14], aside of course from Article 35. Thus, the unlimited power to grant provisional measures will apply when the application is brought before the court of the domicile of the defendant (general jurisdiction – Article 4), the special rules of jurisdiction (for instance, the place of performance of the contract or the place of the harmful event – Article 7), the rules of ancillary jurisdiction (for instance, the court of the domicile of one of the co-defendants – Article 8), the rules of exclusive jurisdiction (for instance, the court of the place of registration of a patent – Article 24), the rules about

12 *The 'Lotus' [France v. Turkey]* PCIJ Series A No 10.

13 Under English case law, provisional orders which produce their effect *in personam*, such as freezing injunctions, disclosure orders or receivership orders, do not raise any issue of public international law or international comity (see e.g. *Masri v. Consolidated Contractors International UK Ltd (No 2)* [2009] 2 WLR 621, per Lord Lawrence Collins). However, in *Société Eram Shipping* [2003] UKHL 30, the House of Lords held that a third party debt order (or garnishee order), as a proprietary remedy which operates by way of attachment of the property, is inconsistent with the comity of the foreign court and infringes principles of international law. This decision implies that such an order cannot be made in respect of a foreign debt even when the court has jurisdiction as to the substance of the matter. This aspect of law of cross-border provisional measures, which does not directly concern the functioning of the Brussels regime, is not entirely straightforward. For scholarly discussion, see R. Fentiman, *International Commercial Litigation* (OUP 2nd ed. 2015), para 18.03–18.04.

14 *Van Uden*, para 22.

prorogation of jurisdiction (for instance, the court designated by the parties in a choice of court agreement – Article 25), or even the rules of jurisdiction for the protection of weaker parties (Articles 10 to 23).

The determination of whether, in a given case, the court has jurisdiction over the substance of the matter appears *prima facie* to involve a simple application of the direct rules of jurisdiction of the Regulation, as in any other case. However, on closer inspection, the matter is not so straightforward. The condition that the court has jurisdiction as to the substance of the case takes a specific meaning when the assessment is done for the purpose of establishing whether the court can grant provisional measures without any restriction. Complex issues which are specific to the matter of provisional measures may arise, some of which will be reviewed here.

First, while the court must assess whether it has jurisdiction over the substance of the case, the difficulty is that provisional measures are often sought *before* the bringing of a substantive claim.[15] As a matter of principle, it does not appear necessary that a claim on the substance has actually been brought before the court for this court to have jurisdiction to grant provisional measures without the need to use Article 35. The test is that the court must have jurisdiction as to the substance of the case, not that the court be actually seized of a substantive claim over which it has jurisdiction. Thus, in effect, the condition of establishing jurisdiction over the substance of the case relates only to a potential claim on the substance. It is only a condition of *putative jurisdiction*. This may create complications, as normally the jurisdiction is assessed by reference to the claims as pleaded by the claimant. When no substantive claim has yet been brought before any court, the jurisdiction over the substance of the claim will have to be assessed by reference to the putative claims that the parties could bring in respect of the dispute.

Second, under the Regulation, it is often the case that more than one court has jurisdiction in relation to the substance of the matter. If there is already a dispute pending before one of these courts, is it still possible to bring an application for provisional measures before another court that would have jurisdiction over the substance of the matter? Take the case where the court of the place of performance of a contract under Article 7(1) of the Regulation is seized with a claim relating to this contract. Is it still possible to seek provisional measures from the court of the domicile of the defendant under Article 4 of the Regulation? In other words, does the *lis pendens* rule (Article 29 of the Regulation) prevent, in such a case, asserting that this other court has jurisdiction as to the substance? The better view is probably that this question should be answered in the affirmative. The jurisdiction on the basis of the heads of jurisdiction of the Regulation must not only be theoretical. Rather, the jurisdiction should also be capable of being *effectively* exercised in relation to the merits of the dispute, in the sense that the

15 Garcimartin, p. 61.

court must have the power and authority, under the Regulation, to rule on the substance of the matter, at the time that it is seized of the matter. If another court is seized in parallel of the same dispute, then the court cannot, as a matter of *lis pendens*, rule on the substance of the case, and this court should not be treated as a court having jurisdiction over the substance of the case.

Third, if no court has yet been seized on the substance of the dispute, it seems that the application for provisional measures can be brought in any of the courts having jurisdiction under the Regulation. But what happens if *after* a request for provisional measures has been brought before one of such courts, the claim on the substance is brought before another court? Would this affect the power of the former court to grant provisional measures? In principle, under the Regulation, jurisdiction is assessed at the time of the bringing of the claim (principle of *perpetuatio fori*).[16] Thus, it should follow that the court having unlimited jurisdiction to grant provisional measures at the time of the bringing of the application should keep this power even if subsequently a claim on the substance is brought before the court of another Member State also having jurisdiction over the substance of the matter.[17] This should however apply only in relation to the provisional measures that were sought in the original application. When a claim is amended, it seems that it is to be treated under the Regulation as having been brought at the time of the amendment.[18]

2.2. RECOGNITION AND ENFORCEMENT OF THE PROVISIONAL MEASURES UNLESS WHEN GRANTED *EX PARTE*

When the provisional measures are granted by a court having jurisdiction over the substance of the case, the decision of the court that grants these measures benefits in principle from the uniform rules of recognition and enforcement of judgments. This is made explicit in Article 2(a) of the Recast Regulation, which provides that for the purpose of the application of the uniform rules on the recognition and enforcement of judgments, the term 'judgment' includes provisional measures '*ordered by a court or tribunal which by virtue of this Regulation has jurisdiction as to the substance of the matter*'. Recital 33 clarifies likewise that '*[w]here provisional, including protective, measures are ordered by a court having jurisdiction as to the substance of the matter, their free circulation should be ensured under this Regulation*'.

---

16 See Opinion of AG Jacobs in Case C-18/02, *Danmarks Rederiforening* [2004] at para 64, noting that *events after proceedings have been brought* cannot affect the attribution of jurisdiction.

17 See however Garcimartin, p. 61, who considers that the measures will have to be revoked or will cease to have effect once proceedings on the substance are brought before another court, unless this court has jurisdiction under Article 35.

18 See R. Fentiman, *International Commercial Litigation*, OUP 2nd ed., para. 11.28 to 11.33.

In order to ensure that the condition as to the jurisdiction of the court of origin is satisfied, Article 42(2)(b)(i) of the Recast Regulation requires, for the enforcement of a decision ordering a provisional measure, that the certificate issued by the court of origin confirms that '*the court has jurisdiction as to the substance of the matter*'. This certificate must be submitted by the party that seeks the direct execution of the decision from the competent enforcement authority in the Member State of enforcement.

The central concept in this matter is therefore, once again, the one of '*jurisdiction as to the substance of the matter*'. In practice, several situations can arise at the stage of enforcement of the provisional measures. Firstly, the provisional measure may have been granted by the actual court which was seized of the claim as to the substance of the matter. In that case, the condition is satisfied, provided of course that the jurisdiction of the court was established. If the defendant challenged the jurisdiction, or did not appear before the court, it is probably required, for the provisional measure to be recognised in the other Member States, that such court has already ruled on its jurisdiction as to the substance of the matter. As long as the court has not ruled on that point, it is doubtful that the parties can obtain the certificate confirming that the court has jurisdiction as to the substance of the matter (Article 42(2)(b)(i)), without which the decision cannot circulate.

Secondly, the provisional measure may have been ordered by a court which was not itself seized on the substance of the matter, but there was another court, in the same Member State, which was so seized. This situation will arise in particular in those Member States which entrust the task of issuing provisional measures to a specific court or magistrate. In that situation, the position is likely to be the same as under the first one, with the proviso that the obligation to certify that the court has jurisdiction as to the substance of the matter does not belong to the court which is seized of the substance of the matter, but to another court or magistrate. The effective application of the Recast Regulation may require an adaption of the judicial practice in some Member States, as the specific magistrates who are competent to grant provisional measures may not be accustomed to rule on the issue of the jurisdiction as to the substance of the matter.

Thirdly, the provisional measure may have been ordered by the court of a Member State when there was no pending suit in that Member State on the substance of the dispute. In that situation, there is room for discussion as to whether the provisional measure is capable of benefitting from the Regulation rules on the recognition and enforcement.[19] In line with what has been explained above, the better view is that this is not an obstacle to the application of these rules. The second paragraph of Article 2(a) requires only that the court of origin has, by virtue of the Regulation, jurisdiction as to the substance of the matter, without requiring that a substantive claim has already been brought before that

19 Heinze p. 607; Honorati p. 539–540; Dickinson p. 545–546.

court. If, therefore, a claim could be sustained based on one of the grounds of jurisdiction in the Regulation, the requirement would appear to be satisfied.

Fourthly, when the court of another Member State was already seized of a claim as to the substance of the matter, the courts of the other Member States should not be regarded as being courts having jurisdiction over the substance of the case. As already explained above, the notion of jurisdiction as to the substance should logically take into account the provisions of the Regulation in respect of *lis pendens*. However, if the court before which an application for provisional measures was made was already seized at the time that proceeding on the substance where brought before the court of another Member State, the provisional measures should freely circulate. By application of the principle of *perpetuario fori*, the court which was competent under Article 35 at the time of the bringing of the application for provisional measures should have the power to issue (and/or to refuse to withdraw) the certificate stating that it has jurisdiction as to the substance of the matter (Article 42(2)(b)(i)).

A further issue arises. Once the court of origin issues the certificate confirming that the court has jurisdiction as to the substance of the matter (under Article 42(2)(b)(i) of the Regulation), is there any room for this point to be reviewed in the Member State of enforcement? In *Mietz*, under the 2001 Regulation, the Court of Justice ruled that the requested court can and must review whether the court of origin has jurisdiction as to the substance and, if it does not, whether the *Van Uden* conditions are satisfied. The same type of control has been accepted by the Court of Justice in respect of provisional measures in the matter of parental responsibility under the Brussels II*bis* Regulation.[20] In both cases, however, the Court was careful to emphasise that the review undertaken by the requested court did not concern as such the jurisdiction of the court of origin: it only concerned '*the extent to which it is possible to seek the enforcement*' of provisional measures with regard to the specific conditions that govern the issue of such measures.[21]

Still more importantly, the Court of Justice stressed in both cases that the ground for the jurisdiction of the court of origin was uncertain and could not be deciphered from the actual terms of the decision.[22] By contrast, under the Recast Regulation, the jurisdiction as to the substance of the matter of the court of origin must be recorded expressly in the certificate issued under Article 42(2)(b)(i). Accordingly, it is doubtful that the Mietz exception to the principle that the jurisdiction of the court of origin cannot be reviewed in the other Member States (Article 45(3)) can still be accepted under the Recast Regulation. Thus, the decision by the court of origin that it has jurisdiction as to the substance of the matter should not be open to review or to challenge by the competent enforcement authority or by the court before which an application for refusal of enforcement is brought pursuant to Art 47 of the Recast Regulation.

---

20 Case C-296/10, *Bianca Purrucker v Guillermo Vallés Pérez* [2010] ECR I-7353.

21 *Mietz* para 49; *Purrucker* para 75.

22 *Mietz* para 50; *Purrucker* para 77.

However, for the authorities of the Member State of enforcement to be bound by the certificate issued in the Member State of origin, this certificate must be established in conformity with the Regulation, including the requirement that it be issued by *'the court of origin'* (Article 53). The certificate must therefore emanate from the court of origin itself, or at least it must have been approved by such a court. The certificate which is issued for instance by the court's clerk, without any review or approval by the body itself which exercises judicial functions, would probably not meet this requirement.

The free circulation of provisional measures is not subject only to the condition that they have been granted by a court having jurisdiction as to the substance of the case. The Recast Regulation has introduced another restriction which was absent from the earlier instruments. The restriction is also found in Article 2(a) of the Recast Regulation, which provides a definition of the notion of 'judgment' for the purpose of the application of the rules of recognition and enforcement of judgments. Pursuant to Article 2(a), the notion of judgment *'does not include a provisional, including protective, measure which is ordered by such a court or tribunal without the defendant being summoned to appear, unless the judgment containing the measure is served on the defendant prior to enforcement'*. To evidence that this condition is satisfied, the party requesting the enforcement of provisional measures must submit to the competent enforcement authority *'proof of service of the judgment'* (Article 42(2)(c) of the Recast Regulation).

As a general requirement under the Recast Regulation, the new system of 'direct enforcement' is subject to the condition that the judgment be served on the person against whom the enforcement is sought prior to the first enforcement measure (Article 43(1)). However, in principle, this formality is *not* required for the enforcement of a provisional measure (Article 43(3)). The effect of Article 2(a) is to introduce an exception to this exception[23]: the formal step of prior service of the decision is still required when the provisional measure has been issued in the Member State of origin without the defendant being summoned to appear or having been served with the decision prior to enforcement. In other words, the European legislator has considered that the abolishing of *exequatur* could not be combined with the suppression of the prior information of the debtor about the contents of the decision, in one form or another.

On this point, the Recast Regulation codifies, in effect, the infamous 1980 *Denilauler* case, where the Court of Justice held that the *'simplified enforcement procedure'* does not apply to *'provisional and protective measures which are ordered or authorized by a court without the party against whom they are directed having been summoned to appear and which are intended to be enforced without prior service on that party'*.[24] This position had however been qualified in subsequent

23 It is quite unfortunate that this exception is not reflected in the text of Article 43(3), which on its own appears misleading.

24 Case C-125/79 *Bernard Denilauler v SNC Couchet Frères* [1980] ECR 1553 para 17.

case law[25], and the domestic courts in some Member States had recently abandoned the restriction altogether.[26] It had been convincingly argued in legal writing that the principle of non-circulation of *ex parte* judgments is outdated and not in accordance with the modern needs of cross-border litigation.[27] In the Proposal for the Recast Regulation, the Commission had proposed to endorse expressly this evolution in the legal thinking: under the terms of the Proposal, the notion of judgment in Article 2(a) was to be defined as *'includ[ing] measures ordered without the defendant being summoned to appear and which are intended to be enforced without prior service of the defendant if the defendant has the right to challenge the measure subsequently under the national law of the Member State of origin'*.[28]

Ultimately, the Council and the Parliament have decided to disregard this evolution of the practice. Taking the exact opposite approach to the one advocated by the Commission, they have defined the notion of judgment as excluding *ex parte* measures, unless the judgment containing the measure is served on the defendant prior to enforcement. This means, in practice, that the judicial process ceases to have the desired *ex parte* character. The 'surprise effect' of the provisional measures is lost, which may sometimes undermine their effectiveness because the person against whom the enforcement is sought will be informed in advance that measures of execution are forthcoming, and will therefore be in a position to take avoidance steps.

When the proceedings have been pursued on an *ex parte* basis in the Member State of origin, it is still possible to proceed to the direct enforcement of the provisional measures under the condition that the judgment containing the measure be *'served on the defendant prior to enforcement'* (Article 2(a)). The text does not specify *how long*, prior to the enforcement, the judgment must have been served on the defendant. In view of this silence, it has been suggested that the applicant could obtain the enforcement of the *ex parte* provisional measure immediately following its service.[29] This is not obvious. With respect to the general requirement of service prior to enforcement under Article 43(1), it is clarified in the Preamble of the Regulation that the service should be effected *'in reasonable time before the first enforcement measure'* (Recital 32). This requirement

---

25 Case C-474/93 *Hengst Import BV v Anna Maria Campese* [1995] ECR I-2113 para 14, where the Court ruled that the judgment that orders provisional measures on an *ex parte* basis is capable of recognition and enforcement under the European rules if *'there could have been an inter partes hearing in the State where it was made before recognition and enforcement were sought'*.

26 See, for example, the decision of the French Court of Cassation in the *Stolzenberg* litigation, which upheld the recognition of an English freezing injunction which had been issued *ex parte* in the course of *inter partes* proceedings on the substance of the matter: Cass civ., 30 June 2004, D., 2004, 2743, noted H Muir Watt [2004] *Rev. crit. DIP* 815.

27 See the detailed analysis of the case law and legal writing in H. Boularbah, *Requête unilatérale et inversion du contentieux* (Larcier 2010), para 955.

28 So, it was enough to show that a challenge could be brought subsequently, which meant that the Commission was proposing to go further than in *Hengst Import*.

29 Garcimartin, p. 67–68.

should logically apply also to the enforcement of *ex parte* provisional measures, as the requirement of prior service of Article 2(a) mirrors the requirement of Article 43(1).

In any event, the requirement of service prior to enforcement will, in practice, mean that the surprise effect of the *ex parte* measure will be lost under the Regulation process.[30]

However, there are possibly two alternative ways in which the surprise effect may be maintained.[31] The first one is alluded to in Recital 33 of the Preamble of the Recast Regulation: while the European regime of free circulation of judgments is said not to apply to *ex parte* provisional measures, '*[t]his should not preclude the recognition and enforcement of such measures under national law*'. Thus, in practice, the claimant must bring an application before the court of the Member State of enforcement, without being able to rely on the principle of direct execution. When the applicable domestic law provides for the enforcement of foreign decisions on the basis of an *ex parte* application, and the local conditions for recognition and enforcement are met, the party who has obtained the provisional measure will be in a position to enforce this measure without prior notice to the defendant.

The reference in Recital 33 to domestic law in this context suggests that the Regulation's procedures for the enforcement of judgments are not exclusive. Yet, prior to the adoption of the Recast Regulation, the prevailing view was that the procedures of the Brussels regime had an exclusive nature[32], in the sense that the claimant who had obtained a judgment from the courts of one Member State could enforce the judgment in the other Member States only by application of the European rules. Support for that view was found in the case law of the Court of Justice.[33] The Brussels regime was treated as a '*closed system which cannot be ignored by the claimant on the basis of considerations of convenience or speed*'.[34]

It is uncertain whether the exclusive nature of the EU enforcement regime has entirely been abandoned.[35] The context suggests that the reference to domestic law

30 Garcimartin, p. 68.

31 See van Drooghenbroeck and De Boe, p. 201, para. 26.

32 A Layton and H Mercer, *European Civil Practice*, 2nd ed. London Thomson 2004, para 24.017; K Kerameus in U Magnus and P Mankowski (ed.), *Brussels I Regulation*, 2nd ed. Munich, Article 38, para 14. Comp. the new edition by I Rueda and G Cuniberti, U Magnus and P Mankowski (ed.), *Brussels Ibis Regulation*, 2016, Article 40, para 12–14.

33 See Case C-42/76 *Jozef de Wolf v Harry Cox BV* [1976] ECR 1759, where the Court ruled that the party who has obtained a judgment in his favor in a Member State cannot bring a fresh claim before the courts of another Member State, relying on the findings of the first court, instead of applying for the enforcement of the first court's judgment under the European rules. Likewise, in the Case C-267/97 *Eric Coursier v Fortis Bank and Martine Coursier, née Bellami* [1999] ECR I-2543, para 25, it was held that the enforcement procedure of the Brussels regime '*constitutes an autonomous and complete system*'.

34 K Kerameus in U Magnus and P Mankowski (ed.), *Brussels I Regulation*, 2nd ed. Munich, Article 38, para 14.

35 See I Rueda and G Cuniberti, U Magnus and P Mankowski (ed.), *Brussels Ibis Regulation*, 2016, Article 40, para 14, who consider that if national enforcement regimes can supplement the Regulation with regard to provisional measures, this should also be the case for other

is confined to the enforcement of provisional measures for reasons that are specific to this matter. Two points support that view. First, the reference to national law is not an unusual occurrence in the matter of provisional and protective measures: at the stage of jurisdiction also, there is an explicit reference referral to domestic law (see above). Second, the permission to use the more liberal regime of enforcement under domestic law in relation to provisional measures may be a specific concession, introduced at the last moment in the text[36], to balance the severe restrictions to the free circulation of provisional measures brought about by the Recast Regulation.

There is a second possible way that needs to be considered to obtain the cross-border enforcement of an *ex parte* provisional measure without the prior notification of the defendant. It is based on the wording of Article 40 of the Recast Regulation. This provision states that *'[a]n enforceable judgment shall carry with it by operation of law the power to proceed to any protective measures which exist under the law of the Member State addressed'*. There is nothing in the provision that excludes provisional measures which are ordered on an *ex parte* basis. Should it still be considered that the restriction under Article 2(a) applies here? It could be argued that the restriction does apply, because under Article 2(a) an *ex parte* provisional measure is not a judgment, and therefore – the argument goes – it cannot be an 'enforceable judgment' under Article 40.

Nevertheless, it could also be argued that the new restriction in the last sentence of Article 2(a) is an exception to the exception provided in Article 43(3) from the general requirement of service in Article 43(1). Indeed, under Article 43(3), the formalities required under Article 43 (including the requirement for the service on the person against whom the enforcement is sought prior to the first enforcement measure) do not apply *'to the enforcement of a protective measure in a judgment where the person seeking enforcement proceeds to protective measures in accordance with Article 40'*. Thus, the party who has obtained a judgment ordering a provisional measure from the court of a Member State is entitled to seek directly in another Member State the execution of a provisional measure *'which exists under the law of the Member State addressed'*.

The application of Article 40 cannot lead, of course, to the circumvention of Article 2(a): if the defendant has not been served with the decision given in the State of origin, it will not be possible to enforce directly the provisional measure that was granted by this decision. But to the extent that the domestic law of the requested State allows, upon the production of the decision given in the State of origin, to grant directly an equivalent provisional measure provided under the local law, the process should be valid under Article 40 of the Recast Regulation. The foreign decision would not be recognised or enforced as such, but

judgments, and that the application of more liberal national regimes would be consistent with the objective of free circulation of judgments.

36 The reference to national law was absent from the Draft Report of 28 June 2011 of the Committee on Legal Affairs.

it could serve as evidence of a fact for its contents and the future possibility of its recognition or enforcement.

The condition of prior information of the defendant introduced in the Recast Regulation is undoubtedly a step backwards from the perspective of the objective of free movement of provisional measures. Yet, during the same period of time, the Court of Justice has continued unabashed with its drive towards the facilitation of the recognition and enforcement of provisional measures, at least when the condition of prior notification of the respondent is satisfied. This is very explicit in the *Meroni* case[37], where the Court of Justice accepted that an asset-freezing injunction ordered by an English court could be enforced against a third party to the proceedings. In that case, the freezing injunction was made against the defendant in England, but also applied to his interests in companies to which the defendant was a beneficial owner. The Court ruled that provided proper notice had been given, these third parties could not rely on the public policy exception to object to the enforcement of the freezing order on the basis that they were not parties to the English proceedings. There was a duty on their part (even as third parties) to use all remedies made available to them in the Member State of origin. This case is part of a new line of case law establishing the principle of exhaustion of remedies in the State of origin.[38]

3. SECOND OPTION: THE COURT DOES NOT HAVE JURISDICTION OVER THE SUBSTANCE OF THE CASE

When the court does not have jurisdiction over the substance of the case under the Regulation, the jurisdiction of the court to grant provisional measures is subject to two conditions relating to the nature of measures that can be ordered and to the requirement of a territorial connection with the forum (A), and the provisional measures do no benefit from the uniform rules on recognition and enforcement of judgment (B).

3.1. LIMITED JURISDICTION TO ORDER PROVISIONAL MEASURES

When the court that is requested to grant provisional measures does not have jurisdiction over the substance of the case, Article 35 of the Regulation comes into play, and provides that provisional measures can be granted under domestic law.

---

37 Case C-559/14 *Rudolfs Meroni v Recoletos Limited.*

38 See A Nuyts, 'Le principe d'épuisement des voires de recours dans l'Etat membre d'origine du jugement', in *Liber Amicorum Nadine Watté*, Bruylant 2017, p. 427 to 460.

Under its terms, Article 35 applies whenever *'the courts of another Member State have jurisdiction as to the substance of the matter'*. The Court of Justice has clarified that the provision also applies when the proceedings as to the substance are to be conducted before arbitrators[39], and when the substance of the matter falls within the *exclusive jurisdiction* of the court of another Member State.[40]

In the Brussels Convention and in the 2001 Regulation, the text of the relevant provision referred to the power of the court to grant provisional measures *'even if*, under this Regulation, *the courts of another Member State have jurisdiction as to the substance of the matter.'* The words *'under this Regulation'* have been deleted in the Recast Regulation. The initial purpose of this change, in the Commission Proposal, was to reflect the fact that the Commission had proposed to refer to the *'courts of another State* or an arbitral tribunal'.[41] This was meant to confirm that the jurisdiction to issue provisional measures exists even if the matter is governed by an arbitral clause, as per the existing case law. In the end, the reference to 'arbitral tribunal' has not been kept in the text, but the words 'under this Regulation' have not been reinstated. The non-inclusion of these words into the Recast Regulation could still serve the purpose of making clear that the application of Article 35 is not subject to the condition that the jurisdiction of the court of another Member State (on the merits of the case) be established under the provisions of the Regulation. Thus, Article 35 could apply even if such jurisdiction derives from domestic law because the defendant is domiciled in a third State (Article 6(1)) or from a convention governing jurisdiction or the recognition or enforcement of judgments in relation to particular matters (Article 71).

Thus, Article 35 applies as soon as the court seised of the application for a provisional measure does not, for whatever reason, have jurisdiction as to the substance of the matter under one of the heads of jurisdiction of the Regulation.[42]

It is not even required that the substance of the (main) dispute falls within the subject-matter scope of the Regulation. As confirmed in the case law[43], it is

---

39 *Van Uden*, para 34.

40 Case C-616/10 *Solvay v. Honeywell Fluorine Products Europe BV* [2012], para 51. This is the case even when the substance of the dispute relates to the registration or validity of a patent: while the jurisdiction of the court of the place of registration of the patent is so intense that it applies regardless of the form of proceedings in which the patent's validity is raised, including when the issue of validity of the patent is raised only incidentally (Case C-4/03 *GAR Gesellschaft für Antriebstechnik mdH v. Luk Lamellen- und Kupplungsbau Beteligungs KG* [2006] ECR I-6509), the exclusive jurisdiction of a court does not catch provisional measures, which can still be sought from the courts of other Member States. See *Solvay*, para 43–50, finding that there is no risk of conflicting decisions between the provisional decision taken by the court before which the interim proceedings have been brought and the decision to be taken on the substance by the court having jurisdiction under Article 24(4) of the 2001 Regulation.

41 Commission's Proposal, Article 31.

42 *Van Uden* and *Solvay* make clear that it does not matter why this is so: the nature and the basis of the jurisdiction of the court (or arbitrators) having jurisdiction as to the substance is not relevant for the application of Article 35.

43 See Case 25/81, *W. V. H.* [1982] ECR 1189; Case 143/78, *De Cavel I* [1979] ECR 1055, para 9; Case 120/79, *De Cavel II* [1980] ECR 731; *Van Uden*, para 33.

enough, for Article 35 to apply, that the provisional measures themselves relate to matters which fall within the subject-matter scope of the Regulation. Thus, an application for provisional measures which, by the nature of the rights which they serve to protect[44], fall within the scope of the Regulation, is governed by Article 35, even though the substance of the dispute between the parties falls outside the scope of the Regulation (eg. because the dispute is concerned with a matter specifically excluded from the scope of the Regulation[45], or because it is subject to an arbitration clause[46]).[47]

The purpose of Article 35 is to allow the court not having jurisdiction as to substance to grant provisional measures that are '*available under the law of that Member State*'. This is seemingly an unfettered reference to domestic law. However, the Court of Justice has placed autonomous limits on the operation of domestic law in order to curtail the use of Article 35 and avoid the circumvention of the jurisdictional scheme of the Regulation.[48]

The starting point for the application of Article 35 remains domestic law. The availability and conditions for the grant of provisional measures are regulated by the law of the forum from which such measures are sought.[49] Article 35 is not a self-standing rule of jurisdiction.[50] It is implicit in *Van Uden* that the jurisdiction of the court is to be founded on the rules of (international) jurisdiction as they apply in the forum State. The Court accepted in *Van Uden* that such rules may include the so-called exorbitant bases of jurisdiction which are otherwise declared inapplicable to establish the jurisdiction on the substance of the matter when the defendant is domiciled in a Member State (Article 5(2)).[51] Thus, in principle, an application for provisional measures can be brought in France based on the French citizenship of the claimant, in Germany on the basis of the presence of a defendant's assets

44 *Van Uden*, para 33.

45 See Case 25/81, *W. V. H.* [1982] ECR 1189; Case 143/78, *De Cavel I* [1979] ECR 1055, para 9.

46 *Van Uden*, para 33.

47 For instance, it has been held that an application for provisional measures which relate to divorce proceedings (the freezing of assets of one of the spouses) is outside the scope of the Brussels regime (*De Cavel II*), while an application for provisional measures relating to maintenance obligations is within the scope of the Brussels regime (because these obligations were (at the time) within the scope of the Brussels Convention (following the adoption of the Maintenance Regulation (No 4/2009), the matter of maintenance obligations arising from a family relationship, parentage, marriage or affinity has been excluded from the scope of the 2001 Regulation (and from the Recast Regulation): see Article 1(2)(e)),even though the application was made between spouses which were involved in divorce proceedings (*De Cavel I*). In other words, to establish whether the provisional measures fall within the scope of the Regulation, reference must be made solely to the matters that are specifically dealt with in the course of the interlocutory proceedings, which implies to scrutinize the interests that are specifically at stake in these proceedings.

48 Dickinson, p. 521.

49 Dickinson, p. 521.

50 See the academic discussion on this point in M. Pertegas Sender in Magnus & Mankowski, Article 31, para 4.

51 The Court of Justice noted that the prohibition in Article 5(2) to rely on the rules of exorbitant jurisdiction '*does not apply to the special regime provided for by Article [35]*', *Van Uden*, para 42.

in Germany (the so-called *forum arresti*), and in England when the defendant is physically present on the English territory when served with the claim form.[52]

However, even when jurisdiction exists under domestic law, the power of the court not having jurisdiction as to substance to issue provisional measures is subject to certain conditions which apply autonomously. There are two basic conditions: the measures must have a provisional or protective nature (3.1.1.), and there must be a territorial connecting link with the forum (3.1.2.).

3.1.1. *The provisional nature of the measures*

The restriction relating to the nature of the measures that can be ordered under Article 35 is explicit in the wording of the provision itself which refers to *'provisional, including protective, measures'*, though the Court of Justice has elaborated certain requirements that flow from this notion.

The basic definition of the notion of provisional and protective measures was provided by the Court of Justice in the 1992 ruling in *Reichert* II, and is still valid under the Recast Regulation: *'The expression 'provisional, including protective, measures' within the meaning of Article [35] must … be understood as referring to measures which, in matters within the scope of the [Regulation], are intended to preserve a factual or legal situation so as to safeguard rights the recognition of which is sought elsewhere from the court having jurisdiction as to the substance of the matter'*.[53]

As this definition makes clear, Article 35 only permits the court to order measures which are intended to *preserve a factual or legal situation*. This means that measures which do not pursue this objective cannot be characterized as provisional and protective.[54]

The objective of preserving the factual or legal situation is associated, in *Reichert II*, with the need to safeguard rights the protection of which is sought from the court having jurisdiction as to the substance of the matter. This formulation may give the impression that the application of Article 35 is subject to the condition that proceedings be brought on the substance of the case, and that the provision ceases to apply once the court has given judgment on the merits. In fact, none of these two apparent limitations seem to have been applied in practice. Article 35 has not been made subject to the condition that the applicant effectively files proceedings on the substance, and the provision has been used as the basis to grant provisional measures in support of the enforcement of the judgment on the substance after such judgment has been issued.[55]

---

52 These are the three classical exorbitant bases of jurisdiction that can be found in the domestic law.

53 Case C-261/90 *Reichert and Kockler v. Dresdner Bank AG* [1992] ECR I-2149, para 34.

54 Thus, in *Reichert II*, the Court found that the *action paulienne* of French law, by which the creditor seeks to set aside a transaction which has been performed in fraud of his rights, is not a provisional measure as it does not seek to preserve the situation.

55 *Masri v. Consolidated Contractors International (UK) Ltd (N°2)* [2008] EWCA Civ 309; [2009] 2 QB 450, at para 106, where the Court of Appeal ruled that post-judgment orders that operate

On the other hand, the Court of Justice has identified, in *Van Uden*, that the notion of a provisional measure implies that the measure cannot be final, in the sense that the court must ensure that it is possible to undo the effect of the measure if the applicant is finally unsuccessful on the substance. This is the condition of '*reversibility*' of the effect of the measures. In *Denilauler*, the Court of Justice noted that the court must '*make its authorisation [of provisional measures] subject to all conditions guaranteeing the provisional or protective character of the measure ordered.*'[56] The Court gave examples of conditions that can be imposed to ensure this provisional character of the order: '*depending on each case and commercial practices [...] the court must be able to place a time-limit on its order or, as regards the nature of the assets of goods subject to the measures contemplated, require bank guarantees or nominate a sequestrator.*'[57]

This specific condition of 'reversibility' appears to be distinct from the general condition that the measure can only seek to preserve the factual or legal situation. While the latter condition is intended to bring a restriction in respect of the *objective* that the measure must seek to achieve (namely, the preservation of the *status quo*), the imposition of limits ensuring the provisional character of the order implies that the *contents* of the measure itself are circumscribed or accompanied by conditions to ensure that its effects can be reversed if necessary (i.e. if the applicant is ultimately unsuccessful). The Court of Justice has further elaborated on the meaning of the latter restriction in *Van Uden*. The Court acknowledged in that case that an order for an interim payment is problematic because, by its very nature, it '*may preempt the decision on the substance of the case*'.[58] As a consequence, such an order cannot constitute a provisional measure unless '*first, repayment to the defendant of the sum awarded is guaranteed if the plaintiff is unsuccessful as regards the substance of his claim and, second, the measure sought relates only to specific assets of the defendant located or to be located within the confines of the territorial jurisdiction of the court to which application is made.*'[59]

In substance, the court requires that the order for provisional measures cannot produce effects which are final and definitive for the defendant. Consequently, there must be a 'guarantee' to be able to return to the *status quo ante* if the decision on the substance goes against the party who has obtained the provisional measure. In relation to an order for interim payment, this implies that there is a guarantee

---

in personam for the purpose of assisting in the enforcement of the judgment, such as freezing orders, disclosure orders or receivership orders, can be characterized as provisional measures under what is now Article 35 because the relief that is sought is intended to safeguard the rights which have been vindicated in the judgment on the substance. The characterization of a post-judgment freezing injunction as a provisional measure under Article 35 has been upheld by the French Court of Cassation in the *Stolzenberg* case: Cass. Civ. 1st 30 June 2004 [2004] D. 2743; [2004] *Rev. crit DIP* 815.

56 Case 125/79*Bernard Denilauler v SNC Couchet Frères* [1980] ECR I-1553, para 15.

57 *Denilauler*, para 15.

58 *Van Uden*, para 46.

59 *Van Uden*, para 47. See also *Mietz*, para 42.

of repayment, and that the order only concerns assets within the territory of the court. As is apparent from the ruling of the Court, the latter condition is designed to ensure compliance with the requirement of reversibility: imposing the condition that assets be located within the territory of the granting court is meant to ensure that the defendant will have access to resources in this territory that guarantee that he will get his money back if he is ultimately successful. For this guarantee to be effective, the assets need to remain within the territory of the forum State, and indeed it is submitted that this condition is implicit in the requirement that the order concerns only assets (to be) located within the confines of the territory of the forum State. To comply with the condition, the court can specify that the order for interim payment can only be executed on assets (to be located) within the territory of the forum State. Nevertheless, there may be other ways to satisfy the condition, such as the provision by the applicant of a collateral or other form of security, including a bank guarantee. Provided that the defendant, if ultimately successful, can have recourse to that security directly in the forum State, it can be considered that some form of assets are located in that territory, and that the *Van Uden* condition is met.

Thus, the presence of assets within the territory of the forum State becomes part of the definition of the notion of provisional measures, but only in relation to an order for an interim payment. The *Van Uden* condition that is discussed here should not be confused with the separate and more general requirement in *Van Uden* that a territorial connection between the subject-matter of the provisional measures and the forum State is needed; the latter condition is further discussed below.

By their very nature, some measures appear *per se* to comply with the condition of reversibility. For instance, freezing orders or attachment orders can be lifted at any time by the court. By themselves, such orders do not affect in any final way the ownership or possession of the assets. However, the effect produced by these orders may sometimes be very serious and far reaching (this is the case for instance in respect of worldwide freezing injunctions), and the requirement to preserve the possibility to go back to the *status quo ante* may justify that guarantees be imposed to ensure that the harm caused to the defendant by the provisional injunction be compensated in the event that the defendant is ultimately successful. However, in respect of such measures, which by their nature appear to be reversible, the court should have some discretion as to whether additional conditions to reinforce the provisional character of the order should be imposed or not.

Other kinds of measures appear to go beyond the requirement of a provisional character of the order. In particular, it has been questioned in legal writing how an order that anticipates the principal relief can ever be properly characterized as a provisional measure.[60] Yet, the Court of Justice has taken the position that such orders are not necessarily excluded from the notion of provisional measures,

---

60 See the very subtle analysis of A Huet, [1989] *Journal de droit international (JDI)* 96.

though they can only comply with the notion if the court imposes strict limits to ensure that the effects of the order can be reversed if necessary, in case the applicant is unsuccessful on the merits. Without such limits, the effect of the measure is not reversible, and it can only be ordered by the court having jurisdiction as to the substance of the matter. It follows from the *Van Uden* decision that in respect of such measures, and in particular an order for interim payment, the court acting under Article 35 has no discretion: it must impose the limits identified by the Court of Justice.

Finally, it should be noted that Recital 25 of the Preamble of the Regulation contains a new interpretation of the notion of provisional measures in the specific context of the gathering of evidence. According to Recital 25, the notion '*should include, for example, protective orders aimed at obtaining information or preserving evidence*'. Reference is made in particular to orders granted in relation to the application of Directive 2004/48/EC on the Enforcement of Intellectual Property Rights. Recital 25 adds that, by contrast, the notion of provisional measures '*should not include measures which are not of a protective nature, such as measures ordering the hearing of a witness.*' It is also emphasized that this is without prejudice to the application of the Evidence Regulation 1206/2001.

This provision reflects the ruling of the Court of Justice in *St Paul Dairy*[61], but also brings some nuances to the matter. In *St Paul Dairy*, the Court ruled that the notion of provisional measures does not cover '*a measure ordering the hearing of a witness for the purpose of enabling the applicant to decide whether to bring a case*'.[62] It has sometimes been suggested that this case implies quite a wide exclusion of evidential measures from the notion of provisional measures.[63] In fact, the meaning of *St Paul Dairy* is that the application of what was then Article 31 of the 2001 Regulation depends on the aim pursued by the applicant and the interests that he seeks to protect. If the applicant can establish that, through the evidential measure, he seeks to preserve a factual or legal situation, or that he can show that there is some interest to protect that goes beyond the mere attempt to decipher whether it is worth bringing an action on the merits, then the evidential measure can be characterized as a provisional measure.

Recital 25 confirms the validity of this approach: in relation to measures such as the hearing of a witness (as in *St Paul Dairy*), it is now specified expressly that such a measure can only have a 'protective' nature. However, it is also confirmed, by reference to the example of intellectual property matters, that the notion of provisional measures can also encompass 'orders aimed at obtaining information'. Recital 25 mentions, in particular, measures that are taken under Article 6 and 7 of Directive 2004/48/CE. Yet, if Article 7 of this Directive relates to measures for 'preserving evidence', Article 6 concerns more generally the *gathering* of evidence,

---

61 Case C-104/03 *St Paul Dairy* [2005] ECR I-3481.

62 *St Paul Dairy*, final para.

63 E Pataut, note in *Rev crit DIP* (2005) 742, at p. 750.

including the collection of banking, financial or commercial documents, when the applicant presents sufficient evidence to support his claim and identify the specified evidence that he is seeking to collect. Ultimately, the position may therefore not be very different from the one that was foreseen in the Commission's Proposal, where there was an explicit rule (in Article 2) stating that provisional measures *'shall include protective measures aimed at obtaining information and evidence'*.

It follows from the foregoing that the exclusion of evidential measures from Article 35 concerns essentially the 'fishing expedition' type of applications, by which the applicant seeks to identify any evidence that may exist (or not) in order to assess whether he wishes to bring proceedings on the substance or on which basis, without any more direct interest in the application. A more direct and specific interest that could be invoked by the applicant to justify the application of Article 35 would be the need to *preserve* the evidence. If there is a risk that the evidence could be destroyed, tampered with or undermined in any way, this should be sufficient to establish that Article 35 applies. Likewise, the provision should apply to the appointment of an expert when there is some urgency that the expert's investigations be carried out. The same should apply to an application for the disclosure of documents: if there is a risk that the documents will not be obtained at a later stage, this again should be sufficient to trigger the application of Article 35. In each of these situations, the evidential measure that is sought appears to fall squarely within 'the preservation function' that *Reichert I* has assigned to provisional measures (see above).

However, in view of Recital 25, the application of Article 35 could be justified in evidential matters beyond the situations where there is a need to preserve the evidence. Article 35 could apply as soon as the intervention of a court other than the court having jurisdiction as to the substance is required to ensure the effectiveness of the measure. For instance, if the effectiveness of the measure depends on the possibility of obtaining an *ex parte* order directly from the court of the place where the order is to be executed, without the other party being informed of the order, then again Article 35 should be available. The reference by Recital 25 to the matter of the enforcement of intellectual property, where the effect of surprise is often paramount for the effectiveness of the measures, confirms the validity of this interpretation. The importance of keeping this option open is still reinforced by the limits placed by the Recast Regulation on the recognition and enforcement of *ex parte* provisional orders, even when they are ordered by the court which has jurisdiction as to the substance of the matter (see above under Article 2(a)).

Recital 25 also states that the interpretation of the notion of provisional measures in this matter is 'without prejudice' to the application of the Evidence Regulation 1206/2001. This point is self-evident, and should not materially affect the relationship between the Evidence Regulation and the Recast Regulation. In particular, the entry into force of the Recast Regulation does not change the decisions in *Lippens*[64] and *Prorail*[65]: the Court of Justice ruled that, when an application is made before the court having jurisdiction as to the substance (which is not the case when Article 35 applies), such court is not required to use the procedures of the Evidence Regulation to collect evidence in another Member State, including when it issues an injunction for the hearing of a witness or the carrying out of an expert investigation on the territory of that Member State.

3.1.2. The territorial restriction

The second condition for the issue of a provisional order under Article 35 of the Regulation is that there must be a territorial connection between the subject-matter of the measures sought and the forum granting them. This condition is not explicit in the text of Article 35. It has been introduced in *Van Uden* as a way to limit 'provisional forum shopping'. According to an often cited passage from *Van Uden*: *'the granting of provisional or protective measures on the basis of Article [35] is conditional on, inter alia, the existence of a real connecting link between the subject-matter of the measures sought and the territorial jurisdiction of the [Member] State before which those measures are sought'.*[66]

As noted above, this condition should not be confused with the requirement that an order for interim payment relates solely to assets located within the territory of the forum State. The latter requirement is part of the definition of the notion of provisional and protective measures for the purpose of ensuring that the effects of such an order are reversible. It is specific to orders for interim payment (or possibly to the category of orders for interim performance of the principal obligation).

The condition that is discussed here is more general, but also more flexible: it is not required that the order relates only to assets within the territory of the forum State, but that there is a 'real connecting link' between the subject-matter of the measures and the territory of the forum State. The Court of Justice has not explained what is meant by 'real connecting link'. Two main approaches have been advocated, reflecting different understanding of the word 'real'.[67] The first one is that there must be a connection between the 'thing' (*res*) which is the subject-matter of the order and the forum State. This interpretation could support the argument that the condition only concerns provisional measures which take effect *in rem*, such as the attachment of assets (for instance, a French *saisie conservatoire*). Orders which operate *in personam*, such as freezing orders or disclosure orders,

---

64 Case C-170/11 *Lippens v. Kortekaas* [2012].

65 Case C-332/11 *ProRail BV v. Xpedys NV* [2013].

66 *Van Uden*, para 40.

67 See H Boularbah, 'Les mesures provisoires en droit commercial international: developpements récents au regard des Conventions de Bruxelles et de Lugano', [1999] *Revue de droit commercial* (R.D.C.) 604, at p. 607; Dickinson, p. 547–548; Heinze, p. 609; Garcimartin, p. 76; R. Fentiman, *International Commercial Litigation* (Oxford:OUP 2010), para 1.85–1.86.

would not be affected by this restriction, or at least the condition would be satisfied as soon as the court has personal jurisdiction over the defendant.[68]

The second interpretation is that the connection of provisional measures with the forum State must be real, i.e. 'effective'.[69] This interpretation implies that the condition has a broader application: it would concern both the orders which take effect *in rem* and the orders which take effect *in personam*. It is suggested that this is the better view, and that the requirement has a wide scope of application which concerns all kinds of provisional measures, irrespective of their specific features under domestic law. The requirement is that the measure itself, whatever its nature, must have a meaningful connection with the forum State to warrant the intervention of the court of that State, as a way to limit provisional forum shopping.[70]

The condition of the 'real connecting link' is clearly satisfied when the measure concerns only assets, persons and/or activities (to be) located entirely within the territory of the forum State, and the order can be enforced entirely locally. By contrast, the condition is clearly *not* satisfied when the measure concerns solely assets, persons or activities located entirely abroad, and the order can only be executed wholly outside the territory of the forum State. For instance, the French Court of Cassation held that the French courts cannot issue an order for the conduct of an expert investigation that is to be carried out entirely in England.[71]

When the measure presents, by its subject-matter (e.g. assets, persons activities or otherwise) a meaningful connection both with the territory of the forum State and with other territories, the court must assess whether the measure has, as a whole, sufficient points of contact with the forum State to establish that the real connecting link requirement is satisfied. There is some form of discretion here. If the court considers that there is a real connecting link, jurisdiction can be confirmed on the basis of Article 35, and under *Van Uden*, the scope of such order is not limited to the territory of the forum State.[72] Provided that the connection

---

68 This approach seems to have been adopted by the English Court of Appeal (Lord Collins) in *Masri v. Consolidated Contractors International (UK) Ltd (N°2)* [2008] EWCA Civ 309; [2009] 2 QB 450, para 106. The Court held that there was in that case a sufficient connecting link between the subject-matter of the measures and the territorial jurisdiction of the United Kingdom 'because of the *in personam* nature of the relief and the court's personal jurisdiction over [the defendant]'.

69 In most languages, the first word in the expression 'real connecting link' is the literal translation of 'real' (in French '*réel*', in German '*reale*', in Dutch '*reële*'), but in the Italian language the word used is '*effettivo*', which denotes the condition of effectiveness of the connection, and not necessarily the requirement of a connection with a 'thing'.

70 This approach seems to have been upheld in *Banco Nacional de Commercio Exterior SNC v. Empresa de Telecommunicaciones de Cuba SA* [2007] Lloyd's Rep 202, where the English Court of Appeal refused to make a worldwide freezing order on the basis that there was no real connecting link between the subject-matter of the measure, directed at assets located abroad, and the English territory.

71 Cass. 11 December 2001, *Virgin Atlantic Airways v. G.I.E. Airbus Industries*, [2002] *Rev. crit DIP* 371, note H. Muir Watt.

72 Unless the order is for an interim payment, which triggers the application of the specific requirement that the order can only concern assets (to be) located within the territory of the forum State: see above.

between the subject-matter of the measure[73] and the court is not insignificant or artificial, the *Van Uden* test is met, and the order may concern assets, persons or activities both within the forum State and in other States.

The question which arises is whether this case law is still valid under the Recast Regulation. As will be further discussed below, Article 2(a) of the Recast Regulation provides that provisional measures that are granted by a court not having jurisdiction over the substance of the case do not benefit from the uniform rules on recognition and enforcement of judgments. The restriction relates, at least apparently, only to the question of recognition and enforcement of the measures, and not to the question of jurisdiction of the court to grant a provisional measure under Article 35. However, Recital 33 of the Regulation casts doubts on the matter. This Recital provides that when the provisional measures are ordered by a court of a Member State not having jurisdiction as to the substance of the matter, *'the effect'* of such measures *'should be confined, under this Regulation, to the territory of that Member State'*. The territorial restriction is formulated in terms of a limitation to the effect of the measures. If this restriction were to be treated as being addressed also to the granting court, it would preclude such court from issuing provisional measures that produce cross-border effects.[74] The restriction would be far more significant than the *Van Uden* requirement of a real connecting link, which does not (as discussed) prohibit the issue of cross-border provisional measures when there is a meaningful connection with the forum State.

At this stage, it is still unclear how Recital 33 should be understood. When referring to the 'effect' of the provisional measure beyond the territory of the forum State, it is possible that Recital 33 means only the issue of the recognition and enforcement of such measures. A cross-border provisional measure may be of interest to the applicant without the need to go through the process of recognition and enforcement of the measure in other Member States. The compliance with the provisional measure may be voluntary, or may be obtained through indirect means of persuasion or even coercion, such as the application of sanctions which can be executed in the forum State. In common law jurisdictions, the sanction for non-compliance with a provisional order can take the form of a finding of contempt of court[75] and in civil law jurisdictions it can lead to the imposition of monetary penalties (*astreintes*). In both cases such sanctions can potentially be executed within the territory of the forum State, or at least can prevent the defendant from

---

73 It is not enough to show that the parties, the dispute or the case as a whole has or have a real connecting link with the *forum* State. *Van Uden* requires that a connection be established between the subject-matter of the measure itself and the *forum* State. This aspect of *Van Uden* is sometimes overlooked in case law. For instance, the condition is not acknowledged in *Masri No 2*.

74 See Hartley, p. 380, para 22.16, who considers that Recital 33 means that *'a UK court with no jurisdiction over the substance cannot grant an extraterritorial asset-freezing order where the defendant is domiciled in another Member State'*.

75 This is the case at least for non-compliance with an injunction directed at a person mandating or prohibiting specific acts.

being present, holding assets or carrying out any activities within the State, which may be a powerful deterrent ensuring compliance with the order.[76]

3.2. RESTRICTION ON THE RECOGNITION AND ENFORCEMENT OF THE PROVISIONAL MEASURES

When the court granting provisional measures does not have jurisdiction over the substance of the case, these measures do not benefit from the uniform rules on the recognition and enforcement of judgments in the Member States.

This restriction is spelt out in Article 2(a) of the Recast Regulation, which provides that, for the purposes of the application of the rules of recognition and enforcement of Chapter III, the term 'judgment' includes the provisional and protective measures ordered by a court *'which by virtue of this Regulation has jurisdiction as to the substance of the matter'*. As is made clear by Recital 33, provisional measures ordered by a court having jurisdiction as to the substance benefit from the 'free circulation' under the Regulation, while by contrast, with respect to measures which are ordered by the court not having jurisdiction as to the substance of the matter, *'the effect of such measures should be confined ... to the territory of that Member State'*.

The principle of non-circulation of provisional measures that are ordered by courts other than those having jurisdiction as to the substance involves a reversal of the case law and practice developed under the Brussels Convention and the 2001 Regulation. In *Denilauler*, the Court of Justice had accepted that provisional measures can be recognized and enforced irrespective of the basis of the jurisdiction of the court of origin.[77] It has sometimes been suggested that this position was reversed in *Mietz*[78], in which the court held that the enforcement of provisional measures is subject to the review by the requested court as to whether (i) the court of origin had jurisdiction as to the substance of the matter or (ii) when this is not the case, that the conditions laid down in *Van Uden* for the issuing of provisional measures are complied with. This uncertainty has been fueled by the Pocar Report on the 2007 Lugano Convention, where it is noted that *'it seems*

---

76 It remains to be seen whether the new system of direct execution (without *exequatur*) under the Recast Regulation can be used in relation to a decision which determines the amount of the payment due by way of penalty (*astreinte*) pursuant to Article 55 of the Regulation when the penalty has been applied for the non-compliance with a cross-border provisional order.

77 Case 125/79*Bernard Denilauler v SNC Couchet Frères*[1980] ECR I-1553. The Court ruled in that case that *'Article [35] does not preclude provisional measures ordered in the State of origin ... from being the subject of recognition and an authorization for enforcement on the conditions laid down'* by the Brussels regime. Therefore, the Court expressly envisages the application of the European rules concerning recognition and enforcement to a decision issued by a court having jurisdiction based on Art 24 (now Art 35), namely a court which does not have jurisdiction as to the substance of the matter.

78 Case C-99/96*Hans-Hermann Mietz v Intership Yachting Sneek BV*[1999] ECR I-2277.

natural that the decisions taken on the basis of the jurisdiction provided for by Art[35] should not, in principle, give rise to recognition and enforcement abroad'.[79]

In fact, however, and contrary to the suggestion in the Pocar Report, in accepting that provisional measures can be enforced when they comply with the *Van Uden* conditions, *Mietz* confirmed in substance that there is no absolute bar against the enforcement of provisional measures that are ordered by a court not having jurisdiction as to the substance of the matter.[80] A further confirmation of this proposition was given in *Italian Leather*, which holds that '*it is unimportant whether the judgments at issue have been delivered in proceedings in interim measures or in proceedings on the substance*', as the notion of '*judgments*' which benefit from the European regime of recognition and enforcement '*has general application*'.[81]

Thus, the Recast Regulation represents, in relation to provisional measures, another step backward in respect of the free circulation of judgments. Article 2(a) has the effect of abolishing the practice consisting of seeking provisional measures in those Member States whose law provides for efficient procedures (such as England or the Netherlands) with the view of seeking to have these measures recognised or enforced in other Member States. This seems to be precisely the practice that the Commission was aiming to end: in the Explanatory Memorandum accompanying its Proposal, the Commission noted that '*given the wide divergence of national law on this issue, the effect of these measures should be limited to the territory of the Member State where they were granted, thereby preventing the risk of abusive forum shopping*'.[82] The intention was therefore to curb the so-called '*provisional forum shopping*' or '*presidential forum shopping*' (as in many Member States, provisional measures are ordered by the President of the court).

Paradoxically, however, the restriction could also have the effect of reinforcing the significance of the diversity of the laws of the Member States in the matter of provisional measures.[83] As courts other than the court hearing the substance of the matter are now precluded from offering their assistance through cross-border measures, the efficient judicial protection of the interests of the parties in the course of the proceedings (and possibly also thereafter) will depend to a greater extent on the initial choice of the claimant between the available courts having jurisdiction. The impact of forum shopping in respect of the substantive claim – *bona fide* or *mala fide* – is still reinforced, as it becomes paramount to bring a substantive claim in a forum that allows for efficient cross-border provisional relief, either pre-judgment or post-judgment.

---

79 [23.12.2009] OJ C319/1, p. 127.

80 As the *Van Uden* conditions apply only to judgments issued by a court not having jurisdiction as to the substance of the matter, and the requirement under *Van Uden* that there is be 'real connecting link' between the court and the object of the measures is not inconsistent with the possibility of enforcement in another Member State. This point is developed very convincingly by Dickinson, p. 531 and 558

81 Case C-80/00*Italian LeatherSpA v WECO Poltermöbel GmbH & Co* [2002] ECR I-4995, para 41.

82 Commission Proposal, p. 9, para. 3.1.

83 This point is made very convincingly by Dickinson, p. 543.

BRUSSELS FALLING: THE RELATIONSHIP BETWEEN THE UK AND EU POST BREXIT[1]

Helena RAULUS
Head of UK Law Societies Brussels Office

1. INTRODUCTION

Currently we are at the post-referendum stage: the UK is still a member of the EU and Brexit, the UK exit from the EU, is being negotiated. At the moment the negotiations are centred on finalising the withdrawal agreement[2] which includes provisions on the rights of the EU citizens to continue to live and reside in the UK as well as the rights of UK citizens in the EU, on the border between Northern Ireland and Ireland, and on budgetary issues. The draft agreement also contains provisions on the transition period, otherwise called the implementation period. The exit date is set for 30 March 2019 – that being the first date when the UK is no longer a member state of the EU.

After 30 March 2019, while the UK will no longer be an EU member state, its status in many respects will be equated with one. The part of the agreement on transition aims to achieve a so-called status quo transition. This means that all EU acquis continues to apply[3], unless otherwise specifically mentioned, after the exit date. The major change will be that the UK will no longer participate in the EU institutional framework: in the EU decision making and judicial bodies, and there will no longer be European Parliament elections in the UK where EU citizens could participate.

However, the new relationship is still to be drafted and negotiated at this point.

---

1 All views expressed in this article are personal and not attributable to the Law Society of England and Wales, the Law Society of Scotland or the Law Society of Northern Ireland or the Joint UK Law Societies Brussels Office.

2 Draft Agreement on the Withdrawal of the United Kingdom of Great Britain and Northern Ireland from the European Union and the European Atomic Energy Community, published on 19.03.2018, https://ec.europa.eu/commission/sites/beta-political/files/draft_agreement_coloured.pdf.

3 Article 121 of the draft Withdrawal Agreement.

On civil justice the UK has stated its desire to continue with civil justice cooperation.[4] This is supported wholly by the legal profession.[5] According to the Government's and the legal profession's assessment, at the very least the UK needs access to the Lugano Convention. However, most on the UK side would prefer to continue with a wider range of EU civil justice cooperation. On the EU side, the response came in March 2017, where the European Council negotiation guidelines do not mention civil justice.[6] They only refer to cooperation in family law. This presumably means that civil justice cooperation in civil and commercial law is to be decided together with other trade issues, with the main question being how ambitious an agreement will be available to the UK in future.

This paper explores ways to find solutions to fitting in civil justice cooperation after Brexit. It argues that Brussels need not fall with Brexit when it comes to UK – EU cooperation. Yet, at the same time this paper recognises that in order to include civil justice cooperation in the framework of the new EU – UK agreement, the new agreement will need to include mechanisms which can guarantee continued convergence. This includes both political and legal mechanisms, and will need to include mechanisms to address the continuation of cooperation where divergences do arise. For that purpose, this paper argues that with Brexit the UK will be moving away from supranational structures, there will be need for different analysis points – points which should not aim for full convergence but rather for the prevention of material divergences.

2. CIVIL JUSTICE COOPERATION IN WITHDRAWAL AND TRANSITION

As mentioned in the introduction, according to the plans laid out in the draft withdrawal agreement, after the initial withdrawal in March 2019 and during the transition period, all EU law continues to apply in the UK. This includes also all the civil justice cooperation instruments, provided that the UK has already opted into them.[7] The complication in this area is the existing UK opt-out, with an opt-in possibility[8], which has allowed the UK to choose whether to participate

---

4 HM Government, Providing a cross-border civil judicial framework, A Future Partnership Paper, 22.08.2017, https://www.gov.uk/government/publications/providing-a-cross-border-civil-judicial-cooperation-framework-a-future-partnership-paper.

5 For the Law Society of England and Wales, see www.lawsociety.org.uk/support-services/brexit-and-the-legal-sector/, the Law Society of Scotland, https://www.lawscot.org.uk/research-and-policy/international-work/brexit/, the UK Law Societies' Brussels Office, www.lawsocieties.eu/brexit/, or the Bar Council of England and Wales, Brexit Papers, https://www.barcouncil.org.uk/media/575175/brexit_paper_4_-_civil_jurisidiction_and_judgements.pdf.

6 European Council guidelines

7 Articles 62 and 63 of the draft Withdrawal Agreement.

8 Protocols 19 and 21 to the Treaty on European Union and Treaty on the Functioning of the European Union.

in EU civil justice instruments. Generally, the UK policy has been to opt-in[9] in the area of civil justice. However, some notable exceptions remain, in particular with respect to the EU rights' framework.[10] The key question for the transition period though, is whether the opt-in, opt-out procedure survives and the UK is able to choose to participate in individual instruments even when it is no longer an EU member state. The answer from the draft withdrawal treaty seems to be no. Articles 62 and 63 of the draft Agreement lists out the instruments that will continue to apply and therefore the status quo is retained only with respect to those areas in which the UK is participating.

The draft agreement also makes it clear that participation in civil justice measures will not continue beyond the end of the transitional period. The draft agreement already lays down provisions on how the running cases will be treated. Article 62 specifically refers to the Rome I and II on choice of law and provides that if the parties had concluded a choice of court agreement, or where the damage arises, before the end of the transition period, Rome I and II continue to apply. This Article is currently in green, which indicates that the parties have reached agreement on it.

Article 63 refers to the various EU instruments setting out recognition and enforcement processes, where the UK is currently participating. The basic proposition is that if the proceedings are instituted during the transition period, the current rules are to be applied as both to the jurisdiction and recognition and enforcement.[11] However, Article 63(3) makes also a special provision for the cases where the parties have agreed on a choice of court clause, which falls under Article 25 of the Brussels I recast or is relating to maintenance and thus in scope of Regulation 4/2009. In March this clause stated that before the end of the transition period, the UK and EU27 courts 'shall apply [the provisions of the agreement] in respect of the assessment of the legal force of the agreements' made by the parties. This provision, though fairly cryptically phrased, seemed to suggest therefore that the choice of court agreements were to be respected even if the dispute arose after the end of the transition period, but where the choice of court agreement is concluded during the transition period. However, Article 63 was then still in white, which means that this was a proposal text and the parties had not agreed to it. According to the latest information, the recognition and enforcement of choice of court agreements will not be as wide-ranging, but that they will be enforced only under the end of the transition period. The final text is not yet released at the date of the writing of the article.

The status quo means that the UK can continue to participate in all agreements that the EU has agreed with third countries.[12] On this basis it is possible to say

9 Even after the EU referendum, the UK has opted into Regulations on taking evidence and service of documents, https://www.parliament.uk/business/publications/written-questions-answers-statements/written-statement/Commons/2017-07-19/HCWS83/

10 To be addressed further below.

11 Article 63 (1) and 63 (3).

12 Article 124 of the draft Withdrawal Agreement.

that withdrawal agreement aims to ensure that the UK will also continue to participate in the Lugano Convention throughout the transition period.

The provisions on the transition period also make it clear that the access to international conventions is granted only because the UK will be participating in EU policies during the transition and that the UK is to be likened to EU member states during the transition.[13] Throughout the draft agreement the UK is equated with the EU member states and it is not called a third country. This means that, as the UK continues to participate in the conventions only as it is to be likened to the EU member states, the UK participation in the international conventions does not continue beyond the end of the transition period, unless (1) the UK chooses to continue to participate in the customs union and single market, and thus is likened to the EU member states, under the new arrangements, or (2) where there is a new agreement between the UK and the third country / countries (and where necessary the EU) that the UK can continue to be party to those conventions. Therefore, in the case of the Lugano Convention, the UK's participation in it will also end, unless there is an agreement between the EU, EFTA and the UK on accession of the UK as a separate entity to the agreement. As the UK would no longer be member of the EU or EFTA, it would also need to get an invitation from one of the contracting parties to join into the Convention. Furthermore, the UK's participation will need to be ratified by the EU as a block and EFTA states.

The withdrawal agreement does not provide provisions going beyond transition on civil justice. Therefore, without a separate agreement on the future relationship, the operation of all EU civil justice measures, including the Lugano Convention, will end, as advertised by the Commission Brexit steering group and DG Justice notice on civil justice cooperation.[14]

3. THE NEED FOR CONTINUED COOPERATION IN RECOGNITION AND ENFORCEMENT OF JUDGMENTS

The UK's legal profession, the Law Societies[15] as well as for example the Bar Council of England and Wales[16] started campaigning on maintaining access to the EU civil justice cooperation in the aftermath of the 2016 referendum result. In particular, the analysis and information from practitioners showed that continued recognition and enforcement of judgments in civil and commercial judgments

13 Article 124 and footnote on p. 177 of the draft Withdrawal Agreement.

14 See for example on civil justice, Commission, notice to stakeholders: withdrawal of the United Kingdom and EU rules in the field of civil justice and private international law, 21.11.2017, available from: https://ec.europa.eu/info/brexit/brexit-preparedness_en.

15 The UK Law Societies report, key legal issues on upcoming negotiations, available from: www.lawsocieties.eu/news/key-legal-issues-for-the-upcoming-eu-uk-negotiations/5061183.article.

16 Bar Council Brexit paper on civil justice, *op cit.* n. 4.

would be of paramount importance for small and medium sized companies, consumers, individuals and for lawyers who are advising them.

It became clear also that there are no corresponding international frameworks which could be readily available. The European system for the recognition and enforcement of judgments has been developed in the context of the Brussels Convention and its transformation into Brussels I Regulation. The Lugano Convention extends the Brussels I framework for the EFTA countries that have close trading links with the EU countries. Besides from these two, there are no other multilateral frameworks on civil and commercial law, which would have an equally wide field of application. The earlier Hague Conference Conventions, such as the 1971 Convention on recognition and enforcement of judgments has only been ratified by Cyprus, the Netherlands, Portugal and Albania.[17] The 2005 Hague Choice of Court Agreements Convention[18] provides a more modern framework and it has already been ratified by the EU, Mexico and Singapore. However, its scope is more limited: it applies only where parties have agreed an exclusive choice of court agreement. This is in no form comparable to the coverage provided by the Brussels I Regulation or Lugano Convention.

Arguably the bilateral conventions[19] that were in force before the Brussels Convention was adopted are not available either. They were retired in 1978 when the UK entered into the Brussels Convention and their resurrection would need an agreement between the parties. However, as the EU has gained exclusive external competence in the area covered by the Brussels I Regulation since that time[20], EU member states can no longer enter into new bilateral conventions with third countries.

The result is that without Brussels I or Lugano, the parties will need to rely in most cases on national law to have their claims enforced. This creates problems in particular in those countries, where there is no method of recognising or enforcing judgments without an international agreement, such as Nordic countries (Finland, Sweden) or Spain. Furthermore, even if the national law would provide for recognition and enforcement of judgments from foreign courts, the procedure in these cases is quite complex and requires time and monetary resources from the parties.

According to the information we have available at the moment, this would also be a problem between the UK and Ireland. The Brussels Convention and the subsequent Regulation have provided a stable solution for recognition and

---

17 Https://www.hcch.net/en/instruments/conventions/status-table/?cid=78.

18 Https://www.hcch.net/en/instruments/conventions/specialised-sections/choice-of-court.

19 Article 24 of the Council Convention on the accession of the United Kingdom of Great Britain and Northern Ireland to the Convention on jurisdiction and the enforcement of judgments in civil and commercial matters and to the Protocol on its interpretation by the Court of Justice, OJ 78/884/EEC.

20 Opinion 1/03 on the competence of the Community to conclude the new Lugano Convention on jurisdiction and recognition and enforcement of judgments in civil and commercial matters, [2006] ECR I-01145.

enforcement of judgments between the UK and the Republic of Ireland. Therefore, this is an issue that has an impact on the border between Northern Ireland and the Republic of Ireland, if the businesses, consumers or individuals cannot easily recognise and enforce the judgments cross-border. Furthermore, as indicated above, the EU has now exclusive competence in the area and therefore it is not possible for the UK and Ireland to solve this question bilaterally.

4. CONTINUED RECOGNITION AND ENFORCEMENT: ALTERNATIVES

While it is clear that continued recognition and enforcement of judgments is needed, what is unclear is how to achieve this. As set out above, the primary choice lies between the UK participation in the EU Brussels I (and the Lugano Convention), and it continuing only within the Lugano Convention. Currently, the UK is naturally participating in both, however, neither is simply available to the UK to continue in, but access to both these needs to be negotiated.

The UK's continued participation in the Brussels I Regulation and other EU civil justice instruments depends on a variety of factors, which stem from the negotiations themselves. The Brussels I Regulation as part of the EU acquis is part of a wider package of the EU's civil justice framework, which includes various other directives and regulations, e.g. the Insolvency, Service of Documents, Taking of Evidence Regulations. Therefore, if the UK were to continue to participate in the Brussels I Regulation, there is at least an expectation that it has access to the other EU instruments on civil justice. Furthermore, the EU acquis has a separate legal arm through the Court of Justice's right to interpret it. The question then becomes what kind of links will be required for the UK to access the EU civil justice acquis.

Yet, it must be noted that the situation is in many ways unprecedented. The current commercial links involving in particular consumers and small and medium sized traders, and the UK's prior strong record of participation in civil justice cooperation, mean that there should be a special consideration for the UK here. Yet, there is no prior example of a non-EU member state participating in the EU civil justice cooperation instruments. Even though the EEA-EFTA states are participating fully in the internal market, civil justice cooperation is not part of the EEA agreement and recognition and enforcement of judgments is dealt with under the Lugano Convention. There are special arrangements with respect to Denmark under the TFEU and TEU under which Denmark can participate in the EU instruments in international level; however, Denmark is not an appropriate model for the UK as it is an EU member state and it fully participates otherwise in the EU institutional structures.

In contrast, access to the Lugano Convention applies on an international level, as the Lugano Convention is a stand-alone instrument, and it has its own protocol on interpretation.

5. CIVIL JUSTICE COOPERATION AND REGULATORY CONVERGENCE: POLITICAL AND LEGAL MECHANISMS

The UK's access to the wider framework of EU civil justice measures will depend on how far it will be possible to form mechanisms to ensure regulatory convergence between the UK and the EU. In civil justice cooperation convergence is important in particular in two ways: (1) where there is harmonisation for instance with respect to the standards – minimum or maximum – achieved commonly, there must be ways to ensure that all parties respect those standards; or (2) where there is continued cooperation on basis of mutual recognition of national decisions, convergence is important as it provides the underpinning for mutual trust, which enables mutual recognition. In other words, with respect to mutual recognition, if the regimes are similar enough, then cooperation can run smoothly as the participating entities can continue to recognise and enforce the decisions as if they were their own decisions. If the regimes are not similar enough, there can be no cooperation as the systems cannot recognise each other's aims or methods.

The crucial issue that then arises is that the UK – EU agreement would need to be deep enough to include regulatory cooperation and various institutional ways to ensure convergence. Mirroring the current arrangements under the EU Treaties or the European Economic Area (EEA) Agreement, the new EU- UK agreement would need to set out both political and legal mechanisms to ensure that there is convergence and address the consequences where there are going to be divergences.

This raises another interesting question, namely whether the new UK relationship with the EU will be situated in the EU, in a supranational framework, in an EEA (type) quasi-supranational framework, or simply in an international framework of cooperation. With regard to civil justice cooperation, the answer to this question will lead either to the UK's assimilation to the EU acquis or to its simple adoption of the Lugano Convention. There is no straight-forward answer to this. On one level, the underlying purpose of Brexit is to take the UK away from the supranational structures of the EU. This would mean that the UK will be situated in the international side of cooperation and therefore the solution would seem to point to the Lugano Convention. However, on another level, the UK Government wants to see a more ambitious solution being reached which would recognise the UK's close existing convergence with the EU. This would point to its assimilation with the EU's civil justice acquis, because the UK has been participating in the EU civil justice cooperation since the time of the Brussels Convention – in particular since the Europeanisation of the civil justice area in the Treaties of Amsterdam, Nice and Lisbon – it should be able to continue in this field. Yet, this option does require that new political and legal links are formed to ensure the necessary mechanisms of convergence.

6. UK ACCESS TO EU COOPERATION: POLITICAL MECHANISMS

The EU, like the UK, will need to be able to review and renew the legislative framework on civil justice. The EU civil justice framework is dynamic and flexible: it is being developed to correspond with the needs of EU cooperation, where, for example, developments take place or e.g. where new ways of enhancing cooperation seem possible, such as insolvency.[21]

In the EU framework, it has been possible to develop a whole framework, or ecosystem, on civil justice cooperation which operates alongside the Brussels I Regulation. The most important examples to date include the Motor Insurance Directive[22] which, in combination with the Brussels I Regulation, provides for possibility for the motor accident victims to litigate against insurers in their own home courts. Other examples are the Insolvency[23], Service of Documents or Taking of Evidence Regulations which operate similarly to the motor insurance framework in conjunction with the Brussels Regulation providing for further clarity in insolvency cases or facilitating the court proceedings prior to the judgments.

As the UK is withdrawing from EU cooperation, in the future there may be parallel initiatives in the UK to deal with similar issues. Ensuring that the EU and the UK initiatives will not diverge too much, and that they move in a similar direction, will require cooperation and dialogue at the political level.

In the EU sphere the political tools that achieve this type of political cooperation and dialogue are relatively straight forward. This is when the EU legislative processes, such as laid out in Article 294 TFEU operate.

Outside the EU, the EEA and the Swiss arrangements on granting access to the single market are the only examples where currently political cooperation exists in this dynamic environment. In both cases there are mechanisms created for a political dialogue through Joint Committees. These Committees are composed of EEA and EU, or Swiss and EU respectively, representatives and this creates the platform to discuss the upcoming initiatives from both parties. Furthermore, in the EEA framework, the EEA-EFTA States are heard when the Commission drafts its initiatives. If the UK were to have access to the EU acquis, some similar institutional arrangement on creating a political link between the UK and EU would need to be created.[24]

There is a further issue that complicates the UK's participation in future EU civil justice cooperation. Previously the UK enjoyed a fairly flexible opt-in / opt-out

---

21 Commission proposal for a directive of the European Parliament and of the Council on preventive restructuring frameworks, second chance and measures to increase the efficiency of restructuring, insolvency and discharge procedures. COM 2016/0724.

22 Motor Insurance Directive 2009/103.

23 Insolvency Regulation 2015/848.

24 There is already a Joint Committee envisaged in the draft withdrawal agreement. The Joint Committee is to discuss the implementation and convergence issues relating to the withdrawal agreement, see Article 31.

regime in civil justice cooperation. As explained above, this mechanism provides that the UK is able to pick and choose which areas of civil justice cooperation it is going to be participating in. One price to be paid for Brexit is likely to be that if the UK is able to continue to participate in the EU civil justice cooperation, it will lose the opt-in opt-out mechanism. This would mean that the UK would either participate in all future EU civil justice mechanisms, or in none. The question would then remain as to what happens with respect to those instruments that the UK did not participate in when it was still a member.[25]

Another crucial problem to be addressed is what to do if there is no consensus between the parties on the upcoming legislation or method of implementation, i.e. where the UK legislative action would diverge from the EU one. This would be the case for example, where the UK does not agree on a piece of upcoming EU legislation and the UK wishes to adopt a different solution. As the UK is no longer an EU state, it would not have power of veto or right to vote on the new EU legislation. The EEA and the Swiss cooperation again provide an example on this – they provide for a possibility to suspend the cooperation where the parties do not agree on common rules. Therefore, it would be likely that the new EU – UK agreement would stipulate a political process, under which the parties decide to suspend cooperation in the specific area as the divergences are too wide (i.e. material divergence, see further below).

In addition, it is possible to prescribe for a dispute settlement mechanism which may have a role as to the interpretation of the question of material divergence. However, it must be noted that there are two considerations here. First, deciding where divergence is too great may often be a political decision rather than a judicial one, unless the new agreement is very clear on the criteria used to determine (material) convergence or divergence. As previous case law from the Court of Justice shows on political issues, such as subsidiarity[26] or EU competences[27], the Court is reluctant to second guess the political decisions taken on the validity of the cooperation. Therefore, the Court of Justice may not be the right forum, but rather this is where there could be a role for an arbitration process between the EU and the UK.

The option of suspending cooperation through a political or (quasi) judicial process may be a dangerous situation for the UK's continued access to the EU civil justice cooperation. This is because, as outlined above, the scope of the Brussels I Regulation is very wide and it underpins the operation of many EU civil justice instruments. Like the present situation faced by Switzerland in relation to the free movement of persons and the continued access to the internal market, it would be

25 The draft Withdrawal Treaty seems to point to the conclusion that the UK is not participating in these instruments, see above.

26 For example, Case C-84/94 UK v Council (Working Time Directive) [1996] ECR I-015755.

27 There are only two successful challenges to the EU competences, Opinion 2/94 on the EC's accession to the ECHR [1994] ECR I-1764, and Case C-376/98 Germany v. European Parliament and Council (tobacco advertising) [2000] ECR I-08419.

inconceivable for the regulation to be applied in a piecemeal fashion. Therefore, in this type of framework the UK would need to mirror any and all proposals which are tied to the Brussels I Regulation, in order to continue to benefit from the recognition and enforcement of judgments regime.

7. UK ACCESS TO EU CIVIL JUSTICE COOPERATION: LEGAL MECHANISMS TO ENSURE CONVERGENCE

Convergence is also achieved by unitary interpretation or a commonly agreed mechanism of interpretation of the adopted instruments. In other words, legal mechanisms can ensure convergence. In the EU context this is provided by the interpretative authority of the Court of Justice.

If the UK were to participate in the EU civil justice area, it would be crucial to decide what kind of links are created between the UK legal systems and the CJEU. The legal mechanism consists of a common framework for interpretation for the courts that are linked together in the agreement.

First, in order to link the legal orders together, there are two models or options. In the EU cooperation model, the CJEU is given the right of interpretation and the final say on the operation of the EU Treaties and secondary law. One solution would be to continue to grant the CJEU jurisdiction in the UK after the withdrawal. However, this would cross one of the red lines currently set out by the UK government in negotiations. Furthermore, this solution can be questioned as the UK will no longer have representation in the Court. Should the Court in such a situation continue to have a role in the UK?[28] This is hardly in accordance with the rule of law. Therefore, while the role of the CJEU remains undisputed on the EU side, on the UK side the direct jurisdiction of the Court is a more complicated matter.

Does this mean that there can be no mechanism, as the CJEU has no direct role? While the answer to this is to be decided by the negotiators, it is possible to point out that alternative approaches may be also adopted. An approach suggested by the UK government would be a joint arbitration mechanism. The examples where this is used are the Comprehensive Economic Trade Agreement (CETA) with Canada or the Ukrainian Association Agreement.

However, it has already been ruled by the CJEU when the EEA was agreed that another court than itself cannot interpret those areas of agreements, where the terms are sufficiently similar to the EU cooperation.[29] Therefore, if the cooperation is to extend to the UK's participation in the EU civil justice cooperation, the CJEU

---

28 The Law Society of England and Wales, UK needs a new dispute settlement mechanism to replace the Court of Justice post-Brexit, www.lawsociety.org.uk/news/press-releases/uk-needs-new-dispute-mechanism-post-brexit-to-replace-court-of-justice/.

29 Opinion 1/91 on the EEA Court [1991] ECR I-6099.

is unlikely to surrender its jurisdiction to a separate body. Furthermore, as the Ukrainian Association Agreement provides that the CJEU is a final arbiter if there is a disagreement between the arbiters, this also would breach one of the red lines of the UK government.

This leaves us with one alternative model for a more extensive level of cooperation. This is again provided by the EEA agreement which provides for a separate EFTA Court and EFTA Surveillance Authority for EEA EFTA parties. The EFTA Court has a similar jurisdiction to the CJEU under the EEA agreement, and the EFTA Surveillance Authority takes on the role of the EU Commission.

On the basis of this model it is possible to consider two alternatives: creating a mechanism for the UK to dock into the EFTA Court for the time being[30] or creating a UK pillar on the enforcement of the agreement. Docking to the EFTA Court would be a rather simple solution. The EFTA Court already exists and even if the judges do not currently have experience over civil justice cooperation, the UK judges who would be appointed to the Court would have. However, this does precipitate UK participation in EFTA and, while this has been under discussion in the UK Parliament, there is not sufficient political support for it at the moment.

This leaves us with the creation of a UK enforcement pillar. It would be possible for the UK Supreme Court to be given a role in the new EU – UK agreement to interpret the agreement. It would even be possible to develop an independent UK body[31], which would have the right to take cases against the UK in the Supreme Court. Finally, it would be possible to give an indirect role to the CJEU, whereby the Supreme Court (and the UK courts in general), would be required to take due account of the CJEU judgments where the agreement provides for similar terms as the EU legal framework.

This type of mechanism would create or forge the necessary link between the EU and the UK legal orders. It should be noted in this context that the UK legal order is particularly receptive to this type of solution. All UK jurisdictions (England and Wales, Scotland and Northern Ireland) prescribe to the notion of precedent. The CJEU judgments are already embedded in the UK case law and the UK courts are used to referring to cases from the CJEU.[32] According to this notion, the case law is developed on the basis of previous judgments and diversions from the case law are only allowed where there are good reasons for it. This means that essentially the case for divergence would arise where there is a parliamentary decision to create legislation to the contrary. In this case though, the problem

30 Advocated by e.g. Judge Baudenbacher, former President of the EFTA Court. See for example the Institute for the Government, Lewis Lloyd, Could the UK sign up to the EFTA Court after Brexit?, available from: https://www.instituteforgovernment.org.uk/blog/could-uk-sign-efta-court-after-brexit-baudenbacher.

31 Withdrawal agreement already perceives this, see Article 152.

32 Even the UK Withdrawal Bill requires the UK courts take account of the CJEU case law, see for example the Institute for the Government, EU Withdrawal Bill: Amendments and debates, available from: https://www.instituteforgovernment.org.uk/explainers/eu-withdrawal-bill-amendments-and-debates.

would be on the side of political convergence rather than legal convergence as the courts are required to follow the legislation set by the Parliament and they would not be able to overturn it.[33] Consequently, if grave or material divergences would arise, the way to solve them would be through the political process outlined above, rather than legal processes.

8. LUGANO CONVENTION AND CONVERGENCE

Compared to the continuing application of the EU acquis, participation in the Lugano Convention would require simply the ensuring of legal convergence. The Convention exists in international law and every change will need to be negotiated and accepted by the parties. The Convention has been revised only once since 1988. The Convention also stands alone, it is not surrounded or supported by other civil justice instruments (apart from individual internal market instruments, which are to be adopted and applied by the EEA States and in some cases Switzerland).

As to the legal convergence, the Lugano Convention provides for Protocol 2, which binds all the parties. According to this, the national courts are to take due account of each other's decisions. This aim is supported by a database of information on the decisions that the national courts are taking under the Lugano Convention. The CJEU has a separate role under the protocol whereby the national courts are to take into consideration the CJEU case law where the terms of the Convention are materially similar to the Brussels I Regulation.

For reasons outlined above, the UK courts and legal systems are particularly well-suited to this type of cooperation. Although common law adopts somewhat different approaches, the notion of precedent and the openness of the UK courts to the solutions adopted by foreign courts means that the UK courts are well placed to take due regard of the judgments from other courts.

However, if the interpretation were to diverge too much, under the Lugano Convention (it being in the international plane), there exists another legal mechanism to intervene. This is done through the use of public policy under Article 34 of the Lugano Convention. To be noted, its use in the Lugano context should be severely limited to those cases where it is simply unacceptable for the courts to recognise and enforce a particular judgment due to a material divergence in the application of the Convention. This should not be developed into a carte blanche to not recognise and enforce judgments in general between the UK, EU and EFTA parties, and can be used only in cases where the interpretation of the courts of one party with regard to a particular clause, or in the context of a particular case, is unacceptable.

Furthermore, if the public policy exception were to be used more frequently, this would mean that the parties would need to set up a discussion on how to bring

[33] This is even now the case because one of the key principles of UK constitutional system is Parliamentary supremacy.

further political alignment so that the Convention remains operable. Therefore, if this level of discrepancy were to arise, it is possible to bring this to the attention of the parties and form an expert group or political platform to solve this. What makes this easier is that the case law under the Lugano Convention is already gathered by the Court of Justice.

9. NOT JUST ANY DIVERGENCE BUT MATERIAL DIVERGENCE?

Perhaps the concept that will be developed due to Brexit is that of material divergence. As the UK withdraws from the EU structures, there may be a possibility to agree on a framework that is close but not assimilated with the legal orders. The EU model on dealing with divergences through supranational doctrines, such as direct effect and supremacy do not apply. Furthermore, the political assimilation to the fullest degree is no longer present.

This convergence could take two forms. First, it is possible to achieve full convergence. That is the parties agree fully on the scope of the revision, the content of the articles, or new instruments, and implement on their sides the new instruments or provisions fully and without any variance. This situation is analogous to how EU regulations are intended to apply. The second situation would be where there is a consensus on the aims, but no identical way of getting there. This situation is analogous to EU directives, in that the parties are left with the discretion on how to achieve these aims. Accordingly, in this situation the parties agree that even though the implementation measures, or legislative initiatives in the case of the EU – UK cooperation under the new agreement, are not identical, even though they fulfil the same aim, there is no material divergence. Thus, the cooperation can continue.

The crucial question here is the level of divergence that can trigger the consequences. As the consequences are severe – such as stopping cooperation in an area – the breach should consequently be serious, not just any breach.

What does a material divergence consist of in the area governed by the Brussels I Regulation or Lugano Convention? In the area of jurisdiction this could be an interpretation which leads to no court having jurisdiction. This is clearly against the aims of the Regulation and the Convention. However, as the Regulation and the Convention are generous in providing alternatives for the parties to bring proceedings in a majority of cases, it is unlikely that this type of problem would arise. The cases where special attention must be had would consist of those where there is a weaker party protection, such as an employment, insurance or consumer dispute. These cases are the most sensitive and could lead to triggering material divergence – or even public policy on recognition and enforcement of the judgments – if the weaker party protection is breached.

Similarly, if there were additional requirements for recognition and enforcement of judgments from the national legislature or from the courts, this could lead to a breach in terms of material divergence. This could also lead to the adoption of reciprocal measures, whereby the parties to the agreement would need to address whether to continue with the cooperation.

10. CONCLUSIONS: SEEKING SOLUTIONS

The Brussels I Convention and the subsequent Regulation has facilitated, to some extent, business moving from arbitration to the use of litigation as a means of dispute settlement. It has provided an alternative route, which is available to the parties to seek a solution. Furthermore, as the Brussels Regulation has facilitated the recognition and enforcement of judgments, it meant that the parties have a true choice – as to the costs and enforceability – in which format to seek the solution to the dispute.

However, as the UK is leaving the EU, the question arises as to whether the parties can still avail themselves of the same options. What has changed since the inception of the Brussels Convention is that through internal market links, UK and EU businesses have been able to take advantage of the openness of cross-border trade on a wholly different scale than before. Cross-border trade has been opened to SMEs and consumers at the same time as it has to larger businesses and multinationals. In particular the potential of e-commerce has been fulfilled.

Yet, in the same space of time, arbitration, which has retained its place in the functioning of big business, has not opened its doors to SMEs. On the contrary, the EU has created its own alternative dispute settlement mechanisms to help SMEs and consumers have access to justice. Additionally, compared to arbitration, litigation is relatively effortless, in particular where it is possible to take the claims to the court of your own domicile or place of business (which the generous jurisdiction provisions of Brussels I allow).

As these trading links exist, and are likely to continue in the future based on the sheer fact of physical proximity, which means that the trading links are more easily established, the recognition and enforcement of judgments in particular – if not the whole area of civil justice cooperation – should continue between the UK and the EU. The question as to how this can be achieved and how to address the potential divergences between the systems that are not similarly assimilated, are solvable, as shown by this chapter, though it must be admitted that this chapter simply provides an outline of some of these solutions.

EUROPEAN PRIVATE INTERNATIONAL LAW AND THE NATIONAL JUDGE. SOME GENERAL REFLECTIONS BY A BELGIAN JUDGE

Ilse COUWENBERG
Judge in the Belgian Court of Cassation, member of the European Judicial Network

1. INTRODUCTION

Fifty years ago the first European instrument in the field of judicial cooperation in civil and commercial matters saw the light of day: the 1968 Brussels Convention on jurisdiction and enforcement of judgments.[1] Its rules, as amended in 2002 by the Brussels I Regulation[2] and in 2015 by the Brussels *Ibis* Regulation[3], very soon became the core of European Private International Law (PIL). Of all the instruments in this field, the 'Brussels rules' are most often applied by the national courts, as evidenced by the numerous preliminary rulings of the Court of Justice of the European Union (CJEU).[4]

The purpose of the 1968 rules was 'to strengthen in the community the legal protection of the people therein established'.[5] The 1999 Tampere Council further explored this idea by introducing the concept of 'one European Area of Justice': an area where citizens can easily enter into cross-border relations and just as

1 The 1968 Brussels Convention on jurisdiction and the enforcement of judgments in civil and commercial matters, [1972] OJ L299/32.

2 Council Regulation (EC) No 44/2001 of 22 December 2000 on jurisdiction and the recognition and enforcement of judgments in civil and commercial matters, [2001] OJ L12/1 (hereafter Brussels I Regulation).

3 Regulation (EU) No 1215/2012 of the European Parliament and of the Council of 12 December 2012 on jurisdiction and the recognition and enforcement of judgments in civil and commercial matters, [2012] OJ L351/1 (hereafter Brussels *Ibis* Regulation).

4 In 2017, 16 of the 24 preliminary rulings on civil law related to the Brussels I rules. This may seem surprising as this Regulation, along with its predecessors, has been in force for 45 years. Statistics can be found via https://eur-lex.europa.eu/collection/eu-law/eu-case-law.html.

5 Recital 2 of the 1968 Brussels Convention.

easily have access to judicial redress in case the relations go awry. The underlying idea is, with the risk of oversimplifying matters, that a Belgian citizen shopping in Brussels, Paris or Milan should always have the same degree of judicial certainty with regard to the competent court, the applicable law and the swift enforcement of a judicial decision.[6]

Since then, ample use has been made of the new judicial basis inserted in the Treaty of Amsterdam, now Article 81 TFEU[7], that allows the European legislator to enact directly binding rules to strengthen this European judicial area. At present more than 20 regulations were adopted, which harmonize large parts of national PIL.[8] More initiatives are planned[9], albeit of a less ambitious nature as the European legislator currently has been focussing on the consolidation and improvement of the existing instruments.[10]

Needless to say that European PIL as it exists today is no longer a topic for the happy few. The European rules on jurisdiction, recognition and enforcement of judgments, on the applicable law or on judicial cooperation in civil, commercial and family matters have penetrated the day-to-day practices of most legal practitioners. At the same time their importance for the national judge cannot be overestimated, for it is the national judge as '*the guardian of the legal order and the judicial system of the European Union*'[11], that has to apply these rules and thus plays an indispensable role in their enforcement and further development.

---

6 Tampere European Council, 15 and 16 October 1999, Presidency Conclusions, nos. 28–39.

7 G. De Groot and J. Kuiper, 'The new provisions on private international law in the Treaty of Lisbon', *Maastricht Journal of International and Comparative law* 2008, 111.

8 See the *Compendium of European Union Legislation on Judicial Cooperation in Civil and Commercial Matters*, edited by the European Commission, whose 2017 edition contains 1054 pages. The Rome III Regulation is the only regulation that was not adopted on the basis of Article 81 TFEU, as it results from enhanced cooperation pursuant to Articles 326–334 TFEU.

9 Communication from the Commission to the European Parliament, the Council, the European Economic and Social Committee of the Regions, The EU Justice Agenda for 2020 – Strengthening Trust, Mobility and Growth within the Union, *COM*(2014) 144 final; Communication from the Commission to the European Parliament, the Council, the European Economic and Social Committee of the Regions, Commission Work Programme 2018 – An agenda for a more united, stronger and more democratic Europe, *COM*(2017) 650 final.

10 See Proposal for a Council Regulation on jurisdiction, the recognition and enforcement of decisions in matrimonial matters and the matters of parental responsibility, and on international child abduction (Recast), *COM*(2016) 411 final; Proposal for a Regulation of the European Parliament and of the Council amending Council Regulation (EC) No 1206/2001 of 28 May 2001 on cooperation between the courts of the Member States in the taking of evidence in civil or commercial matters, *COM*(2018) 378 final; Proposal for a Regulation of the European Parliament and of the Council amending Regulation (EC) No 1393/2007 of the European Parliament and of the Council on the service in the Member States of judicial and extrajudicial documents in civil or commercial matters (service of documents), *COM*(2018) 379 final.

11 CJEU 8 March 2011, *Opinion 1/09*, www.curia.eu, par. 66.

This article will first provide a brief sketch of some of the limits of the European PIL rules (2), followed by an analysis of the tasks (3) and the challenges (4) of the national judge when applying these rules. Finally, some of the 'helplines' offered by the European institutions are identified to facilitate their smooth application (5).

2. NATIONAL PIL IS TO A LARGE EXTENT EUROPEANIZED

PIL is largely Europeanized, but not entirely. Quite a few gaps remain.[12] Accordingly, it is of the utmost importance that the national judge when applying the European PIL rules carefully examines the limits of their scope of application. As will be illustrated by the Brussels *Ibis* Regulation, the territorial scope, the material scope and the temporal scope are relevant.

The Brussels *Ibis* Regulation, like its predecessors the Brussels Convention and the Brussels I Regulation, applies to cross-border disputes[13] in civil and commercial matters. Both concepts have been given an autonomous interpretation by the CJEU. The national judge can thus no longer resolve any discussion between the parties as to the material scope of application of the Brussels I rules by referring to the concepts used in domestic law.

In *Lindner,* a case where all relevant elements were linked to one Member State except for the nationality (and the unknown domicile) of the defendant, the CJEU ruled that this situation can '*raise questions relating to the determination of the international jurisdiction*' and thus should be considered to be an international case. Consequently, one foreign element, even if it is irrelevant for the application of the jurisdiction rules in the case the hand, suffices to qualify a dispute as international, hence entailing the application of the Brussels I jurisdiction rules.[14]

Article 1.1 Brussels *Ibis* Regulation excludes revenue, customs, administrative matters and, pursuant to the consistent case law of the CJEU[15], acts *iure imperii* from its core-concept 'civil and commercial matters'. The nature of the court in which proceedings have been brought is not relevant. Civil claims brought before criminal courts are included.[16] As evidenced by the recent *Pula Parking*

---

12 X. Kramer, 'European Private International Law: the way forward', www.europarl.europa.eu/document/activities/cont/201409/20140924ATT89662/20140924ATT89662EN.pdf.

13 Report Jenard, [1979] OJ C59/8.

14 CJEU 17 November 2011, Case C-327/10, *Lindner,* www.curia.eu.; see also CJEU 1 March 2005, Case C-281/02, *Owusu,* www.curia.eu. For the recognition and enforcement rules it suffices that the judgment (even on a domestic dispute) is to be recognized or enforced in another Member State.

15 The wording 'the liability of the State for acts and omissions in the exercise of State authority (*acta jure imperii*)' was inserted in the Brussels *Ibis* Regulation after the ruling of the CJEU in *Lechouritou* (CJEU 15 February 2007, Case C-292/05, *Lechouritou,* www.curia.eu).

16 CJEU 22 October 2015, Case C-523/14, *Aertssen,* www.curia.eu.

case, the CJEU has been gradually expanding this concept[17], including parking debts issued by a company, entrusted with the administration of public parking spaces.[18]

The national judge who has to rule in a cross-border dispute in a civil or commercial matter as defined by the CJEU, will in any case have to examine whether this dispute does not fall within the scope of one of the exclusions, listed in Article 1.2 Brussels *Ibis* Regulation. Meanwhile most of these topics, like insolvency[19], maintenance obligations[20], successions[21] and matrimonial property regimes[22], have been regulated in new EU Regulations. Consequently, the Brussels *Ibis* Regulation is becoming a residual instrument. If these EU-instruments, in their part clarified and construed by the CJEU, are not applicable it is the Brussels *Ibis* Regulation that revives, not the national PIL Code or otherwise applicable treaties. The latter rules, however, remain applicable to other excluded topics, including the status and capacity of natural persons, social security and most notably arbitration.[23]

As to the scope in time, Article 66 Brussels *Ibis* Regulation limits the application of both the jurisdictional rules and the rules on recognition and enforcement to legal proceedings instituted on or after the 10th of January 2015.[24] Consequently, *exequatur* is still required for judgments rendered in proceedings initiated before

17 An overview of the case law on this concept in P. Rogerson, 'Article 1', in U. Magnus and P. Mankowski (eds.), *ECPIL – Brussels Ibis Regulation*, Cologne, Sellier European Law Publishers 2016, nos. 13–27.

18 CJEU 9 March 2017, Case 551/15, *Pula Parking*, www.curia.eu; see the detailed analysis of this case by B. Hess, 'The Application of the Brussels *Ibis* Regulation in the EU Member States', published in this book.

19 Council Regulation (EC) No 1346/2000 of 29 May 2000 on Insolvency Proceedings, [2000] OJ L160/1 (hereafter Insolvency Regulation) and Regulation (EC) No 2015/848 of the European Parliament and of the Council 20 May 2015 on Insolvency Proceedings, [2015] OJ L141/19 (hereafter Insolvency Recast).

20 Council Regulation (EU) No 4/2009 of 18 December 2008 on jurisdiction, applicable law, recognition and enforcement of decisions and cooperation in matters related to maintenance obligations, [2009] OJ L7/1 (hereafter Maintenance Regulation).

21 Regulation (EU) No 650/2012 of the European Parliament and of the Council of 4 July 2012 on jurisdiction, applicable law and the recognition and enforcement of decisions and acceptance and enforcement of authentic instruments in matters of successions and on the creation of a European certificate of succession, [2012] OJ L201/107 (hereafter Succession Regulation).

22 Council Regulation (EU) No 2016/1103 of 24 June 2016 implementing enhanced cooperation in the area of jurisdiction, applicable law and the recognition and enforcement of decisions in matters of matrimonial property regimes, [2016] OJ L183/1; Council Regulation (EU) No 2016/1104 of 24 June 2016 implementing enhanced cooperation in the area of jurisdiction, applicable law and the recognition and enforcement of decisions in matters of the property consequences of registered partnerships, [2016] OJ L183/30.

23 On the exclusion of arbitration in the Brussels *Ibis* Regulation, see T. Kruger, 'The Disorderly Infiltration of EU Law in Civil Procedure', *Netherlands International Law Review* 2016, 9–11; also CJEU 13 May 2015, Case C-536/13, *Gazprom*, www.curia.eu.

24 Article 66 Brussels *Ibis* Regulation.

this date.[25] The transitional regime was different under the Brussels I Regulation, indicating that the new enforcement rules were applicable, under specified circumstances, for judgments rendered after the date of entry into force of this Regulation (1st of March 2002), but stemming from proceedings instituted before this date.[26] A similar, but not identical, transitional regime still applies under the Brussels II*bis* Regulation[27] and the Maintenance Regulation.[28]

The most predominant limitation of the Brussels I*bis* Regulation relates to its territorial scope. Indeed, most of the jurisdiction rules are only applicable if the defendant has his domicile in a Member State.[29] The proposal by the European Commission in the context of the Recast negotiations to extend the scope of the Brussels rules to all third State defendants[30], resulted in only minor exceptions to this general rule, leading to piecemeal legislation and complicating the task of the national judge.[31]

The Brussels I*bis* Regulation now requires the national judge to make a three-step reasoning: does the dispute fall within its material scope and scope in time; if so, does the defendant have his domicile in a Member States; if not, does the dispute a) fall under one of the heads of exclusive jurisdiction[32] or involve a forum clause in favour of the court of a Member State[33], in which case the domicile of the parties is irrelevant, or b) concern a claim brought by a consumer or employee, domiciled in the EU, against his contracting partner, in which case the domicile of the defendant is irrelevant.[34] For all other jurisdictional grounds, the link with the EU via the domicile of the defendant remains required. Therefore, if the answer to the latter question is negative, the national judge has to determine his jurisdiction to deal with the case at hand according to international conventions, or, if not applicable, the Belgian PIL code.[35] Important to note is that other EU

25 Article 66 Brussels I*bis* Regulation does not define when proceedings are deemed to be instituted, but reference can be made to the criteria of Article 32 Brussels I*bis* Regulation.

26 Article 66 Brussels I Regulation.

27 Council Regulation (EC) No 2201/2003 of 27 November 2003 concerning jurisdiction and recognition and enforcement of judgments in matrimonial matters and the matters of parental responsibility, [2003] OJ L338/1, Article 64 (hereafter Brussels II*bis* Regulation).

28 Article 75 Maintenance Regulation.

29 This includes Denmark, via the 2005 Agreement between the European Community and the Kingdom of Denmark on jurisdiction and the recognition and enforcement of judgments in civil and commercial matters. The necessary legislative amendments in Denmark already entered into force on 1 June 2013.

30 Proposal for a Regulation of 14 December 2010 on jurisdiction and the recognition and enforcement of judgments in civil and commercial matters (Recast), *COM* (2010) 748.

31 T. Kruger, 'The Disorderly Infiltration of EU Law in Civil Procedure', *Netherlands International Law Review* 2016, 5.

32 Article 24 Brussels I*bis* Regulation.

33 Article 25 Brussels I*bis* Regulation.

34 Articles 18.1 and 21.2 Brussels I*bis* Regulation.

35 Law of 10 July 2004 holding the code of private international law, *BS* 27 July 2004; M. Pertegás Sender, 'The Belgian Code on Private International Law: a tour d'horizon', *Iprax* 2005, 53; A. Fiorini, 'The codification of Private International Law: the Belgian experience', *ICLQ* 2005, 499.

instruments, like the Brussels II*bis* Regulation and the Insolvency Regulation, also contain territorial limitations, albeit not always formulated in a similar way.[36]

As to the rules on recognition and enforcement, all Regulations in the field of European procedural law limit these rules to judgments rendered in Member States.[37] Judgments issued by third States can only be enforced according to the national PIL rules or international conventions, resulting in identical decisions being enforced in some Member States and rejected in other Member States.

3. EUROPEAN PIL IN THE NATIONAL JUDICIAL SYSTEM

As said, it is the national judge, as first European judge, who plays a pivotal role in ensuring the day-to-day application of European PIL. As well drafted as they may be, European regulations remain merely theoretical if not properly applied by the national courts. Two questions arise in this respect: a) is the national judge always obliged to apply the European PIL rules and b) does he have to invoke these rules *ex officio* or only per plea of the parties?

3.1. DIRECT EFFECT OF THE EUROPEAN PIL RULES

European PIL Regulations, as with all regulations, have general application, are binding in their entirety, and directly applicable in all Member States.[38] They are automatically included in the Belgian legal order without any need for implementation in or adjustment of the Belgian PIL code, thus rendering parts of this national code obsolete.[39] In order to guide legal practitioners, some of its provisions refer to the relevant Regulations[40] but even without any such explicit referral the European PIL rules take precedence.[41] As they contain clear and precise provisions, the PIL Regulations have direct effect so parties can

36 Articles 6 and 7 Brussels II*bis* Regulation, Article 3 Insolvency Regulation and Article 3 Insolvency Recast.

37 CJEU 20 January 1994, Case C-129/92, *Owens Bank*, *ECR* 1994, I-117.

38 Article 288, §2, TFEU.

39 This is the case when the EU Regulations determine the applicable law in a universal way. Cf. S. Francq, 'Belgium', in J. Basedow, G. Rühl, F. Ferrari and P. De Miguel Asensio (eds.), *Encyclopedia of Private international law*, Cheltenham, Edward Elgar Publ. 2017, 1910.

40 For instance Art. 98, §2 and §4 Belgian PIL Code that refer to the Rome I and Rome II Regulations. However, these references have not been updated after the entering into force of more recent regulations like the Rome III Regulation.

41 For the sake of clarity, confirmed in Art. 2 Belgian PIL Code; see M. Fallon., 'Article 2' in J. Erauw, M. Fallon, E. Guldix, J. Meeusen, M. Pertegás, H. Van Houtte, N. Wattte and P. Wautelet (eds.), *Le Code de Droit International Privé commenté*, Antwerpen, Intersentia 2006, 5–9.

immediately invoke these provisions before the Belgian judge, setting aside, if necessary, any conflicting national provisions.[42]

The odd man out in this system is the Regulation creating a European Enforcement Order (EEO).[43] Its purpose is to create an EEO certificate, allowing a creditor who obtained a judgment on an uncontested claim to enforce this judgment in the other Member States without any *exequatur* needed prior to the enforcement.[44] If the judgment was rendered in default proceedings[45], this so-called 'European passport' can only be issued if the minimum requirements listed in Articles 12 to 19 have been met[46], the latter requiring the procedural law of the court to offer a review in exceptional cases.[47]

Very quickly in Belgian doctrine and jurisprudence a debate emerged on the question as to whether or not the Belgian Procedural Code complied with this requirement and, if not, whether Article 288, §2, TFEU obliged the Belgian judge or legislator to take the necessary steps to establish such a review procedure.[48] In the *Imtech* case[49], the CJEU, with reference to Recital 19 of the Preamble, ruled that the EEO Regulation does not imply an obligation for the Member States to adapt their national rules to these minimum procedural standards. The consequence of not having a review procedure, however, is that Belgian judgments cannot be certified as an EEO.[50] With its Article 19 having no direct effect and imposing

---

42 K. Lenaerts and P. Van Nuffel, *European Union Law*, Sweet & Maxwell, 2011 893, with references to the case law of the CJEU.

43 Regulation (EC) No 805/2004 of the European Parliament and of the Council 21 April 2004 creating a European Enforcement Order for uncontested claims, [2004] OJ L143/15 (hereafter EEO Regulation).

44 See C. Crifo, *Cross-Border Enforcement of Debts in the European Union, Default Judgments, Summary Judgments and Orders for Payment,* Wolters Kluwer 2009, 61–101; P. Gielen, 'Les règlements européens en matière de procédure civile européenne – Règlement (CE) n° 805/2004 du Parlement européen et du Conseil du 21 avril 2004 portant création d'un titre exécutoire européen pour des créances incontestées', in P. Gielen, *La procédure civile européenne* (e-book), Wolters Kluwer 2018, 15–54; also the Practice Guide, drafted by a working group of experts of the EJN, e-justice.europa.eu/content_ejn_s_publications-287-en.do.

45 As defined in Article 3.1 (b) or (c) EEO Regulation.

46 Articles 17 and 18 EEO Regulation have recently been clarified in CJEU 28 February 2018, Case C-289/17, *Collect Inkasso OÜ,* www.curia.eu.

47 Article 19 EEO Regulation states: '*Further to Articles 13 to 18, a judgment can only be certified as a European Enforcement Order if the debtor is entitled, under the law of the Member State of origin, to apply for a review of the judgment where: (a) (...) or (b) the debtor was prevented from objecting to the claim by reason of force majeure, or due to extraordinary circumstances without any fault on his part, provided in either case that he acts promptly*'.

48 See on this debate, I. Couwenberg, 'Brussels I-Vo: *Quo vadis* exequatur?', in *CBR Jaarboek 2012–2013,* Antwerpen, Intersentia 2013, 182–185; P. Gielen, 'Le problème de l'applicabilité du règlement (CE) n° 805/2004 en Belgique', *JLMB* 2010, 1627–1630.

49 CJEU 17 December 2015, Case C-300/14, *Imtech,* www.curia.eu; J. Van Drooghenbroeck and S. Brijs, 'La Belgique sortie du TEE?', *TBH* 2017, 76–86.

50 As was decided by the Antwerp Court of Appeal in its judgment of 27 February 2017 (2013/AR/2511 – not published), following the *Imtech*-ruling.

no obligation on the Member States to take implementing measures, the EEO Regulation can be qualified as an atypical regulation.

3.2 OBLIGATION TO INVOKE THE EUROPEAN PIL RULES *EX OFFICIO*

National practices show that parties in a dispute rarely invoke the applicable European PIL rules. Is the Belgian judge, when confronted with a dispute that falls within the scope of application of one of the EU Regulations, obliged to invoke these rules *ex officio*? In other words: do the European PIL rules have a mandatory character?

Article 28 Brussels I*bis* Regulation obliges the national judge to assess his jurisdiction *ex officio* when the defendant does not appear before the court. When the parties are all present, the court can only verify on its own motion whether the exclusive jurisdiction rules of Article 24 have been violated. A Commission proposal to amend Article 27 imposing on the courts a more general obligation to verify their jurisdiction, was not adopted.[51]

This obligation is formulated differently in the other EU Regulations. According to Article 17 Brussels II*bis* Regulation the court has to declare on its own motion that it has no jurisdiction if it is seized of a case over which it has no jurisdiction and a court of another Member State has jurisdiction under the Brussels II*bis* rules.[52] Hence the judge has to verify his jurisdiction *ex officio* even if the defendant does not contest the judge's competence or if both parties agreed to his jurisdiction.[53] In a Belgian context this obligation is anchored in Article 12 of the Belgian PIL Code.[54]

The EU legislator did not make the application of the European conflict of law rules mandatory.[55] In the absence of CJEU decisions that settle the question unambiguously[56] or a European Code of Private International Law containing a

---

51 I. Queirolo, 'Article 27', in U. Magnus and P. Mankowski (eds.), *ECPIL – Brussels Ibis Regulation*, Cologne, Sellier European Law Publishers 2016, nos. 8–9.

52 See also Article 10 Maintenance Regulation, Article 15 Succession Regulation and Article 4 Insolvency Regulation/Insolvency Recast.

53 P. Mankowski, 'Article 17', in U. Magnus and P. Mankowski (eds.), *ECPIL – Brussels IIbis Regulation*, Cologne, Sellier European Law Publishers 2017, nos. 1–32.

54 M. Traest, 'Artikel 12 – onderzoek van internationale bevoegdheid' in J. Erauw e.a. (eds.), *Le code de droit international privé commenté*, Antwerpen, Intersentia 2006, 70.

55 See M. Requejo Isidro, 'The Application of European Private International Law and the Ascertainment of Foreign Law', to be published in J. Von Hein, E. Kieninger and G. Ruhl (eds.), *How European is European Law*, Intersentia 2018.

56 Cf. Analysis of the CJEU case law made by M. Requejo Isidro, 'The Application of European Private International Law and the Ascertainment of Foreign Law', to be published in J. Von Hein, E. Kieninger and G. Ruhl (eds.), *How European is European Law*, Intersentia 2018, under 3.2.

general rule on whether or not to impose this application[57], the practices between the Member States vary.[58]

As a result of the '*iura novit curia*' principle the Belgian judge has to apply the conflict of laws rules on his own motion when confronted with a dispute of an international dimension. This is valid for domestic, international and European conflict of laws rules.[59] Also the case law of the CJEU confirms that European (PIL) rules must be applied *ex officio* whenever national (conflict of laws) rules are applied *ex officio* or courts are authorized to do so.[60]

Article 15 of the Belgian PIL Code requires the Belgian judge moreover to ascertain the content of foreign law and apply it in the same way the foreign judge would.[61] As will be set out further, the European Judicial Network offers the national judge a firm helping hand in executing this task.

4. CHALLENGES FOR THE NATIONAL JUDGE

The task of being the first European judge is not always an easy one. A 2008 Report 'on the role of the national judge in the European judicial system' showed that most national judges are hesitant to apply European law.[62] Recent studies confirm that European rules, *a fortiori* European PIL rules, are still perceived as being inaccessible, complicated and not always compatible with the national legal systems and domestic procedural rules.[63] The following sore points are mentioned: the quantity of the European instruments makes it difficult to stay '*à jour*', the inaccurate formulation of the rules complicating their correct application, and the lack of information on the court practices in other Member States.

---

57 On the need of a European code of PIL, see M. Czepelak, 'Would we like to have a European Code of Private International Law?', *European Review of Private Law* 2010, 705–728; S. Leible and M. Müller, 'A general part for European private international law? The idea of a 'Rome 0 Regulation', *Yearbook of Private international law* 2012, 137–152.

58 M. Császár, 'On the Mandatory Nature of the EU Private International Conflict of Laws Regulations', http://acta.bibl.u-szeged.hu/36467/1/juridpol_forum_004_001_043-053.pdf.

59 Cass. 17 June 1999 (P.98.0122.F), www.cass.be.

60 CJEU 14 December 1995, Case C-430/93 and C-431/93, *Van Schijndel*, *ECR* 1995, I-4705.

61 Cass. 20 October 2015 (C.14.0338.N), www.cass.be; See S. Geeroms, S., *Foreign law in civil litigation*, Oxford University Press, Oxford 2004, 258–260; S. Francq, 'Belgium', in J. Basedow, G. Rühl, F. FERRARI and P. De Miguel Asensio (eds.), *Encyclopedia of Private international law*, Cheltenham, Edward Elgar Publ. 2017, 1912.

62 Www.europarl.europa.eu/sides/getDoc.do?pubRef=-//EP//TEXT+REPORT+A6-2008-0224+0+DOC+XML+V0//EN.

63 2012 HiiL Report on 'National Judges as European Union Judges', www.hiil.org/publication/national-judges-as-european-union-judges. This was confirmed at the IC²BE seminar of 14 May 2018, held at the Antwerp University, where an assessment was made of the application by the Belgian judges of the Regulations relating to the European Enforcement Order, the European Order for Payment Procedure, the European Small Claims Procedure and the European Account Preservation Order.

Quite a number of national judges feel that their knowledge of EU law is inadequate, admitting that they are not always aware of the existing European rules, potentially applicable to a dispute at hand. This unease is understandable. As said, European legislation expands rapidly. Given their heavy case load, few judges have the time to read the *Official Journal of the European Union* on a daily basis. Most often when European law is invoked, only the rules directly applicable to the problem at hand are being examined, thus losing sight of the overall 'European picture'.

Moreover, a correct application of the EU Regulations is impossible without a thorough and up-to-date knowledge of the existing case law of the CJEU. As the Court follows a hands-on approach as to the interpretation of the concepts of the PIL Regulations[64], numerous and quite detailed preliminary references are rendered, defining the concepts and offering guidelines as to their application. For the national judge it is difficult to survey on an day-to-day basis all the decisions rendered by the CJEU as well as the preliminary references still pending.

The task of the national judge is further, and needlessly, complicated by complex and inaccurate legal drafting. The Brussels I*bis* Regulation offers once more a good example.

Firstly, questions can be raised as to its global structure. Only judges familiar with this instrument know that the Brussels heads of jurisdiction follow a matrix in a descending order of exclusivity and specificity.[65] To determine its jurisdiction as to the case at hand, the court must examine consecutively the heads of exclusive jurisdiction (Article 24), followed by the rule conferring jurisdiction by appearance (Article 26), the protective jurisdiction rules (Articles 10 to 23) and the rules on forum clauses (Article 25). Only in the last instance can the judge consider the specific heads for jurisdiction rules (Article 7) standing on an equal footing with the *forum rei* (Article 4). This is remarkable as the latter rule is generally quoted to be the overall rule of the Regulation. This matrix must be followed, for a judgment rendered in breach of the exclusive or protective jurisdiction rules will not be enforceable in other Member States.[66] It is regrettable that the European legislator did not use the revision of Brussels I to introduce a more logical, user friendly structure for this cornerstone of its jurisdiction rules.

Equally regrettable is the fact that some of the new Brussels I rules are drafted rather carelessly. By way of example, one can mention the new enforcement regime of provisional measures. According to Article 2 Brussels I*bis* Regulation

---

64 An overview of the most recent case law on the Brussels I*bis* Regulation in B. Hess, 'The Application of the Brussels I*bis* Regulation in the EU Member States', published in this book.

65 A. Briggs and P. Rees, *Civil jurisdiction and judgments,* London, Informa 2009, no. 2.10.; G. Van Calster, *European Private International Law,* Oxford, Hart Publishing 2016, 25.

66 Article 45.1 e) Brussels I*bis* Regulation. See. P. Mankowki, 'Article 45', in U. Magnus and P. Mankowski (eds.), *ECPIL – Brussels Ibis Regulation,* Cologne, Sellier European Law Publishers 2016, nos. 91–119.

a provisional measure falls under the scope of the European recognition and enforcement rules if '*ordered by a court or tribunal which by virtue of this Regulation has jurisdiction as to the substance matter*'. Both Article 42 and Recital 33 refer to the court (not) having jurisdiction as to the substance of the matter, without the additional requirement that this jurisdiction should be established '*by virtue of the Regulation*'.[67] Discussion can arise and has arisen[68] whether it suffices for the free circulation of provisional measures that the court has jurisdiction to deal with the merits, even if its jurisdiction is not based on a provision of the Brussels I*bis* Regulation. This discussion will have to be solved first of all by the national judge and eventually by the CJEU, but could have easily been avoided through a more careful legal drafting.

A difficulty of a more general nature is the fact that an increasing number of European PIL instruments, although called 'Regulations', require national implementing legislation to be workable and easily applicable by the national judge. Reference has already been made in this respect to the EEO Regulation.[69]

A similar observation can be made as to the new Brussels I recognition and enforcement regime. It is well known that Brussels I*bis* Regulation abolished *exequatur*.[70] *Exequatur* entailed an intermediate procedure between the judgment rendered in Member State A and its enforcement in Member State B. Under the Brussels I Regulation this was a simplified, formal procedure, conducted in a first stage *ex parte* before the competent court of Member State B and resulting in a declaration of enforceability that allowed the foreign judgement to be enforced in the same way as a domestic judgment. Although perceived to be a lengthy and costly procedure, at least in some Member States[71], it had the advantage of being a well-known procedure, firmly embedded in the legal practice of most Member States and leaving little room for discussion on its application.

Under the Brussels I*bis* Regulation the European recognition and enforcement regime has become more 'messy'.[72] The starting point is that a judgment of a

---

67 This topic is dealt with by A. Nuyts, 'Provisional measures under the Brussels regime', published in this book.

68 Cf. A. Galic, 'Recognition and enforcement of judgments pursuant to the Brussels I*bis* Regulation', *EJTN Civil Justice Seminar*, 12 October 2017 – Portoroz.

69 See under no. 3.1.

70 Article 39 Brussel I*bis* Regulation; X. Kramer, 'Abolition of exequatur under the Brussels I Regulation: effecting and protecting rights in the European judicial area', *NIPR* 2011, 633–641; A. Rodriguez Vazquez, 'Review of the Brussels I Regulation: complete abolition of exequatur', in B. Campuzano Diaz, M. Czepelak, A. Rodriguez Benot and A. Rodriguez Vazquez (eds.), *Latest developments in EU Private International Law*, Intersentia 2011, 153–174.

71 B. Hess, T. Pfeiffer and P. Schlosser, *The Brussels I-Regulation (EC) No 44/2001*, Munich CH Beck, 2008 (also known as the 'Heidelberg Report'), http://ec.europa.eu/civiljustice/news/docs/study_application_brussels_1_en.pdf.

72 M. Wilderspin, 'Recent case law on the Brussels I Recast', *EJTN Civil Justice Seminar*, 17 May 2018 – Zagreb.

Member States is automatically enforceable in all the Member States, under the same conditions as a domestic judgment. The judgment debtor can however, according to Article 46 Brussels *Ibis* Regulation, contest this enforceability by invoking one of the refusal grounds, listed in Article 45. From the wording of the relevant Articles it is difficult to deduce whether, at this stage, only the European grounds or simultaneously the national grounds for the refusal of the enforcement can be examined, as permitted by Article 41 (2), and, more importantly, whether this procedure should take place before the former 'exequatur' judge or the enforcement judge. In other words, is the debtor still obliged to initiate a special European 'reverse *exequatur*' procedure prior to the national enforcement procedure?[73]

The present legal practices in the different Member States show a kaleidoscopic image, that could have been avoided with a more precise drafting of these rules.[74] Now, to achieve legal certainty, Belgian implementing legislation with clear-cut answers is definitely needed.[75]

5. THE EUROPEAN INSTITUTIONS OFFER A HELPING HAND

5.1. CENTRALISATION OF INFORMATION

A frequently voiced complaint, mentioned in the 2008 Report, related to the multitude of European legal sources, complicating the task of the judge to find the relevant European rules in an easy and efficient way. In 2010, the European Commission created in response one central European E-justice portal[76], conceived as a one-stop electronic shop in the area of justice[77] to help legal practitioners

---

73 This question is answered in the affirmative by X. Kramer, 'Cross-border enforcement and the Brussels *Ibis* Regulation: towards a new balance between mutual trust and national control over fundamental rights', *NILR* 2013, 343–373, T. Kruger, 'The Disorderly Infiltration of EU Law in Civil Procedure', *NILR* 2016, 13–14 and A. Galic, 'Recognition and enforcement of judgment pursuant to the Brussels *Ibis* Regulation', *EJTN Civil Justice Seminar* – 12 October 2017 – Portoroz.

74 This was clearly demonstrated at a meeting of the EJN-contact points on the application of the Brussels *Ibis* enforcement rules, held in Brussels on 15 October 2015, and was confirmed at the EJN meeting of 24 June 2018. Some Member States, like Croatia, have installed a procedure prior to the actual national enforcement procedure. Cf. A. Galic, 'Recognition and enforcement of judgment pursuant to the Brussels *Ibis* Regulation', *EJTN Civil Justice Seminar* – 12 October 2017 – Portoroz. Others, like France, designated different courts competent for the application of the refusal of enforcement and the refusal of recognition respectively https://e-justice.europa.eu/content_brussels_i_regulation_recast-350-fr-en.do?member=1#a_3.

75 The Belgian government indicated that the 'court of first instance' is competent, without further clarification.

76 Https://e-justice.europa.eu/home.do?action=home&plang=en&init=true.

77 Https://ec.europa.eu/cefdigital/wiki/display/CEFDIGITAL/2017/05/30/European+e-Justice+Portal.

as well as consumers and businesses in finding answers to their legal questions. Currently, a new *beta* version of this portal is being tested, with an even more user-friendly interface, that will run in parallel with the existing portal until fall 2018.

As to the legal sources, a link is provided to the well-known EUR-Lex database, with access to the Official Journal, EU law, preparatory acts, national transposition measures, international agreements and summaries of EU legislation in all the official EU languages. A further link is made to the N-Lex, an interface that allows one to search on national databases. EU case law in general, including pending preliminary references, can be found on EUR-Lex or on the *Curia* website.[78] A special reference should be made to the ECLI search engine, given that as from October 2017 all the Belgian judgments rendered by the Court of Cassation, the courts of appeal, the courts of first instance, the commercial courts and the labour courts, published on the *Juridat* database[79], will receive an ECLI code.[80]

Noteworthy for European PIL is the link to the Judicial Atlas.[81] This website contains a wealth of information on all the EU instruments adopted in the field of judicial cooperation in civil and commercial matters. The forms, drafted to facilitate the communication between judges and national authorities when applying i.e. the Service Regulation, the Evidence Regulation or the EEO Regulation, can easily be downloaded, completed and sent directly to the competent authority in other Member States. This authority can be located easily, using the search tool specifically designed to this end.

In addition several specialized databases, created or funded by the EU in the field of European PIL, exist: Jure[82], EUPILLAR[83], EUFam's[84] and the envisaged

---

78 Https://curia.europa.eu. A search can be made on case number, name of the parties or date. The subheading 'case law' allows a more detailed search via the search form.

79 Http://jure.juridat.just.fgov.be/JuridatSearchCombined/?lang=nl.

80 Https://e-justice.europa.eu/content_european_case_law_identifier_ecli-175-be-maximizeMS-nl.do?member=1.

81 Https://e-justice.europa.eu/content_european_judicial_atlas_in_civil_matters-321-en.do.

82 Https://eur-lex.europa.eu/collection/n-law/jure.html. Jure is a database created by the European Commission, containing judgments delivered by courts of Contracting States and the CJEU related to the Brussels and Lugano Convention, the Brussels I, Brussels I*bis*, the Brussels II and Brussels II*bis* Regulations, available in their original language.

83 Https://w3.abdn.ac.uk/clsm/eupillar/#/home. EUPILLAR is a database, funded by the EU, containing case law relating to the Brussels I, Brussels II*bis*, Maintenance (including the Hague Maintenance Protocol), Rome I and Rome II Regulations with judgments from the CJEU and national courts of Belgium, Germany, England, Wales, Italy, Poland, Scotland and Spain. The time covered is 1st of March 2002 until 31st of December 2015.

84 Www.eufams.unimi.it. This database contains national case law of Bulgaria, Croatia, Czech Republic, France, Germany, Greece, Italy, Slovakia and Spain from 2004 until 2017 on the Family Law and Succession Regulations.

IC²BE[85], all of them containing EU and Member State case law on different European PIL Regulations.

Nevertheless, the Belgian judges would still benefit from a user-friendly national database focussing primarily on domestic decisions (in Dutch or French, without the need for translation) related to questions of European PIL, with an easy to apply search engine, allowing them to have access to the decisions of colleagues faced with comparable problems. In the existing Belgian database *Juridat* only a small selection of the Belgian case law is published and accessible, providing a distorted and partial picture of the application of EU law by Belgian judges. This database could be inserted in a website, modelled on the French *Lynxlex*[86] or the Dutch *Porta iuris*[87], ideally further complemented with Belgian doctrine in this field as well as the texts of the seminars, organised by the Belgian institute for judicial training (IGO-IFG) or the European Judicial Training Network (EJTN).

5.2. THE PRELIMINARY REFERENCE PROCEDURE

The best know 'helpline' for the national judge struggling with the interpretation of the concepts used in the EU Regulations, is the preliminary reference procedure of Article 267 TFEU, creating on the basis of equality a unique dialogue between the Court of Justice and the national courts. In this procedure again the national judge has to fulfil his role as first European judge, being both the initiator of the proceedings, and, after having received the answer by the CJEU, the final decision-maker.[88]

It is for the national judge to take the initiative. Indeed, the decision to bring a preliminary reference to the CJEU rests solely with the court, not with the parties.[89] The parties may urge the court to do so, but are themselves not entitled to a referral. After the Lisbon Treaty any court of a Member State is entitled to refer questions of interpretation of the PIL Regulations to the CJEU for a preliminary ruling, thus guaranteeing their uniform interpretation. The lower courts may decide that this is needed, because the outcome of a case depends on a point of EU

85 The IC²BE-project aims to assess the working in practice of the 'second generation' of EU Regulations on procedural law for cross-border cases: the European Enforcement Order, the European Order for Payment Procedure, the European Small Claims Procedure and the European Account Preservation Order. It has the objective to create a database of national case law related to these EU-instruments.

86 Https://www.lynxlex.com.

87 Https://www.rechtspraak.nl/SiteCollectionDocuments/Eur*infra*2007NL.pdf.

88 Cf. Intervention of Judge Rosas in the Meeting of Judges at the Court of Justice of the European Union – 27 March 2017 – Luxembourg.

89 CJEU 21 January 2003, Case C-318/01, *Bacardi Martini*, www.curia.eu.

law to which the answer is not clear, but are under no obligation to do so.[90] Those courts that decide in last instance, such as the Belgian Court of Cassation, do not have this discretionary power. They must bring the reference unless there is no reasonable doubt as to the correct application of community law or an identical question has already been decided by the CJEU.[91]

Once the decision is rendered, it remains the national judge that must decide on the original dispute. The referring court is hereby bound by the interpretation given by the CJEU[92] and has to, if necessary, set aside incompatible provisions of national law.[93]

From the statistics one might deduce that the Belgian Court of Cassation seems reluctant to ask questions in the field of European PIL. Indeed, in the past five years only a handful of references were made. This assessment is however not entirely correct. One must take into account that the review by the Belgian Court of Cassation is limited to the points of law that are, in an admissible way, being criticized by the plaintiff.[94] So if no incorrect application of the European PIL rules is invoked or if the appeal before the Court of Cassation is dismissed on grounds of inadmissibility[95], no preliminary reference can be made. Moreover, despite the criteria set out in the *CILFIT* case[96], the decision whether there is reasonable doubt as to the correct application of EU law sometimes requires a judgment call that is not always easy to make, as illustrated by the following case.

In a judgment of the 15th of January 2016 the Court of Cassation had to decide whether it is for the national law to determine if the procedural conduct of a

---

90 Under Belgian law a decision to refer without any other points of law being decided, is not subject to an appeal. Cf. Cass. 30 March 2010 (P.09.1592.N), www.juridat.be.

91 CJEU 6 October 1982, Case 283/81, *CILFIT*, *ECR* 1982, 3415. According to the Recommendations to national courts and tribunals, in relation to the initiating of preliminary ruling proceedings, issued by the ECJ (*OJ* 2017, C 439/1), there is no obligation to refer where 'there is already well-established case-law on the point' or if 'the correct interpretation of the rule in question admits of no reasonable doubt'.

92 The preliminary ruling only has a binding effect for the court and the parties of the referred dispute. However, once the CJEU has decided on an interpretation issue this decision will also be followed by the other national courts of the Member States. Cf. P. Rogerson, 'Article 1', in U. Magnus and P. Mankowski (eds.), *ECPI – Brussels Ibis Regulation*, Cologne, Sellier European Law Publishers 2016, no 127.

93 CJEU 9 March 1978, Case 106/77, *Simmenthal*, www.curia.eu, recently confirmed in CJEU 21 December 2016, Case C-308/15, *Gutiérrez Naranjo*, www.curia.eu.

94 Only exception is the obligation imposed by Article 27 Brussels *Ibis* Regulation to examine on its own motion any violation of the exclusive jurisdiction pursuant to Article 24. See CJEU 15 November 1983, Case 288/82, *Duijnstee*, *ECR* 1983, I-3663; I. Queirolo, 'Article 27', in in U. Magnus and P. Mankowski (eds.), *ECPI – Brussels Ibis Regulation*, Cologne, Sellier European Law Publishers 2016, no 19.

95 CJEU 15 March 2017, Case C-3/16, *Aquino*, www.curia.eu.

96 CJEU 6 October 1982, Case 283/81, *CILFIT*, *ECR* 1982, 3415.

defendant, who failed to attend the proceedings, amounts to non-contestation of the claim as defined in Article 3.1 (b) and (c) of the EEO Regulation. Article 3 makes an express reference to the national law of the Member State seized. However, does this reference imply that it is for the national law to determine whether the defendant in not making an appearance in court, contests or accepts the claim, or is this reference to national law limited to the procedural rules defining how and when the defendant may contest the claim?

The Court of Cassation adhered to the first point of view. It concluded that as in the Belgian legal system default of appearance is considered to be a form of rejection of the claim, a judgment by default cannot be regarded as a judgment on an uncontested claim. Despite the mentioned divergent interpretations, the Court did not see a need to refer a question to the CJEU, qualifying this as a case of *acte clair*.[97] In the *Prebos Servizi* case, rendered only a few months later upon a referral by the court of Bologna, the CJEU took a different stance.[98] It ruled that the fact that under the law of a Member State a default of appearance is taken to mean an acceptance or a contestation of the claim, is irrelevant. The concepts of the EEO, like the concepts of all other PIL Regulations, are autonomous concepts of EU law. Accordingly, the reference to the national law in Article 3 does not relate to the constituent elements of that concept, but is meant to ensure that in order to constitute a valid opposition, the conduct must be in conformity with the procedural requirements of the seized Member State.

Such contradictory rulings can be avoided with a better exchange of information between the courts, especially the courts adjudicating in the last instance, of pending preliminary references to the CJEU. With this aim a new network was created under auspices of the CJEU, the 'Judicial Network of the European Union', that should contribute to the deepening of the cooperation of the CJEU with the Constitutional and Supreme Courts of the Member States.[99] Its first practical manifestation is a website, accessible since the 1st of January 2018 with 3 sections: a) the preliminary rulings portal, that allows the users to consult in all available language versions the entire chain of court documents connected with preliminary references[100], b) a national decision portal, gathering national decisions which did not lead to a preliminary reference but are of great importance in relation to the

97 The Court of Cassation ruled: '*l'interprétation correcte de cette disposition communautaire s'impose avec une telle évidence qu'elle ne laisse place à aucune doute raisonnable, la question préjudicielle proposée par le demandeur ne doit pas être posée à la Cour de justice de l'Union européenne*'. Cf. Cass. 15 January 2016 (C.14.0566.F), conclusion A. Henkes, www.cass.be; *R.W.* 2017-'18, 305; J. Van Drooghenbroeck and S. Brijs, 'La Belgique sortie du TEE?', *TBH* 2017, 76–86.

98 CJEU 16 June 2016, Case C-511/14, *Prebros Servizi*, www.curia.eu.

99 See the introduction by President Lenaerts to the Annual Report 2017 of the CJEU, https://curia.europa.eu/jcms/upload/docs/application/pdf/2018-04/ra_pan_2018.0421_en.pdf.

100 Preliminary references made after the 1st of January 2018 are published, covering all subjects and all referring courts. These documents include the order for reference, the opinion of the

development of EU law, and c) research notes and studies on EU law, comparative law or national law, prepared by the (legal secretaries of the) national courts and the Research and Development Directorate of the CJEU. In the first stage, the access to this website is restricted to members of the participating courts who have been authorized by their courts. However, once fully operation, the access rights will gradually be more widely extended.

5.3. THE EUROPEAN JUDICIAL NETWORK

Not all problems which the national judge encounters when applying the Regulations on judicial cooperation in civil and commercial matters involve the interpretation of their concepts or terms used. Sometimes more practical information is needed, e.g. on the filling in of the forms, annexed to the Brussels *Ibis* Regulation or on how to use videoconferencing when hearing witnesses abroad. As stated, difficulties also occur when, due to the application of the conflict of laws rules, the contents of the law of another Member State needs to be ascertained.

For these problems a helping hand is offered by the European Judicial Network in civil and commercial matters (EJN-civil). This network, of increasing practical and political importance[101], was created in 2001[102] to facilitate and enhance the judicial cooperation between the judges of the Member States[103], and receiving a new impulse in 2009 when it was opened to other legal professions.[104]

The EJN-civil is composed of contact points, designated by the Member States, national 'authorities' with responsibilities for judicial cooperation in this field (mostly magistrates) and representatives of professional associations (bailiffs, lawyers, notaries).[105] These members meet on a regular basis, under the auspices of the European Commission, to discuss the practical and judicial problems, encountered by judges in the context of the judicial cooperation, to search for solutions and to formulate recommendations for envisaged new PIL legislation or recast legislation.

AG, the decision of the CJEU, the subsequent national decision delivered by the referring court and, if available, the various press releases.

101 Cf. Keynote speech of Commissioner for Justice, Consumers and Gender Equality V. Jourova, 'Building a stronger European Judicial Network', Users/admin/Downloads/001%20-%20 170201_Speech-Commissioner-Jourova-EJN-final_EU_EN.pdf.

102 Council Decision 2001/470 of 28 May 2001 establishing a European Judicial Network in civil and commercial matters, [2001] OJ L174/25.

103 All Member States except Denmark.

104 Decision 568/2009/EC of the European Parliament and of the Council of 18 June 2009, [2009] OJ L168 (now Council Decision 2001/470, consolidated version).

105 Article 2 Council Decision 2001/470, consolidated version.

The assistance offered by the EJN-civil to the national judge is twofold. Firstly, the judge can refer all possible questions that arise when applying the European PIL instruments to its national contact point who, if necessary, can further contact the contact point of another Member State or a representative of the European Commission. As indicated, these questions may relate to difficulties related to the application of the Regulations as well as to the contents of another Member State's national law, deemed applicable according to the EU conflict of laws rules.[106] Secondly, the network facilitates the contacts between judges, e.g. in the context of the gathering of evidence abroad pursuant to the Evidence Regulation or the hearing of children as required by the Brussels II*bis* Regulation when deciding on parental access rights.

The procedure itself has deliberately been kept simple and informal: the Belgian judge can refer his question, formulated as precise as possible, by fax, e-mail or telephone to the Belgian contact point.[107] This contact point will transfer this question, if necessary in a translated form, to the foreign member of the network who shall respond without delay and within 15 days at the latest.[108] The obtained information will be transferred to the requesting judge who then has to organize a debate with the parties regarding the received information.

On its website the EJN-civil also distributes freely accessible general information, both on the EU Regulations and the national law of the Member States.[109]

For twenty-two topics, relating to jurisdiction, enforcement, divorce, succession, service of documents, statutory interests, etc., so-called information sheets are published with information on the most important national rules, European rules and international rules. Moreover, this information is accessible in all the official languages of the EU. For example, information on Polish divorce law can easily be found in Swedish.

With the help from specialists from different Member States, the EJN-civil also has drafted a wide range of citizens' and practitioners' guides (on the Brussels II*bis* Regulation, the Small Claims Procedure, the European Order for Payment, the Evidence Regulation, the European Enforcement Order, ...), available in all the official EU-languages.[110] As the word 'practice guide' suggests, it provides step-by-step guidance for those using these instruments for the first time.

---

106 Recital 14 of the Rome III Regulation in this respect explicitly refers to the EJN: '*where the law of another Member State is designated, the European Judicial Network in civil and commercial matters could play a part in assisting the courts with regard to the content of foreign law*'.

107 A judge can find his national contact point by filling in his professional address on the e-justice portal → EJN in civil and commercial matters → judges and other judicial authorities → 'if you wish to contact your contact point'.

108 Article 8 Council Decision 2001/470, consolidated version.

109 Https://e-justice.europa.eu/content_information_on_national_law_information_sheets-439-en.do.

110 Https://e-justice.europa.eu/content_ejn_s_publications-287-en.do.

Some Member States, including Belgium, have a national EJN-section. One of its actual achievements is the electronic newsletter *EUR-Alert!*, distributed since 2011 with the aim of alerting Belgian judges to new EU developments. This newsletter, that can be found on the website of the IGO-IFJ[111], contains a selection of recent EU legislation and jurisprudence of the CJEU, as published in the Official Journal, as well as jurisprudence of the Belgian courts. Regularly, a thematic issue is published with an in-depth analysis of recent developments in European PIL, with which national judges will be confronted sooner or later. A similar initiative, called 'Nieuwsbrief Rechtspraak Europa' exists in the Netherlands.[112]

6. CONCLUSION

The European PIL rules form an integral part of the Belgian legal order. Unfortunately, quite a few Belgian judges still feel uncomfortable when applying these European rules; an unease that can be avoided if better use is made of available tools such as the European e-justice portal, the preliminary reference procedure and the European Judicial Network.

As first European judges, Belgian judges should be prepared to engage in cross-border communication. This communication can take the form of a transfer of national judgments, relating to the European PIL Regulations, to the existing EU data bases, and by referring even more frequently questions to the CJEU. But more importantly, national judges should engage in an increased communication with their colleagues from other Member State through the European networks, as it is one of the most efficient ways to improve their knowledge of European PIL and of each other's legal system.

For, as President Lenaerts of the CJEU quite rightly stated: 'European judicial networks are an indispensable element to guarantee a high quality of European justice'.[113]

---

111 Www.igo-ifj.be/fr/euralert.

112 Https://www.rechtspraak.nl/Organisatie-en-contact/Organisatie/Gerechtshoven/Gerechtshof-Amsterdam/Over-het-gerechtshof/Publicaties.

113 *La Justice européenne en réseau* – Meeting of Judges at the Court of Justice of the European Union on the 27th of March 2017.

www.ingramcontent.com/pod-product-compliance
Ingram Content Group UK Ltd.
Pitfield, Milton Keynes, MK11 3LW, UK
UKHW051928100926
8556IPUK00022B/1431

9 781780 687759